To [illegible]:

My regards -

George

Trade, Agriculture, and Development

Trade, Agriculture, and Development

Edited by

George S. Tolley
Peter A. Zadrozny

Department of Economics
University of Chicago

Ballinger Publishing Company • Cambridge, Mass.
A Subsidiary of J.B. Lippincott Company

Ballinger Studies in Environment and the Urban Economy–under the general editorship of George S. Tolley.

Studies in Environment and the Urban Economy, a special Ballinger series under the general editorship of George S. Tolley of the University of Chicago, is published in the hope that it will be a vehicle for the meaningful synthesis of environmental research.

Other books in this series:

Residential Fuel Policy and the Environment–Alan Cohen, Argonne National Laboratories, Gideon Fishelson and John Gardner, University of Chicago.

Urban Transportation for the Environment–Richard O. Zerbe, Roosevelt University, Kevin Croke, University of Illinois Medical Center.

International Standard Book Number: 0-88410-010-3

Library of Congress Catalog Card Number: 75-2341

Printed in the United States of America

Library of Congress Cataloging in Publication Data

Seminar on Trade, Agriculture, and Development, University of Chicago, 1973.
Trade, agriculture, and development.

"Sponsored by the Agricultural Development Council."
Includes bibliographical references.
1. Economic development–Congresses. 2. Commerce–Congresses. 3. Agriculture–Economic aspects–Congresses. I. Tolley, George S., 1925- ed. II. Agricultural Development Council. III. Title.
HD82.S432 1973 338'.09'04 75-2341
ISBN 0-88410-010-3

Contents

List of Figures ix

List of Tables xi

Foreword xv

Part I
Agricultural Policies in a World Setting 1

Chapter One
Free Trade in Agricultural Products: Possible Effects on Total Output, Prices, and the International Distribution of Output
D. Gale Johnson 3

Free Trade and Subsidization 4
Free Trade and Short Run Effects on the World's Food Supply 5
Free Trade and the Distribution of Consumption 13
Free Trade and the Location of Farm Production 14
Free Trade and the Developing Countries 15
Advantages of Free Trade 19

Chapter Two
The Impact of U.S. Agricultural Policies on

Trade of the Developing Countries
Martin E. Abel 21

Introduction: The Role of U.S. Trade Policies 21
Production and Trade in the Developing Countries 24
Impact of U.S. Agricultural Policies on the Developing Countries 35
The Developing Countries as a Market for U.S. Exports 43
Alternative Agricultural Policies for the United States 44
The Meaning of Agricultural Trade Negotiations with Less Developed Countries 53
Summary and Conclusions 55

Chapter Three
The Impact of Price on Rice Trade in Asia
C. Peter Timmer and Walter P. Falcon 57

Introduction 57
Production and Consumption 60
Trade 77
An Overview 83

Part II
The Analysis of Development Experience 91

Chapter Four
The Interaction of Growth Strategy, Agriculture, and Foreign Trade: The Case of India
John W. Mellor and Uma Lele 93

The Strategy of Growth 94
The Changing Growth and Structure of India's Imports 97
India's Export Performance and Its Determinants 103
India's Policy Constraints on Export Performance 107
Lessons from the Textile Case 110
Conclusions 113

Chapter Five
Agricultural Trade in the Economic Development of Taiwan
Anthony M. Tang and Kuo-shu Liang 115

Introduction 115
Foreign Aid, Agricultural Trade, and Constraints on Taiwan's Growth 118
Postwar Development in Taiwan's Agricultural Exports 134
Domestic Marketing and Price Policy for Agricultural Products 140
Summary and Conclusions 143

Chapter Six
Growth, Capital Import, and Agriculture in Korea
George S. Tolley 147

Typical Near Term Analysis 147
Concept of Moving Long Term Equilibrium 150
The Path of Income as Determined by Short Run Diminishing Returns to Capital Formation 155

Part III
Technology and Trade 167

Chapter Seven
Agricultural Trade: Implications for the Distribution of Gains from Technical Process
Timothy Josling 169

Simple Distribution Model 170
Implications for Other Countries 172
Policy Adjustments 174
The Future of Farm Trade 178

Chapter Eight
Agricultural Trade and Shifting Comparative Advantage
Robert Evenson 181

Technology Transfer: A Specification of the Determinants of Change in Comparative Productivity 182
Comparative Productivity and the International Research System 187
Export Performance in Cereal Grains and Technology Transfer 197
Summary 199

Notes 201

Index 215

List of Contributors 219

About the Editors 221

List of Figures

3-1	Short Run and Long Run Production Function	66
3-2	Relationship Between the Relative Price of Rice to Fertilizer and Fertilizer Applications per Hectare	70
3-3	Net Trade in Rice as a Function of Price, by Countries, Assuming Zero Consumption Response	81
3-4	Net Trade in Rice as a Function of Price	86
3-5	Net Trade in Rice as a Function of Price, for Ceylon and Indonesia and Selected Consumption Response Coefficients	87
5-1	The Two-Sector Constraint Model	127
6-1	The Investment Curve	157
6-2	Ratio of Interest Rate to Marginal Product of Capital and Slope of Investment Curve	159
7-1	Distribution of Gains from Technical Progress in Case of Autarchy	171
7-2	Distribution of Gains from Technical Progress in the Presence of Trade	172
7-3	Distribution of Impact of Technical Progress Abroad	173
7-4	Automatic Redistribution of Impact of Foreign Technical Change by Support Policy	176

List of Figures

List of Tables

1-1	Atlantic Trade Institute Estimates of Consumer and Taxpayer Costs of EEC Farm Program, 1967-68	6
1-2	U.S. Department of Agriculture Estimates of Consumer and Taxpayer Cost of EEC Farm Programs	8
1-3	Price Elasticities of Supply of Farm Products in Industrial Countries	10
1-4	Producer Prices for Farm Products, 1968 or 1968-69	12
2-1	World Trade in Wheat, Rice, and Coarse Grains, 1964-66—Average and Projections to 1980	27
2-2	Cotton Lint Exports as a Percentage of Total Merchandise Exports, Selected Countries, 1966	29
2-3	Cotton Textile Exports as a Percentage of Total Merchandise Exports, Selected Countries, 1968	30
2-4	World Cotton Trade and Textile-Lint Mix, 1952-1967	31
2-5	World Trade in Sugar, 1951-1965	32
2-6	World Trade in Beef, Selected Regions and Years	34
2-7	Nominal and Effective Rates of Protection in the U.S. Farm Production Sector, 1968	36
2-8	World Trade in Wheat and Wheat Flours, 1967	37
2-9	Production and Export of Cotton, United States, 1955-1970	40
2-10	Nominal and Effective Tariff Rates for Selected Commodities, United States, 1962	41
2-11	Weighted Averages of Nominal and Effective Tariffs and Imports from Less Developed Countries, United States, 1964	42

2-12	U.S. Agricultural Exports, by Region and Terms of Sale, 1962 and 1971	44
3-1	Basic Rice Statistics for a Sample of Nine Asian Countries, 1970	59
3-2	Rice Production Function, 1962-70	64
3-3	Relationship Between Relative Price and Fertilizer Applications on Rice, 1970	71
3-4	Rice Consumption Functions, 1962-70	74
3-5	Net Trade in Rice at Different Assumed Ratios of Rice to Fertilizer Prices	79
3-6	Net Trade in Rice at Different Assumed Ratios of Rice to Fertilizer Price	82
3-7	Net Trade in Rice at Different Assumed Ratios of Rice to Fertilizer Price	84
3-8	Net Trade in Rice at Different Assumed Ratios of Rice to Fertilizer Price	85
4-1	Import Performance of Selected Countries by Commodity Groups, 1950-60	98
4-2	Import Performance of Selected Countries by Commodity Groups, 1960-69	99
4-3	Growth Rates of World Exports by Regions and Commodity Groups, 1960-69	104
4-4	Export Performance of Selected Countries by Commodity Groups, 1960-69	106
4-5	Exports of Textiles and Clothing (Excluding Jute Textiles) from Selected Countries, 1953-64	111
5-1	Estimated Values of Parameters *r, s,* and *b,* 1953-1970	122
5-2	Constraints on the Taiwan Economy Without Foreign Capital Transfers: 1953-1970	122
5-3	Constraints on the Taiwan Economy After Foreign Capital Transfers, 1953-1970	126
5-4	Composition of Taiwan's Exports, 1953-1970	131
5-5	Percentage of Total Imports Financed by Agricultural Exports, 1953-1970	131
5-6	Average Annual Rates of Changes in Output, Inputs, and Land Productivity of Taiwan's Agriculture, 1952-1968	132
5-7	Agricultural Labor Force and Outflow Rate of Agricultural Labor, 1952-1970	134
5-8	Exports and Imports as Percentage of GDP, 1951-1970	135

5-9	Major Export Commodities, 1953-1970	136
5-10	Food Balance Sheet of Taiwan	137
5-11	Rates of Capacity Utilization of Selected Manufactures, 1959 and 1970	139
5-12	Average Annual Growth Rates of Real Expenditures on GDP, 1951-1970	140
5-13	Export and Import Values of Agriculture, Forestry, Hunting, and Fishery Products, 1970	140
5-14	Domestic Production, Imports, Exports, Home Demand, Commercial Margin, and Transport Margin of Agricultural, Forestry, and Fishery Products, 1969	141
5-15	Composition of Per Capita Food Consumption, 1970	144
7-1	Impact of EEC Enlargement on Size of European Market and on World Price Levels, 1980	178
7-2	Impact on Selected Countries of the Changes in World Price Levels Arising from EEC Enlargements, 1980	179
8-1	Agricultural Research and Extension, 1965—Interregional Comparisons	188
8-2	Agricultural Research Publications Abstracted in Selected International Abstraction Journals, 1948-1968	189
8-3	Geoclimate Region Research in Cereal Grain Production	194
8-4	Regression Analysis: Geoclimate Yield Determination	196

Foreword

While the roles of agriculture and trade in development have received much attention separately, relatively little attention has been devoted to their interrelationship. Trade has been a vehicle in some of the more successful development experiences, and agricultural commodities have figured both as successful exports and as problem areas on the import side. The authors of this book try to provide an understanding of development in a context that encompasses both agriculture and trade.

In Part One, D. Gale Johnson surveys in Chapter One the impact on less developed countries of a hypothetical worldwide shift to free trade in agricultural products and concludes that even though free trade would permit a more efficient allocation of resources in the long run, the immediate effect would be to lower food production for a decade, with the distribution of food consumption shifting toward high income countries at the expense of the less developed countries. Martin Abel, Chapter Two's author, looks at the impact of less protective U.S. policies on less developed countries and compares the gains (or losses) to less developed countries for various raw and processed commodities. Currently the United States discriminates more against imports of processed primary products than against raw materials and this deprives less developed countries of an important source of export growth. C.P. Timmer and Walter Falcon provide an empirical analysis of the effect of the relative price of rice on the volume of trade of various Asian countries in Chapter Three.

Part Two deals with the analysis of development experience. In Chapter Four, John Mellor and Uma Lele argue that India's development strategy ignored the lessons of comparative advantage: both exports and import substitutes were developed in a way that failed to realize the advantages of producing labor intensive commodities. In Chapter Five, Anthony M. Tang and Kuo-shu Liang review how agricultural exports contributed to Taiwan's successful development: sufficient increases in agricultural productivity were achieved to increase exports of agricultural staples in accordance with import requirements for industrialization. The authors review the role of foreign exchange and domestic savings constraints on growth and trace the composition of exports over the years of development. Whereas Taiwan is often cited as an "ideal" development situation, India was less successful. Drawing on the Korean experience, George S. Tolley argues in Chapter Six that Korea's growth is explained not only by the effect of U.S. expenditures and capital gifts but that economic reforms created differential returns to capital in Korea above the rest of the world, which stimulated an inflow of capital. Tolley concludes that in such a case the constraint on growth is not necessarily a lack of foreign exchange or domestic savings, but may be due to rising costs of capital formation.

In Part Three Timothy Josling and Robert Evenson consider the effect of technological change and technological transfer on agricultural trade. Josling views agricultural protectionism as a way of controlling changes in the income distribution due to trade and the dissemination of technology in Chapter Seven, and Evenson estimates the effects of technological change and technology transfer on comparative advantage in cereal production in the eighth and final chapter.

This volume arises out of papers presented at the Seminar on Trade, Agriculture, and Development, which was sponsored by the Agricultural Development Council and held at the Center for Continuing Education of the University of Chicago on February 13-14, 1973.

Part I

Agricultural Policies in a World Setting

Chapter One

Free Trade in Agricultural Products: Possible Effects on Total Output, Prices, and the International Distribution of Output

D. Gale Johnson

In developing my topic I have, rather heroically, attempted to determine some of the influences on the world food supply if there were free trade in farm products and inputs used in farm production. Using this framework does not imply that I expect free trade to be achieved in the near future or any time. The assumption is a simplification and I have used it because in my efforts to develop the topic I realized that I had never asked myself the question of what would happen to the aggregate food supply of the world if there were free trade in farm products.

In my previous work on the general topic of interferences with agricultural trade I had been mainly concerned with the effects on individual commodities or upon the location of farm production but had never considered the more global effects. Based on fairly extended reading I have not seen the question of the effect of free trade on the world's total supply of food discussed in a direct and explicit manner.[a]

My definition of free trade in farm products and inputs is a simple one, though broader than most definitions: namely that not only are there no barriers at the borders in terms of import duties or quotas but that there are no subsidies to agricultural production, either on outputs or inputs, and that there

Note: An earlier version of this paper was presented at the conference "Expanding World Needs for Food and Fiber and Protection of the Ecosystem," Center for the Study of Democratic Institutions, Santa Barbara, California, August 9-13, 1971. To some degree this chapter reflects the time at which it was first written. However, I have seen no reason to significantly modify the broad framework.

[a]Since the above was written the results of an important effort has been published by the Food and Agricultural Organization of the United Nations, *A World Price Equilibrium Model.*[1] The study was undertaken as a part of the agricultural projections for 1980.[2]

are no export subsidies or taxes. In other words, nothing is done in any country to either encourage or discourage agricultural production. For the latter statement to be factually correct there would have to be free trade in all goods and services.

FREE TRADE AND SUBSIDIZATION

If there were free trade in agricultural products and inputs used in farm production it is probable that, at least during the present decade, world food production would not be increased and might be lower than if the current farm and trade programs were maintained throughout the decade.[b] A significant, though unknown, fraction of the world's output of food is produced in the wrong places with methods of production that are economically inappropriate and at high cost in terms of resources used. In some parts of the world farm production is limited by the lack of opportunities to export and/or governmental policies that have penalized one or several sectors of agriculture.

It is also probable that if there were free trade in farm products that the distribution of world food consumption would shift toward the relatively high income countries of Europe and Japan and away from the low income countries of Asia. Except for the United Kingdom and Ireland, all the countries of Europe (including the USSR and Eastern Europe) significantly restrict the consumption of several food products through the high consumer prices that result from farm price supports. If consumer prices were at the levels that would be possible through free trade, there would be a substantial increase in consumption, especially of animal products. Because of the low price elasticity of demands for grains at the income levels prevailing in Europe and Japan, direct grain consumption as food would increase only slightly but the use of grain for livestock feed would increase substantially.

In Europe and Japan crop production would decline if there were free trade and no other form of subsidization of agriculture. Livestock output would increase, but total farm output might decline. Food consumption would increase in the same areas and the emerging difference would have to be made up with supplies from the rest of the world. It is highly probable that under free trade farm output would increase in North America, Oceania, and Argentina, but it is far from certain that the increase in output in these areas would offset completely the decline in production and the increase in consumption in the other high income regions of the world.

The developing countries of Asia, Africa, and South America could gain from the expansion of export markets for their agricultural products, but they would be able to do so only as they are able to increase their farm output

[b]The results in *World Price Equilibrium Model* for the world (other than the centrally planned economies) projects for 1980 a level of food output under free trade very slightly larger than the projected output with existing (1970) farm prices and policies.

more rapidly than the increase in their own demand or are willing and/or able to restrict their consumption. In many cases the developing countries now have farm and trade policies that mean that their agricultures cannot compete in world markets at present prices and exchange rates.[c] It is not only the trade and agricultural policies of the industrial countries that limit the flow of trade in farm products.

In the longer run a move to free trade in agricultural products and in farm inputs would be of advantage to the world as a whole and to each of its continents. But most of the gain would be in terms of providing a setting in which resources generally could be more effectively used rather than in terms of a significant improvement in the world's food supply or its distribution among countries or groups within countries.

These are the main points I am developing in this chapter. Admittedly I have chosen what might be considered a negative approach to the effect of international trade and other economic relationships on the world food supply. But I think that it is important to realize that there is no simple panacea that will make possible a more rapid increase in the world's food supply, and that many efforts such as research on new varieties, reduction in the costs of purchased inputs, adequate incentives to farmers, and investment in human capital in rural areas are required. It is also important to understand that the agricultural and trade policies of the industrial countries, costly and misguided as they are, have not been and are not now a major barrier to the expansion of agricultural production in the developing countries. I do not, however, want to be interpreted as saying that the policies of the industrial countries have had no adverse effects on the profitability of agricultural production in the developing countries, because I shall later point to some examples where the consequences have been significant.

FREE TRADE AND SHORT RUN EFFECTS ON THE WORLD'S FOOD SUPPLY

With only minor exceptions, most of the agricultural output in the industrial countries of the world is protected by a combination of barriers at the border and domestic price supports and subsidies. The annual cost of such protection to consumers and taxpayers may well approach $40 billion–including about $13 billion in the EEC, almost $10 billion in the United States, at least as much in the USSR as in the United States, and smaller but still significant magnitudes in the rest of Western Europe, Canada, and Japan.[3] In most cases the protection has not been associated with any effort to restrict output.

In the EEC and the United States, where the cost estimates have

[c]Obviously the degree of overvaluation of currencies varies from country to country. In many instances, seemingly high farm prices are required to offset the effects of an overvalued exchange rate.

Table 1-1. Atlantic Trade Institute Estimates of Consumer and Taxpayer Costs of EEC Farm Program, 1967-68

Commodity	Production (1,000 tons)	EEC Prices[a] ($ per ton)	World Prices ($ per ton)	Difference ($ per ton)	Consumer Cost (million dollars)
Wheat	31,168	98.10	58.40	39.70	1,123.7
Rye	4,013	87.30	48.10	39.20	157.3
Barley	15,877	83.00	50.20	32.80	520.8
Oats	8,031	77.70	55.60	22.10	177.5
Potatoes	40,865	33.10	31.40[a]	1.70	69.5
Sugar beets	(48,663)[b]	17.20	13.50[a]	3.70	180.0
Mills	72,476	95.40	70.30[a]	25.10	1,819.1
Eggs	2,257	633.60	387.50	246.10	555.4
Pork	5,026	805.70[c]	528.30[c]	277.40	1,394.2
Beef and veal	3,825	1,154.10[c]	724.20[c]	429.90	1,644.4
Poultry	1,517	723.30[c]	468.70[c]	254.60	386.2
Subtotal					8,028.1
Public expenditures for agricultural programs					6,000.0 - 8,000.0
Less variable levies					2,000.0
Total					12,028.1 - 14,028.1

Source: The Atlantic Institute, *A Future for European Agriculture*, The Atlantic Papers 4 (1970), pp. 8-9 and p. 62.

[a]Prices received by Danish farmers; other prices are either U.S. export prices or U.K. import prices. EEC prices are prices received by EEC farmers.

[b]Not given in original; estimated from price and value data.

[c]Carcass weight.

been worked out in some detail, one can compare the total consumer and treasury costs to the gross domestic product (value added) of agriculture.[d] The gross domestic product of agriculture at market prices in 1968 in the EEC was $23.5 billion and in the United States was $25.0 billion.[4] The costs, through prices above world market levels and payments from treasuries, equalled 55 percent of the value added by agriculture in the EEC and 38 percent in the United States. While the United States has made some effort to restrict the output of farm products, the EEC has not done so except for one or two feeble efforts. And even in the United States it is not clear how much output has been reduced for the major crops (cotton, wheat, and feed grains) nor whether these reductions have not been more than offset by the encouragement of dairy, peanut, rice, and sugar output.

Several years ago Heady and Tweeten estimated that the elimination of U.S. farm programs as of the early 1960s and a return to market prices would have resulted in an increase of total farm output of 2 to 4 percent by the end of a four-year period of adjustment.[5] Two more recent studies of specific farm commodities (cotton and feed grains) indicate that the Heady and Tweeten results are valid for the conditions as of 1973.[6] It is highly probable that if the United States abandoned its farm programs there would be but a very small increase in the U.S. farm output, and one could not rule out the possibility of a decline, though this seems to be quite unlikely.

The accumulated evidence on the elasticity of supply of farm output with respect to price in the industrial countries (see Table 1-3) indicates that the high degree of protection of agriculture in the EEC and the rest of Western Europe has resulted in a substantial expansion of farm output, and that the institution of free trade in agriculture would result in a decline in farm output. In 1959-61 the value of food production in Western Europe, according to USDA estimates, was approximately the same as in the United States and nearly 15 percent of the world total.[7] The total value for all of Europe was about 35 percent of the world total. However, there are so many changes that could be made in the organization of agriculture in Eastern Europe and the USSR that I do not make any inferences about what would happen to food output in that area under free trade. The enormous divergency in producer prices for several major farm products (see Table 1-4) indicates that major declines in output would occur in several industrial countries with free trade. Most of the decline would be in crop products; livestock output would increase.

Another implication of free trade in agricultural products would be that the supply of food aid would diminish. Most of the food aid now available is the result of excess output generated by domestic farm programs in the

---

[d]The estimates of costs were made by valuing farm output at world and domestic prices and adding net treasury expenditures (gross expenditures minus certain taxes or levies) on farm programs. Estimates of EEC costs are given in Tables 1-1 and 1-2. The estimate for the United States was made by the author.

Table 1-2. Department of Agriculture Estimates of Consumer and Taxpayer Cost of EEC Farm Programs[a]

Commodity	Production (1,000 tons)	Quantity Included[b] (1,000 tons)	EEC Price[c] ($ per ton)	World Price[c] ($ per ton)	Difference ($ per ton)	Excess Consumer Cost (1,000 dollars)
Soft wheat	24,507	14,291	107.30	57.90	49.40	705,975
Durum wheat	1,802	1,383	126.64	80.70	45.94	63,535
Barley	12,366	1,061	80.28	56.70	23.58	25,018
Rye	3,475	1,206	93.75	57.48	36.27	43,742
Rice	578	326[d]	179.60	153.40	26.20	8,541
Sugar	5,568	5,910[e]	223.50	78.00	145.50	859,905
Eggs	2,265	2,265	511.40	387.50	123.90	280,633
Poultry	1,495	1,470	723.30	550.00	173.30	254,751
Pork	4,794	4,663	567.10	387.10	180.00	839,340
Beef and veal	6,804	6,684	680.00	388.20	191.80	1,950,391
Butter	1,247	1,145	1,874.40	708.50	1.165.90	1,334,956
Nonfat dry milk	n.a.	92	412.48	165.34	247.14	22,737
Whole dry milk	n.a.	113	863.10	443.12	419.98	47,458
Cheese	1,855	1,746	865.00	632.50	232.50	405,945
Olive oil	353	334	806.20	698.40	107.80	36,005

Subtotal					6,878,932
Less corn & sorghum	12,844	90.10	56.30	33.80	434,127
Excess consumer cost					6,444,805
Cost to taxpayers					
National budgets					5,517,000
FEOGA expenditures					2,433,000
Total cost					14,395,000

Source: G.R. Kruer and B. Bernston, "Cost of the Common Agricultural Policy to the European Economic Community," *Foreign Agricultural Trade of the United States* (October 1969), pp. 7 and 12.

[a]Production and quantity data are for 1966-67 except eggs (1967).

[b]Quantity included in estimate is generally domestic consumption (as food and industrial purposes) less imports; for corn and sorghum only imports are included.

[c]Price data are for 1967-68. Deficiency payments for durum wheat and olive oil are not included in excess consumer costs.

[d]Production in terms of paddy rise: quantity used in calculation is in terms of husked rice.

[e]Includes net imports from French overseas areas.

Table 1-3. Price Elasticities of Supply of Farm Products in Industrial Countries

Country and Commodity (1)	*Dependent Variable* (2)	*Time Period* (3)	*Short Run* (4)	*Intermediate Run* (5)	*Long Run* (6)
United Kingdom					
Crop products	0				0.44
Livestock Products	0				
Feed prices fixed absolutely					0.84
Feed prices fixed relatively					0.37
Agricultural Output	0				
Feed prices fixed absolutely					1.07
Feed prices fixed relatively					0.34
Cereals, all	0				0.9
Grain, all	A	1924-39	0.12		0.52
Grain, all	A	1946-58	0.17		0.30
Wheat	A	1924-39	0.33		0.46
Barley	A	1924-39	0.63		1.75
EEC					
Beef	N	1953-66	0.2 - 0.7		0.7 - 1.8
Livestock (except beef and dairy)	0	1953-66	0.33		2.6 - 4.2
Crop production	0	1953-66	0.37		0.5
Agricultural output	0	1953-66		0.2 - 0.5	
Australia					
Wheat	0	1947-65	0.18	0.82	3.82
Coarse grains	0	1947-65	0.21	0.81	1.54

Beef and veal	O	1947-65	0.16	–	–
Lamb	O	1947-65	0.21	0.94	3.20
Wool	O	1947-65	0.05	0.25	3.59
Dairy	O	1947-63	0.20	0.43	0.46
Netherlands					
Calf production	N	1955-65	0.43		
Broilers	O	1957-65	0.79		
Sows	N	1956-62	0.12		
United States					
Crops	O	1926-59	0.17		1.56
	A	1926-59	0.04		0.10
	Y	1926-59	0.15		1.50
Livestock	O	1926-59	0.38		2.90
	N	1926-59	0.12		1.80
	Y	1926-59	0.26		1.10
Total	O	1926-59	0.25		1.79
Farm Output	O	1952-61	0.46	0.84	2.96
Wheat	A	1909-32	0.48		0.93
Corn	A	1909-32	0.10		0.18
Cotton	A	1909-32	0.27		0.67
Hogs, Spring	N	1949-60	0.82	–	–
Hogs, Fall	N	1949-60	0.56	–	–

Sources: Arthur N. Harlow, *Factors Affecting the Price and Supply of Hogs*, USDA, Tech. Bul. No. 1274, Dec., 1962, pp. 39-40; Luther Tweeten, *Foundations of Farm Policy* (Lincoln, 1970), p. 244; Marc Nerlove, *Dynamics of Supply: Estimation of Farmers' Response to Price* (Baltimore, 1958), pp. 201, 202 and 204; Agricultural Economics Research Institute, *Supply and Demand, Imports and Exports of Selected Agricultural Products in the Netherlands: Forecasts for 1970 and 1975* (The Hague, 1967), pp. 175, 182 and 187; F.H. Gruen, Director of Project, *Long Term Projections of Agricultural Supply and Demand, Australia, 1965 and 1980*, Department of Economics, Monash University, May 1968, p. 178; Institute for Research in Agricultural Economics, Oxford University, *United Kingdom: Projected Level of Demand, Supply, and Imports of Farm Products in 1965 and 1975*, USDA (Washington, D.C., 1962), ERS-Foreign-19, pp. 27-33; (George T. Jones), United Kingdom: *Projected Level of Demand, Supply and Imports of Agricultural Products, 1970, 1975 and 1980*, USDA (Washington, D.C., 1969), pp. 11-13; and George T. Jones, "The Response of the Supply of Agricultural Products in the United Kingdom to Price," *Farm Economist* 10 (1) (1962): 18.

Table 1-4. Producer Prices for Farm Products, 1968 or 1968-69 ($US per 100 kg.)

	Wheat	*Whole Milk*
$ 4 or less	Argentina	--
4-6	Canada	--
6-8	Denmark, UK, US	Denmark, Ireland, Australia[a]
8-10	Ireland, Greece, Sweden, Austria, Spain, Turkey, France, Netherlands	UK, Austria, France,[b] Belgium, Portugal, Spain Netherlands
10-12	Italy, Portugal, USSR	Germany, Italy, Sweden, Switzerland, US
12-14	--	Norway
Over $14	Finland, Japan, Norway, Switzerland	USSR
	Rice (Paddy)	
$ 6 or less	Thailand[b]	
6-8	UAR	
8-10		
10-12	Ceylon, US	
30 or more	Japan[c]	
	Beef Cattle	*Hogs*
$ 30 or less	Argentina[b]	
30-40	Denmark,[b] Yugoslavia	Argentina
40-50	Ireland,[b] UK,[b] Canada[b]	US, Canada, Denmark, UK, Ireland
50-60	US, Norway, Spain	Austria, Spain
60-70	Belgium, France, Germany, Sweden, Switzerland	Germany, Netherlands, Italy, Norway, Greece, Sweden
70-80	Italy	Belgium, Switzerland, France
80-130	--	--
130 or more	USSR	USSR
	Butter	
$100 or less	Australia, Denmark, UK	
100-120	Ireland	
120-140	Sweden, Canada[b]	
140-160	US,[b] Netherlands	
160-180	Germany[b]	
180-200	Belgium	
200-280		
280 or more	Switzerland	

Sources: FAO, *Production Yearbook, 1969* (Vol. 23); International Wheat Council, *Review of the World Grains Situation, 1968-69* and ECE/FAO, *Prices of Agricultural Products and Fertilizers in Europe, 1968-69.*

[a]1967 or 1967-68 price.

[b]Wholesale prices.

[c]Husked rice price of $38.30; converted to paddy price by multiplying by 0.79.

industrial countries. The food provided as aid is output that cannot be sold at existing price support levels and is thus a problem to the area that has generated the excess output. If domestic farm prices were at world market levels, surplus disposal would not be a problem and the offers of food aid would be reduced to minimal levels. In any case, such a situation would only be an extension of recent trends that have seen substantial declines in the volume of food since the mid 1960s.

FREE TRADE AND THE DISTRIBUTION OF CONSUMPTION

Of the world's 3.6 billion population almost one billion live in industrial countries in which the prices consumers pay for food have been increased to a significant degree by the protection of agriculture. The extent of the excess costs imposed on consumers varies significantly from country to country, with the highest rates of consumer exploitation occurring in the USSR, Japan, and the EEC, and the lowest in Ireland and the United Kingdom. The United States, Canada, Australia, and New Zealand treat their consumers with some degree of consideration, though in the United States the taxpayer is shown rather less concern.

The price elasticity of demand for grain products for human use in the industrial countries is low and except for some of the lowest per capita income countries, a reduction in grain prices would have little effect on per capita grain consumption. But for other farm products, especially meat, the price elasticity has a substantial magnitude in the industrial countries. Regier and Goolsby have estimated that the price elasticity of demand for meat is –0.6.[8] This is an estimate for the world as a whole, but appears to be approximately accurate for the industrial countries. Further expansion of meat production would require an increase in the amount of grain per unit of meat output, as the importance of grain-fed livestock would account for a larger fraction of the world's total livestock output.

Thus the reduction in meat prices that would result from free trade in agricultural products would increase the fraction of the world's grain supply that would be used as livestock feed. The net result would be that a larger fraction of the world's grain production would be consumed in the industrial countries. Whether this change would have an adverse effect upon the amount of grain available to the developing countries would depend upon the rate of increase in grain production in the developing countries and the extent of offsetting declines in grain production in the industrial countries due to lower grain prices in Europe if there were free trade.

The various projections made in the last few years by the OECD, FAO, and the USDA have all indicated that by 1980 or 1985 the probable world supply of all grains would exceed demand by a substantial amount *if present agricultural policies are continued.* In other words, these projections are based upon approximately the current degree of protection of agriculture and current relative prices of farm products in the industrial countries. But if the real prices of meat fell by 20 percent (made possible by reducing the cost of feed in the industrial countries) grain consumption by livestock would increase by about 35 million tons over the estimates made by Regier and Goolsby. This estimate does not include any changes that might occur in the central plan economies.

FREE TRADE AND THE LOCATION OF FARM PRODUCTION

In the intermediate run–say up to five years–a move to free trade in farm products would result in a reduction in grain production in Europe and Japan and increases in the United States, Canada, Oceania, and Argentina. As I have argued elsewhere, I believe that free trade would result in about a 10 percent increase in world market prices for the grains.[9] Food aid disposals of wheat have about offset the effects of high support prices in Western Europe in expanding wheat production.

While the United States has made substantial payments to wheat producers, it is probable that wheat output has been held at a level not in excess of what it would have been in the absence of the acreage limitations and subsidies. Canada and Australia have each subsidized wheat production, apparently by about 10 percent. But in both countries some effort has been made in recent years to reduce output, and both countries, especially Canada, have accumulated wheat stocks. Argentina, on the other hand, has imposed a substantial tax upon their wheat output through an explicit export tax and, more recently, by manipulation of the exchange rate. Except for a small fraction of the wheat that moves in international trade, the prospect is that wheat will sell at approximately its feed value. It is almost certain that this would be the case under free trade.

In recent years feed grain prices have been adversely affected by expansion of grain production in Western Europe, by the subsidized feeding of wheat also in Western Europe, and by restrictions on feed grain use in Europe due to high grain and livestock prices. These adverse consequences have been partially offset by pricing policies in Argentina that have restricted production and by some small effect of the U.S. feed grain program on output. If grain prices were at world market levels in Western Europe, grain production would decline but it is probable that other types of feed output would increase. On balance, one might expect about a 10 percent increase in feed grain prices, but this would be offset by some decline in wheat prices if food aid shipments were sharply reduced.

In terms of the basic soil and climatic conditions, the United States and Argentina are in better positions to take advantage of the potential expansion of feed grain demand than either Canada or Australia. Canada's major grain area is relatively too dry to be able to compete with corn production in the United States and Argentina and it apparently lacks sufficient warmth and length of growing season to be a major producer of grain sorghums. Thus unless Canada can reduce its costs of producing wheat so that wheat can compete with feed grains, it may be largely restricted to the market for high quality milling wheat. Australia can probably produce wheat at a price that is competitive with feed grains.

There is no particular reason to expect much change in the location of meat production. Europe should be competitive under free trade. Feed requirements for pork production are apparently lower in much of Western Europe than in the United States. While one could anticipate some change as feed grains became cheaper, it is likely that somewhat lower labor costs would be sufficient to offset the higher grain prices due to transportation costs. Recent changes in ocean transport costs for bulk commodities is clearly an asset to both Western Europe and Japan so far as the maintenance of a livestock economy is concerned.

There would be some shift in dairy production away from the high labor costs of North America. Neither the United States nor Canada appear to be able to compete with Oceania or parts of Western Europe in the production of manufactured dairy products such as cheese and butter. In both countries butter prices have been, until quite recently, about double world prices, and for other manufactured products at least 50 percent higher. Even under such encouragement milk production has not been increasing. However, the output potential of New Zealand and Australia is so small compared to use in the industrial countries that free trade in manufactured dairy products would result in a very substantial increase in world market prices. With free trade among all the industrial countries there would be some reduction in output in North America and parts of Western Europe, but the substantial increase in import prices of dairy products would probably be such as to maintain significant production of such products even in what are now the high cost areas.

FREE TRADE AND THE DEVELOPING COUNTRIES

So far I have primarily considered the changes in the level and location of production in the developing countries. It is time now to consider in some detail what changes might occur in the developing countries if there were something approximating free trade in both farm products and inputs used in farm production. Unfortunately I have relatively little knowledge of the extent of trade barriers to the importation of inputs used in agricultural production. In so many of the developing countries such imports are subject to licensing, often generally imposed because of the lack of convertibility of the currency.

The Economic Research Service of the USDA[10] has described the recent situation with respect to trade in farm inputs in the Far East as follows.

> Total imports of farm inputs by all developing countries of the Far East except communist countries range between $550 million and

> $650 million annually. Fertilizer imports increased from $125 million in 1964 to $335 million in 1968 but have since declined. Farm supplies and equipment received high priority but the shortage of foreign exchange severely restricts the supply of tractors, irrigation equipment, and certain types of fertilizer.

The developing countries, especially those of South Asia, have provided substantially increased quantities of critical farm inputs in recent years. It is also probable that the prices have been more nearly in line with import costs in recent years than during the early part of the 1960s. A study of protection of the Indian production of nitrogen fertilizers indicated that during 1961-63 that the nominal tariff (difference between domestic and import prices) ranged from 34 to more than 70 percent; the effective protection of Indian production of nitrogen varied from 75 to more than 400 percent.[11] However, by the late 1960s the prices paid by Indian farmers for nitrogen fertilizers had declined to about the U.S. level.

A review of the FAO data on fertilizer prices paid by farmers in the developing countries reveals instances of significant subsidies (in Libya, Mali, Dahomey, Pakistan, for example). There are countries in which fertilizer prices are substantially higher than in the United States or Japan but I do not know if the differences reflect high costs of transport and marketing or protection of a local and inefficient fertilizer industry.

In 1964 I wrote the following.[12]

> The protection given agriculture in the industrial countries restricts exports from the less developed countries in one or both of two ways–increasing output and reducing consumption. Only in the United Kingdom have the consumption effects been largely eliminated through use of deficiency payments. If the increase in prices received by producers average 20 to 25 percent and if the increase in prices paid by consumers 15 to 25 percent, even very low elasticities of supply and demand will result in substantial contraction in the demand for exports of less developed regions. If supply elasticities are as low as 0.15 and demand elasticities 0.2, the effect on the value of agricultural imports of the industrial countries would be as much as $3.5-4.5 billion. Some of the increased import demand would be met by developed countries such as Canada and Australia. But if the increase in LDC exports were to be only half that indicated, or about $2 billion, the importance is very great when compared with total LDC exports of agricultural products of approximately $12 billion.

If I were to make a similar calculation at this time, I would obviously opt for a substantially higher elasticity of supply of farm products in the industrial nations. Based on the evidence assembled in Table 1-3, I doubt if the elasticity of supply should be lower than 0.5. This change in assumption would increase the estimated increase in imports of farm products of the industrial countries to perhaps $8 billion. But other assumptions would have to be changed as well, and the most important one is that the developing countries would realize half of the increase in exports. Almost certainly the United States would now obtain a higher fraction of the increase in exports than I had assumed at that time and the same would undoubtedly be true of Australia and perhaps also of Canada.

One factor not taken into account in the above quotation is the extent to which a number of developing countries have price supports for certain key agricultural products–supports that hold the prices above world market levels. To some degree the price supports above world market levels are offset by overvalued currencies. But even so a number of developing countries have producer prices for grains that must fall substantially before these countries can compete effectively in international markets without the use of export subsidies. In four countries that have had considerable expansion of wheat production due to the introduction of high yielding varieties–Mexico, India, Pakistan and Turkey–the wholesale price in 1969 ranged from a low of $101 per ton in Pakistan to a high of $127 per ton in Mexico.[13] In the same year Australian wheat was landed in the U.K. at $66 per ton. Quality problems are also involved for wheat.[e]

In some countries the same situation prevails with respect to rice. In 1969 the wholesale price of rice in Pakistan was $255 per ton compared to the export price received by Thailand of $184.[15] India, however, has maintained the internal price below world market prices and at times by as much as one-fourth. The Philippines have kept their wholesale prices near world market levels.

Another point that needs to be made is that not all the agricultural exports from the developing countries are subjected to major degrees of protection in the industrial countries. According to an FAO tabulation of LDC exports to the rest of the world, cotton accounted for approximately one-tenth

[e]Rojko and Mackie[14] estimate that if the Green Revolution is accelerated so that wheat production in the less developed regions reaches 105 million tons in 1980 rather than 84 million tons that would be projected on the basis of recent growth rates, South Asia would shift from being a net importer of wheat to a net export of seven million tons. But they add

> However, several important developments would be necessary for this shift to occur:
>
> (1) Wheat produced in South Asia (mainly India and Pakistan) would have to be of a quality acceptable in international trade. For the most part, this region produces soft wheat of a quality not suited to present baking technology.
>
> (2) Substantial export subsidies would be needed for South Asia to sell wheat at international price levels, because South Asia's producer prices would be relatively high compared with the world trade price. This subsidy cost could be between $300 and $400 million.

of such exports in 1962-64.[16] The major restraint on the growth of exports of cotton is competition from synthetics and not trade barriers. Oilseeds and their products made up about the same proportion of LDC agricultural exports, and trade barriers, other than preferential arrangements, are not nearly as severe as on grains. Rubber is also an important LDC export, accounting for about 10 percent of the total, and here also the major difficulty is competition with synthetic rubber rather than trade barriers. The situation with respect to bananas (3 percent of LDC exports) and coffee, tea, and cocoa beans (30 percent) is mixed, with a number of countries permitting free or nearly free entry while other countries impose quotas or have high tariffs or internal taxes. In general the United States has the freest entry while the USSR has the most restrictive for this group of farm products.

Thus more than half the 1962-64 agricultural exports from LDCs to the rest of the world were not subject to major trade restraints due to the desire to protect domestic production in the industrial countries. While there would be some increase in exports by reducing trade barriers—whether direct ones or indirect ones through high internal prices—true free trade would probably have only modest effects on exports for this group of products. Major gains in exports would occur in sugar, which accounted for one-fourth of total exports to the rest of the world. Annual sugar exports from developing countries might increase by $500 to $800 million. The other major products that would be affected by achievement of free trade would be the grains, meats, wool, and tobacco.

I do not have strong grounds for revising the earlier estimate that free trade would increase LDC agricultural exports to the rest of the world by about $2 billion annually.[f] Sugar might account for 35 to 40 percent of the increase. To realize the remaining increase of about $1.2 billion would require substantial output expansion in the developing countries. In several cases the output expansion would be in response to significantly lower producer prices than now prevail, unless substantial export subsidies are utilized and accepted by the industrial countries.

An annual increase of $2 billion in LDC agricultural exports is not an insignificant increase when viewed from the standpoint of the LDCs. The method of estimating the increase in exports did not reflect any gain in the value of exports due to a change in terms of trade. Other things being equal, there should be some improvement in the terms of trade for the LDC agricultural exports. I have estimated that the increase in world prices for agricultural products would be relatively modest as a result of free trade and the modification of domestic farm policies.[18] However, an increase of 5 to 10 percent in

---

[f]Data in *A World Price Equilibrium Model* indicate that LDC net farm exports to the rest of the world might increase by $4 billion as of 1980 due to free trade. About half the difference is due to projected rice imports by the centrally planned economies; much of the remainder represents the LDC share in expanded international trade in food products between 1970 and 1980.[17]

world market prices would be reflected not only in the value of the increased exports but on the quantity exported before. A 5 percent increase in real prices would add something like $600 million to the value of LDC exports.

The long run gain in LDC exports due to free trade could be much greater than indicated above. With the present domestic farm and trade policies of the industrial nations, an LDC does not have much incentive to invest in new or different farm products for the export market. With present farm and trade programs there can be no reasonable certainty that a given potential export market can ever be realized. The industrial countries have shown considerable ingenuity in closing out some markets through redefining quotas or tariffs or offering preferential arrangements to others, or by application of sanitary or health regulations, or by subsidizing domestic production to compete with imports.

If there were free trade in both farm outputs and inputs, the developing countries would be in a much better position to make the investments and arrangements required to meet potential export demands than is now the case. The current trade and farm policies of the industrial countries clearly inhibit the developing countries from shifting resources to meet prospective demands in the industrial areas. A decision made in Brussels or London or Washington can overnight destroy a potential export market.

ADVANTAGES OF FREE TRADE

It cannot be said that one of the advantages of free trade in farm products and farm inputs would be an increase in the world's supply of food. In the short and intermediate run it is more probable that the aggregate quantity of food would decline. Furthermore, free trade would probably result in a somewhat larger fraction of the world's available supply of food's being consumed in the industrial countries that now have very high consumer prices. The major readjustment in consumption would be the added amount of grains that would be converted into livestock products. There would be a decline in the amount of food supplied to the developing countries by the industrial countries under noncommercial terms since the pressure to dispose of unwanted surpluses would disappear.

Are these reasons why there should not be free trade in farm products? I think the answer to that question is clearly in the negative. All the projections made by FAO, OECD, and the USDA indicate that the world's capacity to produce grain will exceed the world's demand for grain for the foreseeable future at approximately the current level of prices. Part of that grain is being produced in the wrong places and some areas are being discouraged from expanding production because of the prospects of low grain prices for years to come. World free trade would greatly reduce the risk that faces the developing countries if the full potentials for expanding grain production are fully realized in this decade.

With present farm and trade policies of the industrial countries, the realization of wheat production of 105 million tons in the developing countries by 1980 (indicated as a possibility by Rojko and Mackie) might constitute a near disaster for South Asia rather than a source of increased well being. Under these assumptions South Asia would shift from being a significant net importer to a net exporter at a level of seven million tons of wheat. The potential export market would almost certainly not be available. These countries could not compete with the treasuries of the EEC or the United States or Canada and Australia for the remaining export markets for wheat.

True, some of the problems faced by the developing countries of South Asia would be of their own making if they maintained their domestic wheat prices at recent levels in the face of rapid growth in wheat output. But suppose the expansion in wheat production to the 105 million ton level could be achieved at the world price of wheat that would prevail if there were free trade and that seven million tons were available for export? Either the South Asia developing countries would have to permit wheat prices in their own markets to fall to the level that would produce an output just equal to the self-sufficiency level or they would have to engage in large scale export subsidies. Either solution would be somewhat unsatisfactory!

Obviously I do not know if the scenario as outlined by Rojko and Mackie has any possibility of being realized, but it is clear that the present farm and trade policies of the industrial countries, if such possibilities were realized, would force all the adjustments upon the developing countries. Free trade would permit an accommodation to such good fortune in a way that would benefit the developing countries of South Asia with only a very modest impingement upon the interests of grain farmers in the industrial countries. And some of the losses of grain farmers in the industrial countries would be offset by gains realized by livestock farmers.

The major advantage of free trade in farm products, for both industrial and developing countries, is the standard economic argument: namely that under free trade nations can make efficient use of their resources. In several cases the current international prices of farm products do not provide a satisfactory guide for the efficient allocation of resources. Nor do the international markets for farm products—buffeted as they are by variable levies, import quotas, export subsidies, and other regulations—provide any reasonable degree of certainty that an available export surplus can be disposed of under satisfactory conditions.

If present policy trends continue, the developing countries may well find themselves by the end of the decade with as many distortions in resource use in agriculture as the industrial countries now have. Given the models that they have available to them, and the major difficulties that they confront in taking advantage of the possibilities of either exporting or importing farm products, such an outcome should surprise no one.

Chapter Two

The Impact of U.S. Agricultural Policies on Trade of the Developing Countries

Martin E. Abel

INTRODUCTION: THE ROLE OF U.S. TRADE POLICIES

We are concerned here with the interactions of agricultural developments in the developing countries and in the United States. It is difficult to deal with such a broad topic in the space of one relatively short chapter. I have chosen, therefore, to focus my remarks on developments in the production, consumption, and trade of a set of commodities that both the developing countries and the United States produce and in which the developing countries have a significant export interest. Emphasis will be on the role of U.S. agricultural trade policies as they affect the world market potential for these products.

We are not concerned with a group of noncompetitive commodities–those produced and exported by the developing countries and imported but not produced by the United States; these are mainly tropical products such as coffee, cocoa, tea, bananas, spices, etc. While the value of noncompetitive agricultural imports by the United States is fairly large (amounting to $2.1 billion in fiscal year 1971 or 37 percent of total U.S. agricultural imports), there are few trade issues involved. Unlike many other developed countries, the United States does not subject imports of noncompetitive

Note: This paper builds on an earlier one, "The Developing Countries and United States Agriculture," prepared for the Atlantic Council of the United States study, "U.S. Agriculture in a World Context."

I would like to thank a number of persons for helpful comments and suggestions during the writing of this paper; namely, Willard W. Cochrane, Vernon W. Ruttan, James P. Houck, W.B. Sundquist, Lauren Soth, and P.G.H. Barter.

commodities to significant levels of tariff and nontariff protection, or to domestic excise taxes.[a]

The major competitive commodities that have been or are likely to be in the trade picture for both the United States and the developing countries are grains, oilseeds and products, cotton, fruits and vegetables, sugar, tobacco, and meats. Our concern is not just with the raw forms of these products, but also with semiprocessed and processed products based on them. For many agricultural products, the degree of trade protection employed by the United States is higher for processed than for raw products. This means that present trading practices by the United States discourage processing of agricultural products in the developing countries. This is an important trade issue of our time.

There is one large topic in the trade area—generalized trade preferences for the developing countries granted by the developed countries—that is not covered in this chapter. This has been an important item of discussion for some time and was a major item at the UNCTAD II conference in New Delhi in 1968. It was generally agreed that the question should receive serious study and efforts should be made to move toward a general system of trade preferences by the developed countries for products from the less developed countries. The argument for this kind of reverse discrimination for a very broad range of commodities can be viewed more as a foreign aid issue than one of trade. The main concern is with the transfer of resources from rich to poor nations, which can be done in many ways. Generalized trade preferences is one such way. Since we consider this topic to fall more appropriately in the foreign aid rather than in the trade field, we will not discuss the topic here.

However, foreign aid prospects are relevant to our discussion in one important sense: the less foreign aid available to the developing countries, the more pressure there is for them to increase their export earnings. The developing countries are keenly interested in increasing their access to foreign exchange in order to pay for needed capital imports and service past debts. Basically there are four ways by which this can be done: (1) increase the volume of economic aid and private capital transfers from the rich to the poor nations; (2) relieve the developing countries of part of their debt burden; (3) increase commercial exports from the developing to the developed countries; and (4) follow policies of import substitution that make the developing countries less dependent on imports.

The prospects for significant increases in flows of foreign aid and private capital to the developing countries in the 1970s are not bright. The Pearson Commission Report[1] refers to a sense of "weariness" in the richer countries toward foreign aid.

---

[a]There is one exception to this statement. Some of the tariffs applied to processed forms of noncompetitive agricultural products do discriminate against the processing of these products being done by the less developed exporters.

> The signs are not propitious. In the last years of [the 1960s], the volume of foreign official aid has been stagnant. At no time during this period has it kept pace with the growth of national product in the wealthy nations. In fact, the commitments by the United States, which has been much the largest provider of aid funds, are declining. There, and in some other developed countries, we have encountered a spirit of disenchantment.

With no increase in the annual flow of foreign aid in sight, and a decline being possible, the annual flow of *net* aid from the developed to the developing countries will decline. This is so because the levels of interest and principal repayments on old debts are scheduled to grow rapidly. Let us illustrate how critical this problem is likely to become with the following data from the Pearson Commission Report:

Debt Service as Percentage of Gross Lending, 1965-67 and 1977

	Africa	*Europe*	*East Asia*	*South Asia and Middle East*	*Latin America*
1965-67	73	92	52	40	87
1977 with gross flow of new lending unchanged	121	109	134	97	130

These debt figures refer to the flow of supplier's credits, private and governmental loans, and loans of international agencies, but exclude grants or direct private investment. Clearly, the debt burden is rising and is projected to equal or exceed gross foreign aid lending in all developing nations of the world by the end of the 1970s. *Thus, the 1970s, rather than being the "N-th Development Decade," could very well be the "Decade of Debt Crisis."*

There are two ways out of this problem, assuming the level of gross aid cannot be increased. One is to provide debt relief to the developing countries either through cancellation or rescheduling of old debts. This has the effect of increasing the flow of net aid. This has been done in the past and it is inevitable that more of it will be done in the future. But if the donor nations are already in an "owly" mood with respect to foreign aid, the prospects of the developing countries' not being able to meet their debt obligations will make them even more parsimonious.

The other alternative is to facilitate a larger and growing volume of exports from the developing to the developed countries. While there is a great deal that would have to be done by both groups of countries to bring this about (much more than is possible to discuss here) we will focus on what the United States could do to increase the flow of exports from the developing countries, particularly the flow of agricultural products based primarily on agricultural raw materials.

Further import substitution, particularly for nonagricultural products, does not represent a viable alternative. Many developing countries have already pushed such policies to the point where long term economic growth and development have been adversely affected.[2] However, there are ample opportunities for developing countries to increase their agricultural production in an efficient manner and reduce somewhat their dependence on agricultural imports. Increased production can be accomplished by a shift in agricultural growth based on traditional resource use to one that is science (technology) based. This, of course, requires the development of agricultural research institutions capable of producing a steady stream of technologies that are economically viable in the developing countries.

PRODUCTION AND TRADE IN THE DEVELOPING COUNTRIES

The purpose of this section is to indicate (1) the importance of grains, oilseeds and products, cotton, sugar, fruits and vegetables, meats, and tobacco in world trade; (2) the importance of these commodities in the total value of exports from the developing countries; (3) the extent to which world trade in them is likely to expand; and (4) the position the United States occupies in world markets as either an exporter or importer of these commodities. From such a perspective we can get a rough idea of the importance of U.S. trade and trade policies to the export interests of the developing countries.

Grains

We are concerned here with wheat, rice, and coarse grains. In 1965, four developing countries—Burma, Cambodia, Thailand, and Argentina—depended on grain exports for 20 percent or more of their total export earnings; in Burma and Cambodia, rice accounted for over 50 percent of export earnings.[3] Thus, the number of developing countries which depend heavily on grain exports is small. On the other hand, there are a large number which have become or could become grain exporters.

Since about 1965 there has been a marked increase in grain production in a number of developing countries, particularly in wheat and rice. The basis for this expansion has been the development and adoption of new, higher yielding varieties of grain, and favorable grain prices. At the same time, excess production capacity continues to exist in the developed, grain exporting countries, while some major developed grain importing countries like the EC continue to increase their output. As a result there has been a downward pressure on world grain prices in recent years. But one should view these price developments in a longer term context. World grain prices at the end of the decade of the 1960s were at about the same level as at the beginning of that decade. Yet wide swings in prices occurred during this period.

Let's look at rice, which of all the grains exhibited the widest price swings in the 1960s. In 1961 the f.o.b. Bangkok export price of Thai white rice 100 percent was about $135 per metric ton. World rice prices rose sharply in the 1966-68 period; the price for the same grade of rice reached a peak of $250 per ton in October 1967. But by April 1971 the price had fallen to $120 per ton.[4] There was a similar, though less pronounced swing in wheat prices. The Canadian export price for wheat averaged $64 per metric ton during 1959-1961. Export prices reached a high of $71 per ton in 1966 and were back down to $64 per ton in 1969.[5]

There were two important factors in the world grain picture—one transitory and one permanent—that gave rise to the roller coaster behavior of grain prices, and both operated in the developing countries. The transitory element in the picture consisted of two parts: (1) the unprecedented droughts in South Asia during the 1965-66 and 1966-67 crop years, which required record levels of food aid; and (2) the sharp increases in rice imports by South Vietnam in 1966 and 1967, which put considerable pressure on world rice prices.

The more permanent aspect of the grain situation in the developing countries can also be looked at in two parts. During the 1950s and the first half of the 1960s, grain production per capita in the developing countries was increasing at a modest rate, but not fast enough to keep pace with the rate of growth in demand.[6] Consequently, grain imports by the less developed countries increased steadily. Starting in about 1965, the new high yielding varieties of wheat and rice began to be used in many developing countries. And, by the end of the decade, several countries had experienced sharp increases in production of these crops, reducing the need for imports and in some cases contributing to export supplies. In a number of countries significant increases in the production of maize, sorghum, and millets were also experienced.

At the same time, the major developed grain exporting countries continue to have more grain production capacity than can be utilized at current domestic and world prices. For example, in the late 1960s and early 1970s, wheat production in the United States, Canada, and Australia was sharply curtailed in response to sagging exports and growing stocks. It is generally agreed that rapid technological change in grain production in many developing countries and surplus production potential in the developed grain exporting countries will continue in the 1970s.

World trade in coarse grains grew at a fairly rapid rate in the 1950s and 1960s because of the rapid rates of economic growth and growth in the demand for livestock products in the developed countries. These forces for growth in the trade of coarse grains can also be expected to continue in the future.

What are the trade prospects in grain for the coming decade? A recent study by the Economic Research Service of the U.S. Department of Agriculture projects world grain production, consumption, and trade to 1980.[7] Trade data for the 1964-66 period and projections to 1980 are summarized in Table 2-1. The study concludes that

> *For wheat:*
>
> Import demand will be sluggish in the developed area but potentially strong in the LDCs if concessional terms of trade are available. Increased feed use of wheat would reduce downward pressures on prices. Some increase in the share of the world market would be possible for LDC exporters, largely Argentina. Accelerated wheat production in the LDCs could lead to an improved export earnings position if major developed exporters moderated the price effect by withdrawing exportable supplies from the world market. Subsidy costs and quality factors could offset potential export earnings in South Asia.
>
> *For rice:*
>
> The Green Revolution would result in lower world import demand, a demand centered in the LDCs. Import demand in the developed area is expected to rise moderately but the increase is small relative to potential supplies for export—from both developed and less developed exporters. Consequently, continued downward pressure on prices is expected. Since most of the market for the LDC exporters is within the LDCs, prospects for export earnings from rice are poor, particularly under accelerated growth in rice production in the importing LDCs.
>
> *For coarse grains:*
>
> Import demand in developed areas, particularly Japan, is expected to be strong. Given concessional terms of trade, import demand of the LDCs could increase sharply as a result of a rapidly expanding livestock industry in these countries. Lower internal grain prices in developed importing areas, particularly the EC, could give trade an additional boost. Some LDC exporters might not fully share in the expansion because their port facilities are limited in handling large cargo vessels. On the other hand, maintenance of very high internal prices through limited access could lead to self-sufficiency in total grains in the EC, thereby lowering export prospects.

Thus the prospects for growth of grain exports from the developing countries are mixed. For wheat and rice especially, much hinges on the policies followed by the developed grain exporting countries. We will return to this subject in a later section with specific reference to the United States.

Table 2-1. World Trade in Wheat, Rice, and Coarse Grains, 1964-66—Average and Projections to 1980

Region	Wheat			Coarse Grains			Rice		
	1964-66	*1980A*[a]	*1980B*[b]	*1964-66*	*1980A*[a]	*1980B*[b]	*1964-66*	*1980A*[a]	*1980B*[b]
	million metric tons						1,000 metric tons		
United States	21.2	19.3	14.8	21.8	30.0	21.0	1,527	2,063	147
Canada	13.8	11.9	8.7	.7	1.1	.4	–45	–64	–66
Central Am. & Mexico	–1.0	–2.3	–2.1	.7	–2.2	–.7	–367	–503	–394
E. South America	–3.0	–4.9	–5.0	.2	1.0	3.0	382	158	379
W. South America	–1.2	–3.4	–3.5	–.1	–1.2	–1.2	–71	–22	100
Argentina	5.1	5.2	6.2	5.2	7.0	8.4	29	43	81
N. Africa	–3.6	–8.9	–9.6	.1	–1.0	–.4	341	538	662
E. Africa	–.3	–.7	–.7	–.1	1.2	3.3	–177	–454	–437
W. Africa	–.6	–1.5	–1.6	.1	–2.8	–2.2	–428	–791	–637
So. Africa, Rep. of	–.4	–.5	–.5	.5	3.9	3.4	–73	–132	–137
W. Asia	–1.9	–5.0	–4.3	–.5	–2.8	–2.6	–354	–575	–464
S. Asia	–9.3	–2.4	7.1	–1.3	–2.8	–2.4	–1,137	–770	–117
S.E. Asia	–.2	–.4	–.4	1.3	1.6	2.9	2,419	2,480	2,791
E. Asia & Pacific Is.	–2.1	–4.2	–4.4	–.3	–3.7	–1.3	–1,728	–1,627	–1,046
Australia & New Zealand	6.3	7.8	6.8	.7	2.8	2.7	71	158	140
Eastern Europe	–5.7	–1.8	–1.8	–.4	1.1	1.0	–290	–354	–367
USSR	–2.4	4.6	4.6	.3	.7	.6	–247	–266	–287
Communist Asia	–5.7	–6.1	–6.1	.1	–.3	–.4	903	768	574
Japan	–3.6	–6.5	–6.5	–6.0	–16.7	–17.2	–750	–170	–365
E.C.	1.3	3.9	2.4	–11.9	–10.0	–9.3	–199	–302	–336
United Kingdom	–4.3	–4.5	–4.6	–3.5	–1.7	–2.9	–109	–134	–140
Other Western Europe	–1.3	.5	.6	–5.6	–5.1	–6.2	–29	–40	–82

Source: Rojko, Urban, and Naive, *op. cit.*

[a]Assumes a continuation of present food and fiber policies, allowing for moderate gains in productivity in the less developed countries.

[b]Assumes that agricultural productivity and economic growth in the less developed countries would be higher than projected under 1980A.

Oilseeds and Products[8]

Oilseeds and products are important export crops for many developing countries. In 1965, exports of oilseeds, oil nuts, and animal and vegetable oils accounted for more than 20 percent of export earnings in fifteen countries. In seven of these countries these products accounted for more than 50 percent of total export earnings.

World prices of various oilseeds and vegetable oils have followed generally similar patterns since World War II. Prices were relatively high in the early 1950s, declined from about 1951-52 until the early 1960s, and exhibited some upward movement in the mid and late 1960s.

On the other hand, there has been rather continuous growth in the value of world trade in oilseeds and vegetable oils. Between 1951 and 1965 world trade in oilseeds and oil nuts increased from 5.0 to 12.2 million tons. Trade in vegetable oils went from 1.8 to 3.9 million tons during the same period. Most of this growth has been in oilseeds and vegetable oils produced in the temperate zone developed countries; the exports from tropical less developed countries have not fared that well. Within the category of oilseeds and oil nuts, soybeans, cottonseed, rape and mustard seed, and sesame seed had the most rapid rate of increase in trade. On the other hand, ground nuts, palm and palm kernel, and copra—commodities important to the developing countries—had either no growth or suffered some decline in world trade. A similar pattern existed for vegetable oils, although the picture was a little less pessimistic for the developing countries as there was a modest increase in exports of ground nut and coconut oil while exports of palm oil and palm kernel oil declined or remained about constant.

Looking to the future (1980),[9] production of major oilseeds is expected to increase steadily. In terms of oil equivalent, world production is expected to grow by 3.5 percent a year through 1980. A slightly faster rate of growth is expected in the developed than in the developing countries. For vegetable oils, prices are expected to decline by as much as 20 percent. Of equal importance to many developing countries, growth in their domestic consumption will hold down exportable supplies. On the other hand, import demands for oil cake, particularly in the developed countries, are expected to increase at a substantial rate. Since production of oil cake in the developing countries will increase faster than domestic demands, exportable supplies of oil cake should increase.

Cotton[10]

Cotton is another agricultural commodity which is a major earner of foreign exchange for a number of developing countries, and a potential earner of foreign exchange in a number of other less developed countries. In 1966, fifteen developing countries earned more than 10 percent of their total export earnings from lint cotton. Of these, cotton accounted for more than 20 percent of total exports in eight countries, and for more than 50 percent of total exports in three countries (Table 2-2).

Table 2-2. Cotton Lint Exports as a Percentage of Total Merchandise Exports, Selected Countries, 1966

Country	*Percent*
Chad	77.2
United Arab Republic	55.0
Syria	51.6
Sudan	49.9
Nicaragua	41.5
Turkey	25.8
Uganda	22.9
Tanzania	20.9
Guatemala	19.2
Afghanistan	17.0
Mozambique	15.4
Central African Republic	14.6
Mexico	13.5
El Salvador	12.6
Peru	11.1
Cameroon	7.3
Pakistan	6.9
Greece	6.7
Brazil	6.4
USSR	4.2
Honduras	4.0
Paraguay	3.8
Togo	3.1
Iran	2.9
Angola	1.7
Kenya	1.4
United States	1.4
Costa Rica	1.4
Nigeria	1.2

Source: Richard S. Magleby and Edmond Missiaen, *World Demand for Cotton in 1980 with Emphasis on Trade by Less Developed Countries* FAER No. 000, ERS, USDA, January 1971.

A number of other countries depend heavily on cotton textiles for foreign exchange earnings. In 1968, cotton textiles accounted for 15 percent or more of total exports in four countries: Hong Kong, UAR, Portugal, and Pakistan (Table 2-3). The combined exports of lint cotton and cotton textiles accounted for about 75 percent of total exports from the UAR. The prospects for future world trade in lint cotton and cotton textiles are of significant interest to a large number of developing countries.

Table 2-3. Cotton Textile Exports as a Percentage of Total Merchandise Exports, Selected Countries, 1968

Country	*Percent*
Hong Kong	20.5
United Arab Republic	19.3
Portugal	15.4
Pakistan	15.3
Taiwan	8.1
India	7.2
South Korea	4.6
Israel	3.3
Japan	3.1
Greece	2.6
Poland	1.5
EC (total)	1.2
Turkey	1.0
United Kingdom	0.8
Mexico	0.7
United States	0.7

Source: Magleby and Missiaen, *op. cit.*

While cotton use has increased from 7.7 million metric tons in 1952 to 11.4 million metric tons in 1968, its share in total fibers used for textiles declined from 73 to 57 percent during the same period. This was the result of proportionately greater growth in the use of man-made fibers.

World prices of cotton declined sharply in the 1950s and continued to decline at a moderate rate in the 1960s. In 1952 the price of strict middling 1-1/16 in. cotton at Liverpool was about 38 cents a pound. By 1960 it was down to 30-1/2 cents a pound, and declined further to about 28 cents a pound for the 1970-71 crop year.

World cotton trade has grown steadily over the years in both volume and value, despite the decline in world cotton prices. The volume of total cotton exports (lint and textiles) went from 3.4 million tons in 1952 to 5.4 million tons in 1967 (Table 2-4). Textile exports had a faster rate of growth—from 0.8 to 1.6 million tons—than lint cotton, which went from 2.6 to 3.8 million tons. In 1967, world exports of lint cotton and cotton textiles were valued at $6.1 billion.

The developing countries are very interested in exporting cotton textiles rather than lint cotton because of the increased possibilities for earning foreign exchange and expanding domestic income and employment. The value of cotton textiles over the value of lint cotton ranges from over 1.5 times for yarn to 3 to 6 times for clothing exports.

The long term outlook for world cotton trade is reasonably favorable. While prices are expected to decline slightly in the 1970s, world cotton

Table 2-4. World Cotton Trade and Textile-Lint Mix, 1952-1967

Calendar Year	Exports			Share of Total		
	Textiles	Lint[a]	Total	Textiles	Lint	Total
Volume	*Thousand metric tons*			*Percent*		
1952	798	2,617	3,415	23	77	100
1953	795	2,681	3,476	23	77	100
1954	883	2,949	3,832	23	77	100
1955	843	2,838	3,681	23	77	100
1956	893	3,084	3,977	22	78	100
1957	960	3,395	4,355	22	78	100
1958	871	2,930	3,801	23	77	100
1959	1,045	3,325	4,370	24	76	100
1960	1,219	3,943	5,162	24	76	100
1961	1,133	3,729	4,862	23	77	100
1962	1,133	3,508	4,641	24	76	100
1963	1,168	3,705	4,873	24	76	100
1964	1,480[b]	3,890	5,370	24	76	100
1965	1,462[b]	3,778	5,240	28	72	100
1966	1,579[b]	3,917	5,496	29	71	100
1967	1,556[b]	3,813	5,369	29	71	100
Value	*Million dollars*			*Percent*		
1952-58	(not available)			(not available)		
1959	n.a.	1,891	n.a.	n.a.	n.a.	n.a.
1960	3,100	2,569	5,669	55	45	100
1961	3,020	2,362	5,382	56	44	100
1962	3,030	2,054	5,084	60	40	100
1963	3,190	2,257	5,447	59	41	100
1964	3,470	2,372	5,842	59	41	100
1965	3,600	2,295	5,895	61	39	100
1966	3,790	2,307	6,097	62	38	100
1967	3,815	2,238	6,053	63	37	100

Source: Magleby and Missiaen, *op. cit.*

[a]Volume data 1952-65 are USDA/FAS. Other figures and all lint value data are FAO.

[b]These data are more conclusive of clothing than previously.

production, consumption, and trade are expected to grow at a moderately rapid rate. Rojko and Mackie[11] conclude:

> The LDCs would increase their share of world cotton lint and textile exports by 1980, and the developed countries would increase their net imports. . . . The greatest changes for the LDCs are

projected for cotton textile trade. . . . net cotton textile imports of the developed [areas] should increase from a little over 100,000 tons in 1965-67 to almost 600,000 tons in 1980.

Sugar

The volume of world trade in sugar has grown steadily from a level of 10.5 million tons in 1951 to 18.5 million tons in 1965. On the other hand, world prices of sugar varied considerably during this same period (Table 2-5), giving rise to significant variation in the value of world trade.

In 1965, some fourteen countries[b] depended upon sugar for over 20 percent of their total export earnings. In eight of these countries[c] sugar accounted for over 50 percent of total export earnings. Sugar exports were valued at $2.6 billion or about 7.0 percent of world agricultural trade in 1965.

Regionally, Latin America, Australia, New Zealand, South Africa, Eastern Europe, and other East Asian countries accounted for 73 percent of world sugar exports in 1964. Latin America alone accounted for 45 percent of

Table 2-5. World Trade in Sugar, 1951-1965

Year	*Volume*	*Price per Metric ton*
	1000 metric tons	*U.S. dollars*
1951	10,542	116.1
1952	10,960	110.0
1953	12,728	97.4
1954	13,042	99.0
1955	14,177	95.1
1956	13,549	95.4
1957	14,791	116.4
1958	14,902	99.8
1959	14,174	94.5
1960	17,039	89.5
1961	19,902	92.7
1962	18,763	93.9
1963	17,255	135.7
1964	16,771	135.0
1965	18,476	102.4

Source: Arthur B. Mackie and J. Lawrence Blum, *World Trade in Selected Agricultural Commodities, 1951-65; Vol. IV–Sugar, Fruits, and Vegetables*, FAER No. 44, ERS, USDA, June 1968.

---

[b]Fiji, Mauritius, Reunion, Antigua, Barbados, Cuba, Dominican Republic, Guadeloupe, Guyana, British Honduras, Jamaica, Martinique, Philippines, and Taiwan.

[c]The first eight countries listed in footnote b.

world sugar exports. The major importers are the United States, Japan, Western Europe, and the USSR: they accounted for 65 percent of world imports of sugar. The United States is the second largest importer in this group, accounting for 20 percent of world sugar imports.

Most of the major, developed importers have followed high domestic price policies aimed at ensuring a high degree of self-sufficiency in sugar. While the world demand for sugar can be expected to grow at a modest rate, the future trade prospects depend heavily on future sugar policies in the developed countries. We will return to a more detailed discussion of this matter for the United States in a later section.

Fruits and Vegetables

As discussed earlier, we concentrate here on those fruits and vegetables that are produced in both the developed and developing countries. This eliminates from our discussion such important tropical fruits as bananas and pineapples.

In 1965 there were twenty developing countries in which exports of fruits and vegetables accounted for 20 percent or more of their total exports.[12] World trade in fruits and nuts increased from 6.1 million tons in 1951 to 15.2 million tons in 1965. During the same period, trade in vegetables went from 3.1 to 10.9 million metric tons. These commodities have experienced rapid growth in world trade and future trade prospects are also bright.

The major importers of fruits and vegetables are the United States, Western Europe, and Eastern Europe. These three areas accounted for 74 percent of world imports of fresh fruits and 71 percent of vegetable imports in 1964. Western Europe is by far the biggest importing region, accounting for 57 percent of total world imports of fruits and vegetables.

Meats

World trade in meats has increased rapidly. We will focus on trade in beef, since this is the meat that is generally of most interest to the developing countries. Between 1954 and 1969, total world exports of beef went up from 530,000 to 1,857,902 tons, or by 350 percent (Table 2-6).

Among the developing regions of the world, beef exports expanded most rapidly in Central and South America. Exports from Central America increased eighteen-fold; from Argentina nearly four-fold; from Uruguay by over two-fold; and from other South American countries by 120-fold. Africa is the only other developing region of the world where beef exports increased significantly: from 20,000 tons in 1954 to 45,596 tons in 1969. In value terms, beef exports in 1969 from Central America, South America, and Africa were $97, $333, and $30 million, respectively.

Europe and the United States are the major beef importers. Imports into Europe increased from 380,000 tons in 1954 to 1,203,952 tons in 1969, or

Table 2-6. World Trade in Beef, Selected Regions and Years

Region	Exports		Imports	
	1954	1969	1954	1969
	(metric tons)			
Europe	167,000	695,823	380,000	1,203,952
Canada	8,400	21,522	1,500	49,252
U.S.	5,900	7,609	7,800	470,160
Central America	5,700	100,925	7,700	18,773
South America	–	–	15,000	26,362[a]
Argentina	105,200	404,570		
Uruguay	45,100	106,461		
Other So. Am.	700	84,175		
Asia	–	1,844	11,000	74,342
Africa	20,000	45,596	18,000	43,439
Oceania	175,000	389,377	2,000	3,544[a]
World	530,000	1,857,902	500,000	1,887,120

Source: *FAO Yearbook of Trade*, various issues.
[a]Numbers are for 1968.

by nearly 320 percent. U.S. imports during the same period went from 7,800 to 470,160 tons—an increase of 600 percent. Imports in Asia also increased rapidly, from 11,000 to 74,342 tons, or by 675 percent.

The United States has been and is likely to continue to be a major importer of beef. In 1969 the value of beef imports into the United States was $483 million. Policies affecting U.S. meat imports have an important bearing on the export earning potential of a large number of developing countries exporting beef.

The above data are for fresh, chilled, and frozen beef only. They do not include U.S. imports of beef in processed form. Unfortunately, the available data do not permit us to look at the world trade picture for processed beef separately from all processed meats. However, we should keep in mind that processed beef is also a significant import item for the United States.

Tobacco

World trade in tobacco has grown steadily during the past two decades. World exports increased from 620,000 metric tons in 1951 to one million metric tons in 1969, or by 5.5 percent a year. Between 1959 and 1969 quantities exported increased by 3.3 percent a year while the value of exports increased by 3.7 percent, indicating a modest rise in world tobacco prices. The United States accounted for 26 percent of world exports in 1969.

Europe is by far the largest importing region, accounting for 68 percent of world imports in 1969. The United States accounted for 10 percent.

The principal tobacco exporting less developed countries are Cuba, Dominican Republic, India, Indonesia, Philippines, Turkey, Rhodesia, Malawi, and Zambia. (Mainland China also exports significant quantities.) Based on historical trends, one would expect world trade in tobacco to continue to grow at a moderate rate.

IMPACT OF U.S. AGRICULTURAL POLICIES ON THE DEVELOPING COUNTRIES

The developing countries probably have at least one overriding common interest: to increase foreign exchange earnings from trade, especially from primary products. But while the bulk of trade in these products is from the developing to the developed countries, we have to be mindful that all poor countries are not exporters of the commodities being considered; some are net importers. Thus it is difficult for a country like the United States to be all things to all developing countries with respect to its present or future agricultural trade policies. Changes in trade policies that increase U.S. imports and raise world prices would be beneficial to the less developed exporters, but would work against the interest of the less developed importers.

In addition, many less developed countries are striving to reduce their dependence on agricultural imports. In the process they have supported domestic prices of some commodities at well above world levels. Thus the developing countries are contributing to distortions in world prices of certain agricultural commodities.

In a world in which trade is distorted by policies of both the developed and developing countries, it is difficult to define quantitative norms of good economic behavior. Of course we can invoke the principles of comparative advantage and free trade. However, it is difficult to estimate what a world operating on these principles would look like, and unrealistic to think that such a world would come to pass very quickly. What we can do is to estimate, however roughly, the impact of changes in U.S. agricultural trade policies on the volume and value of world trade, and on the value of agricultural exports from the developing countries.

To examine the impact of U.S. agricultural policies on the agricultural trade of developing countries we have to do three things: (1) assess the comparative advantage of the United States in the production of each of the commodities or commodity groups with which we are concerned; (2) determine the extent to which U.S. agricultural trade policies restrict exports from developing countries; and (3) evaluate the benefit to developing countries from less restrictive policies by the United States. We will concern ourselves with policies that encourage U.S. exports as well as those that restrict imports.

We can get a fairly good, though not precise, idea of the extent to which agricultural production in the United States is insulated from world markets by looking at both the nominal and effective degrees of protection for different commodities. The nominal rate of protection tells us the extent to which tariff and nontariff barriers, payments to producers, etc., keep domestic product prices above world prices. The effective rate of protection given to a particular product depends not only on the levels of tariff and nontariff protection of the final product, but also on the value added in production and the tariff and nontariff protection given to production inputs.

In a recent study, Wipf[13] has calculated the levels of nominal and effective rates of protection for a number of agricultural products at the farm level in 1968. These data are presented in Table 2-7. Four commodities stand out as having very high rates of effective protection: sugar (662.2 percent), cotton (100.8 percent), food grains (143.5 percent), and dairy products (48.2 percent). Of these, we are interested in all but dairy products. The other products that we are concerned with in this chapter—oilseeds, fruits and vegetables, meats, and tobacco—do not appear to have excessively high rates of protection. If we accept these measures as a rough guide to the competitive position of the United States in world agricultural trade, we can focus our analysis on wheat, rice, sugar, and cotton. While it would appear that the United States has a comparative advantage in oilseeds (primarily soybeans), we could

Table 2-7. Nominal and Effective Rates of Protection in the U.S. Farm Production Sector, 1968

Farm level sector	*Total Nominal*	*Total Effective*	*Effective Tariff*	*Effective Nontariff*
			(percent)	
Meat animals	7.5	13.8	13.2	0.6
Poultry and eggs	0.8	−19.6	−16.6	−3.0
Farm dairy products	16.8	48.2	−3.4	51.6
Other livestock products	2.5	3.3	3.5	−0.2
Food grains	8.4	143.5	2.7	146.2
Feed crops	0.4	8.1	0.0	8.1
Cotton	0.3	100.8	−1.3	102.1
Tobacco	17.0	28.2	24.5	3.7
Oil-bearing crops	11.3	16.4	−0.8	17.2
Vegetables	12.4	17.9	20.8	−2.9
Fruits	8.4	9.1	11.8	−2.7
Tree nuts	20.1	25.5	35.2	−9.7
Sugar and syrup crops	195.8	662.2	72.2	590.0

Source: Larry J. Wipf, "Tariffs, Nontariff Distortions, and Effective Protection in U.S. Agriculture," *American Journal of Agricultural Economics* 53 (3) (August 1971).

add peanuts to our list because they are a highly protected commodity. In 1968 the nominal and effective rates of protection on peanuts were 69.3 and 204.0 percent respectively.[14]

Wheat

With the exception of Argentina, and possibly Mexico, the developing countries have not historically had a significant interest in wheat exports. They have, in the main, been importers (Table 2-8). In the 1960s, most of the U.S. wheat exports were to the developing countries under government programs, mainly P.L. 480. About 70 percent of wheat exports were under government programs in the first half of the decade, and between 50 and 60 percent during the last half. Thus the developing countries, being mainly importers of wheat, benefited greatly from the soft terms under which they received wheat from the United States.

In recent years a large number of developing countries have increased their wheat production through the use of the new high yielding varieties, related production inputs, and price support programs. These develop-

Table 2-8. World Trade in Wheat and Wheat Flours, 1967

Region	*Imports*	*Exports*
	(1000 metric tons)	
Europe	18,077	12,112
USSR	418	6,802
Canada	–	7,333
U.S.	38	13,774
Mexico	1	253
Other Central America and Caribbean	1,990	–
Argentina	–	2,462
Uruguay	–	68
Other So. America	4,566	–
N. Asia	1,709	62
S. Asia	3,734	2
S.E. Asia[a]	2,403	111
E. Asia[b]	10,308	82
Africa	3,914	71
Oceania	931	5,343
Total	48,039	48,697

Source: *Trade Yearbook, 1970,* FAO, Rome 1971.

[a]Includes Republic of North Vietnam.

[b]Includes Mainland China, Mongolia, and Republic of North Vietnam.

ments have greatly reduced the need for imports in several of these countries and have even created some small exportable surpluses. In the main, however, it does not look as though the traditional developing country importers of wheat will contribute significantly to world wheat exports.

Growing domestic demands resulting from increases in population and per capita incomes will keep pace with increased production. Those few countries which have produced or will produce exportable surpluses will find difficulty selling in world markets because (a) they lack adequate marketing and grading facilities, and (b) their domestic prices are well above world levels, requiring costly export subsidies.[15] Nonetheless, increased self-sufficiency in wheat for a number of the historically large wheat importing countries in the developing world will sharply reduce the size of world wheat trade and U.S. exports.

Needed adjustments in wheat production and consumption in the United States as well as in the other developed exporting countries and Western Europe would call for, among other things, pricing of wheat basically as a feed grain. If this were done, the effective supply of feed grains would be expanded and world prices would probably move downward. It is difficult to judge the extent of this downward pressure because we do not know by how much wheat production would decline with the decline in prices. In any event, bringing about more competitive pricing of wheat in many of the developed countries would affect the world market prices for feed grains and the market prospects for the developing countries which are feed grain exporters. This would tend to work against the interests of those developing countries which are now or have the potential of becoming major exporters of coarse grains such as Mexico, Argentina, Brazil, Kenya, Thailand, and Indonesia.

Sugar

Of all the agricultural commodities that the United States imports from the developing countries, sugar undoubtedly is the most protected. Detailed descriptions of the U.S. sugar program can be found in Johnson[16] and Horton[17] and will not be repeated here. We are interested in looking at the cost of sugar programs and what alternative programs would mean both to the United States and to the developing countries.

Over the last 40 years the United States has relied increasingly on domestic sugar production. During the period 1925-29 about 37 percent of U.S. sugar consumption was produced on the mainland, Puerto Rico, Hawaii, and the Virgin Islands. By the late 1960s, about 60 percent of U.S. consumption came from these same sources. As Johnson points out: "the net effect of the sugar acts has been to reserve all—or more than all—of the growth in domestic use for domestic producers."[18]

The United States is a very high cost producer of sugar. Various estimates have been made of U.S. production, consumption, and imports under alternative price and program assumptions. They all point to substantial gains to both the United States and the developing countries from a more liberal U.S. sugar policy. Johnson has estimated that in 1970 the U.S. sugar program cost U.S. consumers and taxpayers $1 billion, compared with total cash receipts from sugar cane and sugar beets in domestic areas of $700 million.[19] Thus U.S. consumers and taxpayers could afford to completely subsidize domestic producers for not producing at all and still be left with a substantial net benefit.

It has been estimated that if the United States were to follow a completely free trade policy for sugar, the domestically produced share of consumption would decline from 60 percent to 20 percent. Free trade in sugar would increase the gross earnings of less developed countries by about $400 million[20]—not an insignificant sum.

Harry Johnson,[21] refining some earlier work by Snape,[22] has estimated that in 1959 if the United States had allowed free imports of sugar but made a deficiency payment to domestic producers, the increased consumption and imports of sugar would be worth about $250 million to the developing country exporters. The assumptions about deficiency payments are less extreme from the point of view of domestic producers than a totally free trade situation; yet they illustrate once again the large gains to U.S. consumers and sugar exporters from more liberal import policies without imposing undue burdens on domestic producers.

Cotton

Cotton is also one of the highly protected agricultural commodities in the United States. It is estimated that in 1968 the effective rate of protection for U.S. cotton production was just over 100 percent. U.S. production and exports have declined in recent years (Table 2-9) to the point where production has been around ten million bales a year and exports about three million bales. This has worked to the benefit of developing country exporters.

Under a situation of no government programs for cotton in the United States and a domestic farm price of 19.5 cents a pound, production is estimated at 9.4 million bales, lower than the level prevailing in recent years.[23] Under such conditions exports would be at a modest level, probably not over 1.5 million bales. Such further reduction in U.S. cotton exports would add to the foreign exchange earnings of a large number of developing countries with exportable supplies of cotton.

Rice

The United States has been the largest exporter of rice in recent years, accounting for nearly 30 percent of world exports in 1968 and 1969. Italy, Australia, and very recently Japan are the only other developed countries which export any significant amount of rice, and their exports are small. Both the nominal and effective rates of protection for U.S. rice producers have been very high—36.4 and 120.4 percent respectively in 1963.[24]

Table 2-9. Production and Export of Cotton, United States, 1955-1970

Year	*Production*[a]	*Exports*[a]
	(million bales)	
1955	14.7	2.3
1956	13.3	7.9
1957	11.0	6.0
1958	11.5	2.9
1959	14.6	7.4
1960	14.3	6.9
1961	14.3	5.1
1962	14.9	3.4
1963	15.3	5.8
1964	15.2	4.2
1965	15.0	3.0
1966	9.6	4.8
1967	7.5	4.4
1968	11.0	2.4
1969	10.0	2.9
1970	10.3	3.7

Source: Agricultural Statistics, 1971, USDA, Washington, D.C., 1971.
[a]500 pound bales.

The level of rice production in the United States is controlled through acreage restrictions, and domestic prices are well above world market levels; thus sizeable export subsidies are required for commercial exports. Even more important, exports under the P.L. 480 program have accounted for 38 to 57 percent of total rice exports between 1961 and 1970. The United States is the largest competitor the developing rice exporting countries face. And, they are not competing with U.S. rice producers, but with the U.S. Treasury.

On a milled basis, farm prices of long grain rice have averaged about $220 per metric ton. The export subsidy has been running at $44 per metric ton, or about 20 percent of the domestic price.[25] Continued protection of domestic rice production and aggressive use of export subsidies provide stiff competition for the less developed exporters. Because of its dominant position in world rice trade, the United States can exert considerable influence on the level of world prices and export earnings of rice.

Estimates of rice production in the United States under free market conditions are difficult to come by.[26] It is the author's best guess that, given the outlook for relatively low world prices in the 1970s, production in the United States would decline somewhat under a free market situation, U.S. exports would decline, and the position of less developed rice exporting countries would improve.

Effective Rates of Protection on Processed Agricultural Products

Access to the markets for raw agricultural products in developed countries such as the United States by the developing countries is only one part of a larger set of agricultural trade issues. Another is the ability of the developing countries to penetrate the market in the United States for semimanufactured and manufactured products based on agricultural raw materials. The developing nations would like to do as much processing as possible of the raw product, for this generates much needed employment and incomes domestically, and increases the value of and the foreign exchange earnings from agricultural exports.

It is typical for developed countries to have higher degrees of protection for manufactured products than for raw materials, and the United States is no exception. Tariff structure of this type bias imports in favor of raw materials and provides added protection to domestic manufacture in the developed countries. In other words, the effective rate of protection for manufactured products can be much larger (or smaller) than the value of the nominal tariff. This is illustrated in Table 2-10 for a few commodities: the effective tariff rate is about two to three times the nominal tariff for some of the commodities listed and ten times higher for one product, coconut oil. The

Table 2-10. Nominal and Effective Tariff Rates for Selected Commodities, United States, 1962

Item	*Nominal Tariff*	*Effective Tariff*
	(percent)	
Thread and yarn	11.7	31.8
Textile fabrics	24.1	50.6
Hosiery	25.6	48.7
Clothing	25.1	35.9
Other textile articles	19.0	22.7
Shoes	16.6	25.3
Coconut oil (refined)	5.7	57.5
Jute fabrics	3.1	5.3
Cigarettes	47.2	89.0
Hard fiber mfg.	15.1	38.0

Source: Bela Belassa, "Tariff Protection in Industrial Countries: An Evaluation," *The Journal of Political Economy* LXXIII (6) (December 1965); and Harry G. Johnson, *Economic Policies Toward Less Developed Countries*, Washington, D.C.: The Brookings Institution, 1967.

effective rate of protection is further enhanced when nontariff trade barriers such as quotas are employed in addition to tariffs.

To further illustrate the point, Belassa[27] calculated the effective rates of protection for 22 primary products for the United States, the United Kingdom, the European Community, Sweden, and Japan. The commodities covered in the study are: meat, fish, fruits, vegetables, cocoa, leather, ground nuts, copra, palm kernel, palm oil, rubber, wood, pulpwood, wool, cotton, jute, sisal and henequen, iron, copper, aluminum, lead, and zinc. Four stages of processing were considered. The results for the United States are presented in Table 2-11.

Clearly the degree of protection, both nominal and effective, increases rapidly as we move to higher stages of processing. Furthermore, the distribution of imports by stage of processing follows from the nature of protection. Of the total value of the 22 commodities imported by the United States from the developing countries in all stages of processing, over one-half—56.6 percent—was imported in the primary stage. An additional 33.2 percent was imported with the first stage of processing. Only 10.2 percent was imported in the third and fourth stages of processing. Clearly, the United States (and other industrialized countries as well) is discriminating against the import of processed products from the developing countries.

All this is not insignificant for the developing countries, which are hungry for foreign exchange and are not getting as much as they need or want in the form of economic aid. In 1964 the value of U.S. imports from developing countries of the 22 commodities Belassa studied amounted to $2.3 billion. The amount is even larger today. Removal of discrimination by developed countries against imports of processed primary products should be given serious attention in future trade negotiations.

Table 2-11. Weighted Averages of Nominal and Effective Tariffs and Imports from Less Developed Countries, United States, 1964

Stage of Processing	*Nominal Tariff*	*Effective Tariff*	*Value of Imports*	*Distribution of Imports*
	(percent)		*($mil)*	*(percent)*
I	4.0		1,311.1	56.6
II	6.0	19.5	768.9	33.2
III	16.6	30.7	114.9	4.9
IV	24.0	42.7	123.7[a]	5.3[a]
Total			2,318.6	100.0

Source: Bela Belassa, "Tariff Protection in Industrial Nations and Its Effects on the Export of Processed Goods from Developing Countries," *Canadian Journal of Economics* (August 1968).

[a]A fifth stage of processing was listed for value of imports. The amount of trade in this category was small ($7.1 million) and it was added to stage IV.

THE DEVELOPING COUNTRIES AS A MARKET FOR U.S. EXPORTS

The interest of the United States in promoting economic development in the less developed countries should go beyond moral and political considerations; economic benefits should not be overlooked. Certainly, changes in U.S. trade policies that would stimulate imports of agricultural raw materials and processed agricultural commodities from the developing countries would contribute to their earning of foreign exchange and their ability to finance imports and future development.

There has been a positive association between the rate of economic growth in developing countries and growth of U.S. agricultural exports to them, to say nothing of nonagricultural products. Mackie[28] has shown that between 1955-56 and 1961-62 there was a positive relationship between the rate of growth of national income in the developing countries and the rate of growth of commercial imports of agricultural products from the United States. For all developing countries, national income grew at 4.0 percent a year, total agricultural imports from the United States by 11.0 percent, and commercial agricultural imports by 8.4 percent.

One group of developing countries[d] with a rapid rate of growth of national income of 8.1 percent per year had a rate of growth for total agricultural imports of 7.6 percent a year while commercial imports grew at 14.0 percent a year. On the other hand, the remaining low income countries had annual average growth rates of 2.4 percent for national income, 13.0 percent for total agricultural imports from the United States, and 2.8 percent for commercial agricultural imports. Furthermore, an analysis of agricultural imports from the United States by a group of 24 countries in the 1959-1961 period showed that the proportion of commercial imports was positively associated with the levels of per capita incomes in these nations.

During the 1960s, U.S. agricultural exports to the developing countries continued to grow at a rapid rate. In general, exports under government programs (mainly P.L. 480) declined while commercial exports rose rapidly (Table 2-12). From 1962 to 1971, agricultural exports under government programs declined from $1,512.8 million to $1,057.1 million. On the other hand, total commercial exports increased from $3,518.6 million to $6,637.8 million, or by 7.3 percent a year. Asia was the only region of the world to which exports under government programs increased. In general, commercial exports to the developing countries increased at a faster rate than commercial exports to the developed countries: by 7.1 percent a year for exports to Latin America and the Caribbean, by 13.6 percent a year to Asia (excluding Japan), and by 12.1 percent a year to Africa. *In fact, the less developed regions of the world accounted for 43 percent of the growth in U.S. commercial agricultural exports during the 1962-1971 period.*

---

[d]Japan, Venezuela, Israel, Chile, Cyprus, Ghana, Iraq, Thailand, and Mexico.

Table 2-12. U.S. Agricultural Exports, by Region and Terms of Sale, 1962 and 1971

	Government Programs		*Commercial*	
Region	*1962*	*1971*	*1962*	*1971*
	(million dollars)			
Latin America and Caribbean	148.9	110.3	288.8	535.3
Asia (excluding Japan)	663.1	761.9	251.0	792.1
Africa	310.9	115.7	63.6	177.9
Total	1,512.8	1,057.1	3,518.6	6,637.8

Source: *Foreign Agricultural Trade of the United States*, ERS, USDA.

The United States should not overlook the rapid growth of its agricultural exports to the developing countries. There is evidence of a strong association between rapid economic development in the poor countries and rapid growth in their agricultural imports, particularly commercial imports. To the extent that the United States pursues trade and aid policies that contribute to economic growth in the less developed countries, it is helping to build markets for U.S. farm and nonfarm products.

ALTERNATIVE AGRICULTURAL POLICIES FOR THE UNITED STATES

We confine our discussion of changes in agricultural policies to wheat, rice, cotton, and sugar—commodities that are of great importance in the export trade of developing countries and that are highly protected in the United States. More general discussions of U.S. agricultural policies and their impact on world agricultural trade can be found elsewhere.[29]

Guiding Principles

Before turning to a discussion of specific commodities, we should spell out certain guiding principles that will be employed in the discussion of agricultural trade policies.

First. The welfare of consumers should be a major concern of trade policy. The improvement of consumer welfare is one of the major underpinnings of the arguments in favor of freer trade. We can further argue that trade policies that place a relatively heavy burden on the poor compared with the rich represent one of the worst forms of protectionism. The "ability to pay" argument, which is sometimes applied to domestic policy considerations, should also be applied to foreign trade and aid policies. As one author has commented about the highly protectionist U.S. sugar program, "to the extent that sugar quotas can be justified as a form of foreign aid they appear to be a case of 'poor people in rich countries giving money to rich people in poor countries.' "[30] Another writer[31] has pointed out that it is one of the ironies of protectionism that the burden of such policies falls on the very poor and the very rich:

> The man who eats Kobe beef and the one who eats at McDonald's have something in common, just as the one with the $25 English cotton shirt and the one with the $1.95 discount house shirt from Hong Kong. Both are consumers for whom the mass market is not large enough to activate the U.S. production process, and in the absence of imports they would be forced into less satisfactory consumption patterns.

The rich can afford it, but the poor cannot.

Second. Trade policies should promote efficient use of resources from the point of view of national output and productivity. This, after all, is what the free trade argument is all about. In moving from a protectionist set of policies to ones that are more free trade oriented, one has to keep in mind the kinds of resource adjustments that could be expected to occur and their impact on total output and productivity. In particular, special attention has to be given to moving resources out of inefficient production processes into efficient ones.

Third. The benefits to producers from past agricultural programs have been capitalized into the value of land or allotments. Policies that would reduce prices received (without compensating income payments) would, in the short run, lead to lower incomes based on current land values and, in the longer run, to lower land prices. This would represent a depreciation of an important capital asset. If there is a real saving to consumers and taxpayers from more liberal agricultural trade policy, considerations of fairness and political feasibility might dictate compensation to producers for part or all of the capital losses associated with a liberalization of trade policies and resulting adjustments of resource use in agriculture. But unlike present income transfers, which perpetuate inefficient resource use, this would be a compensation that would bring about desired resource adjustments.

Fourth. There are those who would argue, with considerable justification, that there are surplus resources employed in U.S. agriculture, and shifting resources out of the production of one set of agricultural commodities into the production of others is merely shuffling around redundant resources. In the short run this is probably true. But in the long run something of value would be accomplished: resources would be moved into the production of those agricultural commodities in which the United States has a comparative advantage and for which world markets are growing at reasonably rapid rates—e.g., feed grains and soybeans. And, with competitive prices, the United States would assure itself of a "fair" share of this growth. There would undoubtedly still be a need for controlling output of U.S. agriculture after all these resource adjustments took place. But with more efficient resource use, the cost to society of withholding a given amount of resources from production in agriculture and meeting a given income objective for farmers would be less than it presently is.

Fifth. Changes in U.S. trade policies that are clearly to the benefit of the United States should not be made conditional upon actions by other countries. We have been conditioned to think in terms of balanced, multilateral trade negotiations, primarily concerning tariffs. But if it is clearly in the national interest to change some agricultural policies, one cannot justify asking other countries to do something of "equal value" in return. Furthermore, tenacious adherence to a reciprocity approach provides opponents to trade liberalization with a justification for continuing protectionist policies.

Sixth. Changes in agricultural policies are always difficult; they are especially so when the removal of a significant degree of protection is involved. It is doubtful that much can be achieved by relying solely on voluntary surrender of such protection. But decisions should be made. And, they should take into account the interests of consumers, taxpayers, and national economic growth, as well as those of the agricultural producers concerned. This means that responsibility for agricultural policy changes that lead to trade liberalization should rest at sufficiently high levels of government to permit the views of all the aforementioned groups to be fairly represented.

Policy Alternatives

With these principles in mind, let's now look at some policy alternatives for the four commodities in which we are principally interested: wheat, rice, cotton, and sugar.

From the point of view of the developing countries, movements toward less protectionist wheat policies in the United States present some vexing problems. We will highlight these problems by assuming that the United States moves toward a set of policies for wheat that lower domestic and world market prices and make wheat competitive with feed grains for feed uses, as some have suggested.

First. With the exception of Argentina and possibly Mexico, the developing countries do not have a major export interest in wheat. Thus, actions on the part of the United States that would lower world wheat prices would adversely affect only a few developing countries.

Second. Since most developing countries are net wheat importers, lower world prices would work to their benefit by reducing their import bill. However, the extent of this benefit must be tempered by the fact that many developing countries have availed themselves of the new wheat technology, have succeeded in expanding their production, and have substantially reduced their reliance on wheat imports. These developments are likely to continue in the future and this is one of the reasons why export prospects for wheat are not bright. Thus, one would have to think of the benefits of lower world wheat prices to the developing countries in terms of a lower import level than prevailed in, say, the 1960s.

Third. To the extent that lower wheat prices lowered the price of feed grains in world markets, this would work against the interests of developing countries which have a stake in feed grain exports. To them, the United States would become an even more awesome competitor in the world feed grain market.

Thus, it is difficult, if not impossible, to come to any conclusion about the net benefit to the developing countries of less protectionist U.S. wheat policies that lowered world wheat and feed grain prices. How does one weigh the benefits of lower world grain prices to less developed net grain importers against the losses to less developed grain exporters?

What about the benefit to domestic consumers and taxpayers from lower wheat prices? Certainly consumers would gain; but the gain to taxpayers is not obvious, or at least not overwhelmingly so. There is excess production capacity in both wheat and feed grains at current prices. And this would continue to exist, at modestly lower prices. There would continue to be a need to control grain output. In this situation, expanded production of wheat would call for less production of feed grains. There is no obviously large saving in government program costs from pricing wheat competitively with feed grains at current or even modestly lower support rates for feed grains.

Wheat. Some have argued that the current level of support for wheat is above that which is required to withhold current acreage from production; i.e., there is a net income transfer to producers. This net income transfer might be eliminated, but it wouldn't affect output levels, only incomes of wheat producers. This is a domestic policy consideration, however, which has little bearing on trade.

We are left then with one policy consideration for wheat that may have some significance for agricultural trade. The one agricultural commodity in which the United States does not have surplus production capacity is beef. To the extent that land currently could be shifted into forage and beef production, U.S. consumers would be better off and, in the long run, so would taxpayers.

The value of land presently in wheat production reflects past high prices of wheat. A combination of somewhat lower wheat prices (including payments), lower acreage allotments for wheat, and payments to producers for all or part of the cost of shifting land out of wheat into forage production should be considered. The amount of resource adjustment that can be achieved and its cost is a matter for careful study.

Rice. The situation for rice is more clear-cut than for wheat. Its production in the United States is highly protected, the United States is a major exporter competing directly with less developed rice exporters, and reduced production in the United States would greatly expand the export market for low cost producers in the developing countries.

Adjustment of acreage out of rice production would, to a large extent, free resources for the production of commodities for which there are no surpluses, and additional output would be welcomed at home and for export—e.g., beef and soybeans.

The United States should move toward a policy for rice under which production would take place at competitive, world market prices. During a transition period, rice producers should be compensated for losses in land values as a dual result of shifting land out of rice production and the lower rice prices. In the long run there would be some benefit to domestic consumers, appreciable benefit to taxpayers, and substantial benefit to the rice exporting less developed countries.

Cotton. The case of cotton appears to be quite different from that of either wheat or rice. The United States has ceased to be a major factor in the world cotton market; at the same time, it has become a major importer of cotton textiles. As we have seen, world market prices for cotton in the United States would reduce production in and exports from the United States. This would be a benefit to the less developed countries. Reliance on world market prices to guide production of cotton is recommended, with resource adjustment payments similar to those for wheat and rice. But the United States should go beyond questions of lint cotton production and trade: it has high rates of effective protection against imports of cotton manufactures through the use of tariffs and quotas. It is in the area of manufactures rather than lint cotton that the developing countries have the greatest export interest in the U.S. market.

Clearly, the efforts of United States textile manufacturers to limit cotton textile imports indicate that the U.S. industry is not fully competitive with foreign suppliers. The present voluntary import quotas on textiles attest to this fact. Every effort should be made to liberalize textile imports into the United States. Mindful of the dislocation that such liberalization would cause to the domestic industry, consideration should be given to financial assistance to relocate textile workers to other industries and for manufacturers to shift investments, where feasible, to other lines of production.

Sugar. The case of sugar is in a category all by itself when it comes to the degree of protection afforded domestic producers. In addition, there is the procedure by which the United States allocates sugar quotas to foreign suppliers. The United States should dispense with all quota allocations, making the U.S. market for sugar available to all suppliers on an equal basis.[e] Furthermore, the United States should move to a free market price for both domestic consumers and producers. As we have seen, the savings would be great enough to buy U.S. producers out and still have a net benefit to the economy to show for the effort. If it were not politically possible to move to a free market, even in the long run, it would still be beneficial to U.S. consumers and taxpayers (and to developing country exporters) for the United States to move to a deficiency payment system, which would support a limited amount of domestic production but allow domestic market prices to decline to world levels.

In the short run, resources freed from the production of wheat, rice, cotton, and sugar as a result of less protectionist policies would go into the production of other commodities and put downward pressure on their prices. The extent to which this occurs is a matter for detailed analysis. In the longer run, however, we would be producing agricultural commodities that have high and more rapidly growing domestic demands: feed grains, soybeans, beef, etc. This would aid in adjusting resources and help the United States better meet its domestic needs, as well as stimulate exports.

One Final Comment. The United States has had quotas on meat imports for several years. They have recently been suspended because of the high domestic meat prices. While it can be argued that these quotas have not been overly restrictive, they nonetheless should be suspended permanently to the benefit of U.S. consumers and meat exporters.

The previous discussion on proposed policy changes for wheat, rice, cotton, and sugar is primarily, though not entirely, in the context of an idealized economic world—one which does not give full weight to the politics of American agriculture (and agriculture in other developed countries as well). When one considers some of the political realities, there does not appear to be much hope for moving away from high levels of protection afforded domestic producers.

Clearly the producers of the commodities in question have had sufficient political power to get and retain the present set of policies. And there is no evidence to indicate that they have lost, in any measurable degree, the political power to protect present programs. In fact, the growing mood of protectionism in many quarters of the United States—both in and out of

[e]If, for political reasons, the United States deems it undesirable to trade with a country, then trade should be restricted for all commodities, not just one commodity like sugar.

agriculture is working to strengthen rather than reduce protective agricultural policies.

The main beneficiaries of more liberal agricultural trade policies, in the context of this chapter, are domestic consumers and taxpayers, and the developing countries. Yet none of these groups has the political strength or willingness to focus on specific policy questions of the type we have discussed and bring about policy changes.

All this argues in favor of basically more of the same: economic rationality does not carry a high premium. This is not to say that efforts should not be made to put forth arguments in favor of the benefits to be derived from more efficient resource use and trade policies. But we should recognize that much more than the logical merits of alternative agricultural policies will be needed to bring them into being.

Food and Fiber Assistance Programs—P.L. 480

Exports of agricultural commodities under P.L. 480 have been an important factor in U.S. trade and of considerable importance to the developing countries. The developing countries benefited from food and fiber imports that required very little foreign exchange, and the P.L. 480 program helped to export some of the United States surplus agricultural production (capacity).

In the early 1960s, exports of agricultural commodities under P.L. 480 were valued at about $1.5 billion; they rose to $1.6 billion in 1966 and have been around $1.0 billion in recent years. The major commodities involved have been wheat and wheat products, rice, cotton, and dairy products.[32]

The decline in exports under the P.L. 480 program reflects two basic developments in the developing countries. One is that several developing countries have achieved rapid rates of economic development, have ceased to be eligible for the soft credit terms of the P.L. 480 program, and have become commercial importers. The other is that a number of formerly large recipients of P.L. 480 have benefited from the Green Revolution and now require less in the way of imports. This has been particularly true for a country such as India and for a commodity such as wheat.

With continued progress in agricultural development in the developing countries there will be a smaller market for P.L. 480 commodities in the 1970s than there was in the 1960s. Nevertheless, there will be a need for commodity assistance to the developing countries. Droughts, typhoons, floods, and wars will still occur in the developing nations, causing dislocation in their agricultural production. There will be need for temporary food assistance. Further, not all developing countries are going to become "rich" and self-sufficient in agricultural production in either the near or distant future. There will probably always be countries who could benefit from food and fiber assistance on a long term basis.

It is recommended that the United States continue to supply such assistance, whether under bilateral programs such as P.L. 480 or through multilateral international programs. But because of the limited and uncertain size of this market, food and fiber assistance should be provided out of a commodity reserve for that purpose; it should not be viewed as a surplus disposal program, as it has been through most of the life of the P.L. 480 program.

Since the P.L. 480 market has been so important for wheat, rice, and cotton, and since the commercial as well as P.L. 480 export prospects for them are not bright, there is all the more reason for policies that will adjust resources out of the production of these commodities.

Commodity Price Stabilization

One cannot discuss the interests of developing countries in exporting agricultural commodities without at least referring to the problem of commodity price instability in world markets. This has been a subject of a great deal of discussion and study, the main thrust of which has been to establish international commodity agreements that would stabilize prices and foreign exchange earnings of exporters.[33]

The exports of primary commodities account for a very large proportion of total exports from the developing countries. And, most of these exports are to the developed countries. The following is a good summary of the problem.[34]

> With limited but important exceptions [world commodity markets] have shown two major unfavorable characteristics. First, their absorptive capacity has grown only slowly, so that increased sales have often been possible only at falling prices. Second, these markets have been subject to particularly wide price fluctuations which themselves sometimes contribute to adverse longer-term trends.
>
> Demand for most primary products is growing relatively slowly as a result of both technological developments and changes in consumer spending patterns. Moreover, world trade in primary products, and particularly in agricultural products, has been held back by the protection given by industrial countries to their own primary producers. As a result, world commodity markets have in some cases taken on the characteristics of unstable residual markets bearing a disproportionate share of attempted adjustments between production and consumption in domestic as well as international markets.
>
> The necessary remedial action has to extend over a broad front. Commodity arrangements have a part to play. To be effective, these will need to be associated with action by the less developed countries in the field of development policy and of domestic and external financial policies. Industrial countries could make a major contribution by providing access to their markets and opening their

domestic primary production to international competition, as well as by the extension of financial assistance of a high and stable level of aggregate demand.

We have argued for less protectionist policies by the United States for some agricultural commodities. This would either provide the developed countries with greater access to the U.S. market or spare them from undue competition from subsidized U.S. exports. While these policy changes would significantly increase the size of the market for a number of exports from the developing countries, they would not necessarily lead to greater stability in world prices and export earnings.

First. There is considerable evidence to indicate that instability in world markets for primary products results primarily from fluctuations in supply rather than demand.[35] This being the case, some form of effective control over output or management of the quantities marketed would be required to stabilize prices. That the developing countries have been unable to do this, except in a few cases, is one of the reasons there have been so few successful international commodity agreements. This is particularly true when price stabilization efforts have also involved attempts to raise world prices. The near term prospects for improvements in this situation are not bright.

Second. Stabilization of world market prices does not necessarily lead to stabilization or increases in foreign exchange earnings.[36] Much depends on the price elasticities of demands for the products in question.

Third. While it has been generally assumed that fluctuating world prices of primary products have been detrimental to the development interests of the poor countries, a recent study concludes that "the statistical evidence . . . appears to contradict the consensus that export fluctuations inflict significant damage on the stability and growth of the average underdeveloped country."[37] The same author does not, however, jump to the conclusion that this is no place for price stabilization schemes. Rather, he suggests a careful analysis of each proposal.[38]

While international commodity arrangements for stabilizing world prices (and earnings) do not appear to be all that has been claimed for them, and the history of negotiating successful agreements has not been good, there are reasons why the United States should take a sympathetic posture with respect to the developing countries' interests in such arrangements. There are a number of agricultural commodities that face intense competition from synthetics—e.g., cotton and jute. With wide swings in their prices, synthetics are substituted for the primary product during periods of high prices, but the reverse does not occur when primary product prices fall. Thus there tends to be a cumulative loss of markets. Stabilization of primary product prices at modest levels would tend to lessen the inroads made by synthetic prices. For other products, the developing countries do not have the financial resources to store commodities and follow orderly marketing practices. To the extent that market conditions are such as to stabilize (and possibly increase) earnings from stabilizing marketings, the United States ought to support efforts to achieve this goal.

Finally, in some cases the developing countries have too many resources locked into the production of a few primary commodities. Sensible efforts to diversify their output mix should be encouraged as this may add stability to total export earnings. The present International Coffee Agreement provides for restructuring of the agricultural sector. The United States should encourage and provide financial support to such efforts.

The above recommended changes in domestic U.S. agricultural policies and suggested U.S. posture with respect to food aid and international commodity agreements are in general, though not complete, accord with the recent recommendations of several high level groups within government.[39] For the commodities concerned, however, the recommendations to the U.S. government in both the extent of resource adjustment suggested and explicit means for bringing these adjustments about. Furthermore, the interests of U.S. consumers and taxpayers have been treated in a more explicit manner.

Also, trade can be treated as either an alternative or, hopefully, as a complement to foreign aid. Certain U.S. agricultural policies loom large in this arena: the developing countries have much to gain from alternative policies which provide a more liberal trade environment.

There is ample opportunity for the United States, through significant changes in its policies for a few agricultural products and for a few manufactured products based primarily on raw agricultural products, to (1) improve the lot of domestic consumers and taxpayers, (2) contribute to more efficient domestic resource use and stimulate total domestic economic growth, (3) contribute to the economic development of numerous poor countries, and (4) indirectly expand the market for U.S. farm and nonfarm products in the poor regions of the world.

THE MEANING OF AGRICULTURAL TRADE NEGOTIATIONS WITH LESS DEVELOPED COUNTRIES

Our discussion of agricultural trade policies of the United States as they affect trade with the developing countries involves changes in domestic agricultural policies in order to bring about changes in trade policies. Historically, international trade negotiations have primarily dealt with tariff barriers. An institutional mechanism (GATT) has provided clearly defined procedures for carrying out these negotiations. But no such institution exists for negotiating nontariff barriers, particularly those that are an integral part of domestic agricultural policies. Schnittker[40] has said:

> I am pessimistic to the core about "negotiating major elements of domestic agricultural policies." Here again, we move from a conventional stance associated with tariff negotiations to a situation where such an approach is scarcely applicable. About 10 years ago, it came to be generally understood that domestic agricultural policies may and do interfere with an efficient and fair world trade pattern, just as excessive and uneven tariffs do. So, people said, let's negotiate. Such a stance neglects entirely the sensitive political nature of agricultural policies in most countries, even where farmers represent a very small percentage of the population.

The above quotation refers mainly to the developed countries where, with respect to domestic and foreign agricultural policies, none is without sin—some are just more sinful than others. In such a situation, domestic political considerations aside, there is or should be a mutual interest among countries to move toward less trade restrictive agricultural policies. One can visualize a "give and take" approach for all the countries, although the actual trade results might be hard to predict with any reasonable degree of precision.

But when we look at agricultural trade relations between a major developed country such as the United States and the developing nations we have quite a different situation. In the first place, most developing countries are not that far away from the period of colonial rule that they don't feel strongly about past exploitation of their economies by the developed, ex-colonial powers. Second, the economic development of the less developed countries is dependent upon export earnings of primary products, thus the "irrational" and trade restrictive policies of most of the developed countries are a matter of serious, immediate concern.[41] Third, because the developing countries are poor and disadvantaged, they would argue that the developed countries have moral, political, and economic obligations to assist them in their development through economic aid and expanded trade opportunities. This the developed countries should do as a matter of course, without extracting concessions from the developing countries.

A poor trade policy is just that, and policies should be improved as quickly as possible. The fact that most developing countries also follow restrictive trade policies, they would argue, is a matter of necessity in order to husband scarce foreign exchange. Less restrictive trade policies by the developed countries would expand exports from the less developed countries, increase their foreign exchange earnings, and lead to a liberalization of their import policies.

In the situation described above it is difficult to imagine the United States changing certain of its agricultural policies in favor of the developing countries on the basis of concessions granted to the United States by the poor nations. This does not mean that in a process of discussions between the United States and the less developed countries that certain understandings could not be reached concerning improvements in the domestic economic and trade policies of the developing countries that might result from expanded exports. *But these should be understandings, and not commitments.* At present the UNCTAD and FAO provide well suited institutional frameworks within which such discussions could take place.

It would seem then that the benefits to the United States from less protectionist agricultural policies are the main justification for changing U.S. agricultural policies. This being the case, unilateral action by the United States is called for—action that is not only independent of steps taken by the developing countries, but may also be independent of any actions or lack of actions by other developed countries. The negotiation of trade policies between the developed countries as a group and the less developed countries as another block generates numerous reasons for inaction. This was evident in UNCTAD I and especially in UNCTAD II, where there was a high degree of polarization between rich and poor countries. This approach should be avoided, except for those trade questions where there is a clear advantage to a multilateral approach.

Unilateral action by the United States would have one very important implication for future multilateral negotiations: it would demonstrate that a leading industrial country has both the will and the ability to rationalize its agricultural policies; and it would support those legitimate claims of the developing countries with respect to their disadvantages in world trade. This could well strengthen the present case for other developed countries to liberalize their agricultural trade policies, which would be of general benefit to world agricultural trade.

SUMMARY AND CONCLUSIONS

We have looked at world trade in a number of agricultural commodities in which the United States and the developing countries have competitive interests. Of these, four stand out as being highly protected in the United States: wheat, rice, cotton, and sugar. With respect to rice and sugar, the developing countries stand to gain much from less protective U.S. policies. The benefits to be gained by the developing countries from less protective U.S. wheat and cotton policies is less clear.

While a case can be made to alter domestic agricultural policies for these four commodities in ways that will liberalize trade, benefit the developing countries, and benefit domestic consumers and taxpayers, it is not at all clear that the freer trade forces have sufficient political power to overcome the interests of specific producer groups and other forces for protection of U.S. markets from foreign competition. Nonetheless, continued efforts should be made to put forth the case for more efficient resource use in U.S. agriculture and the benefits of less protectionist agricultural trade policies. The odds for success in these fields is not high, but the battle is worth fighting.

We have also seen that the United States (as well as other developed countries) discriminates more against imports of processed primary products than it does against imports of raw materials. This tends to deprive developing countries of an important source of export growth.

We also looked at two other issues of concern to the developing countries: food aid and commodity price stabilization. The future levels of food aid are not likely to be as high as they were during the past decade. The developing countries are making progress toward meeting more of their domestic food needs, or are gaining the economic capacity to import food and fiber on commercial terms. There will continue to be a need for food and fiber assistance; but such aid should be geared to the needs of the recipient countries and not be used as a method of surplus disposal by the United States.

There has long been a desire on the part of developing countries to stabilize world prices of agricultural products through the use of international commodity agreements. There have been a few successful agreements and many ill-fated ones. The United States should support efforts to develop realistic international commodity agreements that bring stability to world prices or to export earnings of developing countries. Naturally care must be taken to stabilize prices at realistic levels so that some agricultural products are not replaced by synthetic substitutes and surplus production is avoided.

There is ample opportunity for the United States–through significant changes in its policies for a few agricultural products and for a few manufactured products based primarily on raw agricultural products–to (1) improve the lot of domestic consumers and taxpayers, (2) contribute to more efficient domestic resource use and stimulate total domestic economic growth, (3) contribute to the economic development of numerous poor countries, and (4) indirectly expand the market for U.S. farm and nonfarm products in the poor regions of the world.

There does not now exist an international forum adequately suited for the discussion and "negotiation" of national agricultural production and trade policies. This is true among the developed countries as well as between developed and developing countries. Such an institution is badly needed. But until one comes into existence, the United States should make efforts unilaterally to alter those of its agricultural policies that are clearly harmful both to the trade and development interests of the developing countries, as well as to domestic consumers, taxpayers, economic growth, and efficiency of resource use.

Chapter Three

The Impact of Price on Rice Trade in Asia

C. Peter Timmer and
Walter P. Falcon

INTRODUCTION

No other commodity in the world is as important to its society as rice is in Asia. Especially for the lower income, agriculturally dominated countries such as Indonesia, Ceylon, Burma, Thailand, and the Philippines, rice production and distribution provide the great bulk of employment opportunities and incomes. And its consumption provides the great bulk of the calorie and protein intake. It is little wonder then that a stable and low retail rice price is viewed as a major objective of nearly all Asian governments; many have fallen by failing in this task.

To achieve this objective and others, many countries resort to importing rice to supplement their domestic production. This is a precarious situation, however, as it places the fulfillment of a major political objective in the hands of relatively unstable and uncontrollable international market forces. Recently only about 3.5 percent of world rice production has moved in international trade, and even this small amount is differentiated by two significant factors. First, perhaps one-third or more of this rice moves on

Note: This essay is Working Paper No. 3 of the Stanford Rice Projects, a 27-month study of the political economy of rice in Asia. Funding is provided by the United States Agency for International Development under Contract No. CM-ASIA-C-73-39; however, the views expressed are not necessarily those of the sponsoring agency.

We wish to acknowledge helpful comments from the following people without implicating them in either the point of view or results: William O. Jones, Bruce Johnston, Raj Krishna, Scott Pearson, Vernon Ruttan, Lance Taylor, and the participants at the ADC/RTN Seminar on Trade and Development organized by George Tolley where some of these results first felt the cold February winds of Chicago. We would also like to thank Anne Thomson for her efforts in the difficult task of data collection.

concessionary terms or direct government-to-government contracts. Second, taste preferences for long grain versus short grain rice varieties are quite marked, with Japan and South Korea preferring the latter and most of the rest of Asia the former. Thus, relatively minor fluctuations in production can cause very wide swings in quantities of rice entering the international market and demanded from it. When bad weather affects much of monsoon Asia simultaneously, as it is wont to do, rice supplies in the international market shrink quickly and prices skyrocket. This has happened frequently enough in the past two decades that self-sufficiency in rice has become a second major objective of most importing countries.

There are obvious contradictions in the two objectives of stable, low prices and self-sufficiency, and significant differences from country to country in how the contradictions are resolved. It is the resolution, however, that ultimately determines a country's import and export level of rice and thus the pattern of international trade in rice. It is this trade that we wish to understand.

Diversity

Table 3-1 provides an overview of basic rice statistics for a sample of nine East and Southeast Asian countries: Japan, South Korea, Taiwan, Malaysia, Sri Lanka (Ceylon), Indonesia, Thailand, the Philippines, and Burma. Despite the uniformity of region and the important place rice occupies in the economies and societies of all nine countries, the dominant impression from Table 3-1 is diversity. Japan, with a low per capita consumption level, was in 1970 an exporter of similar magnitude to Burma and Thailand, which have the highest consumption levels. Thailand's per capita consumption is double Japan's. Paddy yields vary three-fold from the meagre 1.7 tons per hectare in Burma to 5.64 tons in Japan, and the other countries in between are strung out fairly evenly. Also, the prices vary tremendously from one country to another. The relative price of rice to fertilizer is seven times higher in Japan than in Indonesia. The diversity is also apparent in retail prices, although the difficulty of finding meaningful exchange rates makes this comparison somewhat more difficult.

Given this great diversity, this chapter is in many ways only an intermediate product: it builds on and extends earlier results with respect to the impact of rice and fertilizer prices on production.[a] The earlier results are extended in two directions. First, the production results themselves are extended by further analysis of alternative functional specifications. The results are somewhat neater but not drastically different. Second, instead of holding consumption constant while varying production levels via the rice price-fertilizer price ratio, consumption levels are now linked to price changes as well. This involves determining a consumption function for rice for the nine countries in the sample.

---

[a]See Timmer and Falcon (13). Parts of this earlier paper were discussed at the Bellagio, Italy, Conference on "Agriculture in Development Theory," May 23-29, 1973, as well as the ADC/RTN Workshop at Chicago, February 13-14, 1973.

Table 3-1. Basic Rice Statistics for a Sample of Nine Asian Countries, 1970

Country	*Production*	*Imports/ (Exports)*	*Change in Stocks*	*Consumption*	*Population*	*Per Capita Consumption*	*Relative Price of Rice to Fertilizer*	*Retail Price*	*Paddy Yield*
		(000 metric tons)			*(000)*	*(kg.)*		*($/ton)*	*(ton/ha.)*
Japan	11,674	(770)	(268)	11,172	103,390	108	1.43	501	5.64
South Korea	3,939	737	0	4,676	31,147	150	1.00	286	4.55
Taiwan	2,290	(5)	(5)	2,290	14,040	163	0.45	178	4.16
Malaysia	930	266	102	1,094	9,140	120	0.43	219	2.72
Ceylon	993	534	0	1,527	12,514	122	0.70	101	2.64
Indonesia	11,420	950	238	12,132	115,590	105	0.30	92	2.14
Thailand	8,758	(1064)	0	7,694	35,390	217	0.20	130	1.97
Philippines	3,473	0	0	3,473	36,880	94	0.40	118	1.72
Burma	5,550	(640)	0	4,910	27,580	178	0.20	65	1.70

Source: Basic data from various sources; see Timmer and Falcon[13].

PRODUCTION AND CONSUMPTION

Just as with the rice production functions, the ideal would be separate estimates of reaction parameters for each country based on econometric analysis of national time series data. Since the time series are too short and the production and consumption data of dubious accuracy for several countries, this direct approach is ruled out for the time being.[b] This chapter is an intermediate product in the sense that the questions and point of view were suggested by an earlier paper, but a truly finished product will require extensive national data, which are not likely to be available for at least another year. In the meantime, this chapter will attempt to provide a fuller analysis of the impact of price on rice trade, especially by including consumption reactions, but without any pretense that the results are definitive.

The primary analytical tool used to investigate the structure of production and consumption within and among these nine Asian countries is analysis of covariance. The production and consumption data for the nine years 1962 through 1970 for each country are pooled to form an overall data set containing 81 observations. The intent is not to assume that all nine countries are drawn from a single "Asian" universe but to use statistical procedures to sort out similarities and differences.

The treatment of production and consumption are somewhat different. Since annual data for farmgate rice and fertilizer prices are not available, it is necessary to estimate production response to price indirectly, through the physical production function. What is needed are time series on inputs and rice production. Such data on many inputs—especially labor, physical capital, and irrigation—are not available, but reasonably reliable data on fertilizer and acreage fortunately are available. The production function is estimated with these two inputs as continuous arguments. Since several variables are omitted from the estimated production function, the resulting coefficients for acreage and fertilizer suffer from specification bias. By introducing separate intercepts (and slopes) for individual countries or groups of countries, the analysis of covariance estimates are designed to circumvent this problem. The resulting coefficients, when compared with the coefficients from the simple production functions, strongly support the hypothesis that substantial bias existed and that the analysis of covariance removes a good deal of it.

With reasonable estimates of the short run response of production to fertilizer it is possible to determine what the production response to changes in the relative price of rice to fertilizer would be by assuming farmers react rationally. Although it is not possible to test this assumption for the entire nine-year sample, cross-country results for 1970 indicate the assumption is

[b]A major goal of The Stanford Rice Project is collection of the most accurate data possible for each country in order to permit direct estimation of reasonable supply and demand functions.

reasonable enough for the purposes at hand. Still, it must be remembered that the short run supply function for the nine countries is synthetic in the sense that it derives from profit maximization conditions for a directly estimated production function.

When stated this way, it is obvious that the consumption function for rice must be estimated in a different fashion. Since utility is not directly observable (or at least reported), the indirect route of estimating a utility function, where prices need not enter, and then constructing a derived demand function for rice by assuming utility maximization is not open to us. The demand function must be estimated directly.

But direct estimation raises many of the problems that could be finessed on the production side by resorting to a physical production function. In the first instance it means the assumption of maximizing behavior must be statistically tested. Although it is easy to believe such behavior is pervasive, it is often hard to find statistical evidence of it, due to the masking effect of a large number of factors entering into the consumption process. Second, it becomes necessary to compare directly price and income levels across countries, rather than relying on neutral quantities such as hectares and nutrient tons. The Houthakker-Weisskoff approach of working only with double log functions in first differences—thus avoiding exchange rates altogether—is not suitable here.[c] Different *levels* in rice consumption and prices are as important, or more so, than changes. Indeed, we bring to the research the strong suspicion that the vastly different rice consumption levels per capita in Asia are largely accounted for by historic and current price and income levels rather than by taste differences. The Houthakker-Weisskoff formulation cannot address this issue, nor can it permit the price and income elasticities to be functionally dependent on the levels of these variables. Since retail rice prices vary from around $50 per metric ton to $500 per metric ton in the sample, and per capita incomes from $50 to $1,500, constant price and income elasticities seem unlikely.[d]

A further constraint on the consumption function arises from its intended use. Not only must the function fit the wide range of data for the various countries as they exist in reality, but it must also provide reasonable consumption parameters when, for instance, the retail rice price in Burma is assumed to be the level of Japan and vice versa. Although a number of functional forms are tested in the empirical analysis of consumption section, a log-inverse function is used in the simulation runs because it yields a consistently

[c]See Houthakker (16) and Weisskoff (14).

[d]The same argument might also be made for the production functions due to the great variation in per hectare fertilizer applications, types of seeds, irrigation, land quality, sunlight, etc. However, analysis of covariance sorts out a great deal of these differences, even to permitting different response coefficients, and this procedure is awkward in the Houthakker-Weisskoff formulation.

negative price elasticity that declines (in absolute magnitude) at higher price levels.[e]

The impact of rice and fertilizer prices on levels and patterns of international trade in rice is determined by generating national production and consumption levels at various prices. The difference between production and consumption, corrected for 1970 stock changes, equals trade. The simulation equations are calibrated on a 1970 basis, the last year of the data sample. The intent in producing the synthetic trade values is not predictive in the narrow sense: that is, it is not suggested that if 1971 price levels were plugged into the equations, they would yield good estimates of 1971 trade levels and patterns. Too much depends on weather and, more importantly for the overall rice research project, on deliberate government policies. The purpose of the synthetic trade values is analytical. In particular, they are very suggestive in analyzing the role of price policy in achieving self-sufficiency in rice—a major political goal (or achievement) of almost all the countries in the sample. The comparative national price structure of self-sufficiency in the absence of other changes is very revealing about the real goals of rice policy and the constraints governments are under in achieving them.

This chapter, then, is an intermediate product in a third sense. The rice research project is interested in policy formulation, implementation, and impact, but none of these takes place in a vacuum. Some of the external constraints are economic, some technical, and some political, cultural, and social. This is an attempt to understand the economic and technical constraints in a cross-national setting. The exericse is interesting and productive in itself, but the results are only part of a larger whole.

Production

Since the ultimate purpose of estimating the technical production functions is the derivation of a synthetic supply function for rice with the relative price of rice to fertilizer as the primary argument, it is sufficient to concentrate attention on the relevant parameter in the production function—the output elasticity with respect to fertlizer input. As a starting point we use a simple Cobb-Douglas function:

$Q = A H^{\alpha} F^{\beta}$, where

Q = rice production

H = area harvested

F = fertilizer application

---

[e]The log-inverse function takes the form $\log C = \frac{\gamma}{P}$, where C is consumption and P is price. When γ is positive, the price elasticity is negative but approaches zero as P increases.

Application of standard profit maximization procedures yields an equally simple expression relating rice production to the relative price of rice to fertilizer:

$$Q = B P^{\frac{\beta}{1-\beta}} \text{, where}$$

$$P = \text{Ratio of rice to fertilizer prices}$$

$$B = A\beta H^{\alpha}$$

Clearly, β is the critical parameter for the trade simulation runs. But the rather single-minded concentration on the magnitude of β and its subsequent impact on production levels as prices vary is not intended to downgrade a number of other very important factors that influence rice production. Area expansion, especially of technically irrigated area, is still open to a number of countries in Asia. Further use and development of high yielding varieties, pesticides, and herbicides seem clearly in the immediate future for most of the low yield countries.

But these aspects of rice production are not treated further because the primary interest at this stage is the relatively short run impact of prices on consumption, production, and trade patterns. Expansion of acreage, new irrigation works, and better distribution of high yielding varieties are not directly affected in the short run by prices (except perhaps in a permissive way). However, if developments in these fields are induced by higher relative prices for rice, the estimates of response of output to price changes will be *understated.* The concern here is only with response to fertilizer, and short run response at that.

Table 3-2 presents the results of several different specifications of the rice production function. As Equation P-I shows, nearly 94 percent of the variation in total rice production for the nine countries during the 1962-70 period is accounted for by variations in area harvested and fertilizer applications. An equivalent yield equation, not shown, indicates that over 70 percent of yield variations are accounted for by the same two variables. Impressive as these results appear, they should be kept in perspective. The fact that these two inputs, area and fertilizer, account for 94 percent of variations in rice production does not mean that they cause this much of the variation. Other variables that are essential to achieving any output at all may be used more or less in tandem with these two variables, and hence their contribution is captured by the output coefficient of one or the other of the included inputs. This is the specification bias problem mentioned earlier.

It is easy to see how it might work. For most of these Asian countries, expansion of land area under rice means a concomitant expansion of labor inputs; they are basically labor surplus and land scarce countries. Hence the exclusion of labor from the production function probably accounts for some of the large output coefficient attached to area harvested (although a separate

Table 3-2. Rice Production Function, 1962-70[a]

Equation Number	Independent variables and coefficients					
	R^2	A_o	A_i	F	F_i	H
P-I	0.9372	−1.049 (−3.2)	–	0.251 (12.4)	–	0.867 (32.6)
P-II	0.9952	−2.377 (−2.6)	*	0.123 (4.9)	–	1.202 (10.1)
P-III	0.9973	−3.769 (−2.8)	*	0.028 (0.8)	*	1.473 (9.8)
P-IV	0.9955	−2.413 (−2.7)	*	0.109 (4.3)	*	1.222 (10.4)

*Country specific coefficients.

Country	Equation P-II	Equation P-III		Equation P-IV		Equation P-V			
	A_i	A_i	F_i	A_i	F_i	A_i	F_i	H_i	R^2
Japan	0.627	−5.561	0.467	−1.929		−2.557	0.441	0.730	0.6595
	(4.0)	(−2.0)	(2.4)	(−1.5)		(−0.6)	(3.1)	(1.8)	
So. Korea	0.779	−0.542	0.157	−1.494	0.181	−5.652	0.172	1.684	0.5082
	(3.4)	(−0.4)	(1.5)	(−1.3)	(2.0)	(−0.8)	(1.1)	(1.6)	
Taiwan	0.865	−2.481	0.333	−1.301		4.943	0.440	−0.354	0.9060
	(3.3)	(−1.5)	(2.5)	(−1.2)		(1.5)	(7.2)	(−0.7)	
Malaysia	0.736	3.070	−0.134	0.809		−0.346	0.023	1.173	0.9808
	(2.3)	(2.4)	(−1.5)	(2.6)		(−0.8)	(0.2)	(4.6)	
Ceylon	0.468	−2.943	0.370	0.537		−8.306	0.261	1.974	0.8429
	(1.6)	(−1.7)	(2.6)	(1.9)		(−2.8)	(1.0)	(4.5)	
Indonesia	−0.273	−0.496	0.028	−0.248		−2.988	0.083	1.293	0.8870
	(−3.9)	(0.6)	(0.4)	(−3.5)		(−1.1)	(1.1)	(3.3)	
Thailand	−0.191	−1.345	0.111	−0.176		−3.602	0.150	1.286	0.9841
	(−3.7)	(−2.8)	(2.3)	(−3.4)		(−3.1)	(9.3)	(9.2)	
Philippines	−0.369	−3.570	0.301	−0.329		5.815	0.330	−0.162	0.9235
	(−3.8)	(−4.7)	(4.4)	(−3.4)		(1.3)	(8.5)	(−0.3)	
Burma	b	b	b	b		−10.083	0.037	2.208	0.8009
						(−2.6)	(1.7)	(4.8)	

[a] All functions were estimated in double logarithmic form. Thus both dependent and independent variables shown are logarithms. Numbers in parentheses are t-statistics. There are 81 observations (nine countries for nine years).

[b] A separate intercept for Burma was dropped from Equations III, IV, and V to avoid a singular matrix. Its effect is included in A_o.

labor coefficient for several of these countries would probably be near zero). Similarly, fertilizer inputs are correlated with a number of other output raising inputs–e.g., higher yielding seeds, better water control, better management practices, etc. Thus the value of β in Equation P-I of 0.251 is too large to use as an estimate of the pure response to fertilizer in the short run.

On the other hand, to the extent that the other yield raising inputs continue to be associated with fertilizer inputs as in the past, the coefficient of 0.251 is not such a bad estimate of the longer run potential for rice intensification. But this longer run potential cannot be achieved by higher fertilizer applications alone. Figure 3-1 shows that the longer run potential can be achieved only by moving from one short run response function to another higher one and from there to yet another. The succession of short run functions depends on all the "other" factors determining rice production: seed with higher fertilizer response potential linked with better water control and farmer knowledge.

Although all the evidence is not in, price induced shifts along the short run response function seem to have their longer run counterparts. Hayami and Ruttan have argued along similar lines for movements along their metaproduction function.[f] This longer run potential of price policy to draw along the

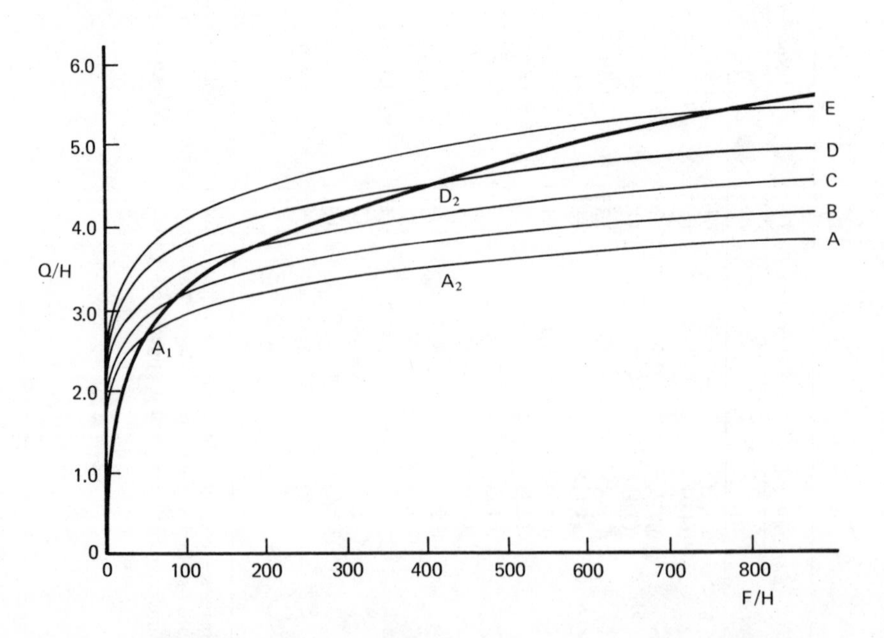

Figure 3-1. Short Run and Long Run Production Function

[f]See Hayami and Ruttan (4), pp. 82 ff.

essential ingredients of agricultural modernization is fascinating and, needless to say, controversial. However, it is not the process that most interests us here. We wish to concentrate on movements along the short run response functions when the other factors are held more or less constant.

In the absence of satisfactory input data for the missing factors of production—labor, capital, management—the only means by which they can be held more or less constant is through analysis of covariance estimates of the production function. In the present context this means the production function for the entire sample of nine countries and nine years must be estimated with separate intercept terms. These will tend to capture the pervasive differences among countries in utilization of the missing inputs. The procedure was originally used in the economics literature to correct for "management bias," the bias resulting from exclusion of this nonobservable input, but it is also largely applicable to the present problem.[g]

Equation P-II reports the statistical results of the analysis of covariance specification. The separate intercept terms are individually highly significant and their range and magnitudes accord with general expectations. Five of the countries are on higher short run response functions than Burma (whose effect is captured in the overall intercept A_o, and hence it serves as the reference base): Japan, South Korea, Taiwan, Malaysia, and Ceylon. The three lowest yielding countries—Indonesia, Thailand, and the Philippines—are on lower response functions. The arithmetic antilog of the intercept for Taiwan is more than three times higher than that for the Philippines, to look at the extremes. That is, the factors *not included* in the continuous arguments of the production function account for a three-fold shift in yields from the lowest response function to the highest. This is ample evidence that those factors, although excluded, are very important in the production process. Of course some of them, such as hours of summer sunshine, are not transferable from one country to another. Others, such as a high proportion of land under controlled irrigation, are transferable only at major investment costs. And still others, such as high yielding seeds, may be transferable at relatively modest costs in adaptive research and extension efforts.

But again, these issues are not of major concern here. Interest continues to focus on the value of β, the fertilizer response coefficient. With many yield increasing factors now captured by the separate country intercepts, this coefficient should drop substantially. And it does, from 0.251 in Equation P-I to 0.123 in Equation P-II. The *pure* short run effect of increasing fertilizer by 10 percent is an increase in output of only 1.23 percent—a value just half the long run elasticity. Figure 3-1 has been drawn using these two coefficients to illustrate the rather dramatic difference between short run and long run

[g]For further discussion of specification bias, management bias, and analysis of covariance techniques as a corrective, see Griliches (3), Hoch (5), Mundlak (9), and Timmer (11).

responses. In the short run, Indonesia, for instance, must move along the lightly drawn function A, whereas Taiwan can move along function E. Even if Indonesia were to apply equal amounts of fertilizer per hectare in the short run, its yields would not equal Taiwan's. On the other hand, extremely high prices for rice relative to fertilizer such as exist in Japan might make it profitable to use fertilizer so intensively that Japan's rice farms would outyield Taiwan's even though Japan is on a lower short run response function than Taiwan.

It is this role of price in determining where on the short run response function a country is located that should be explored further. In Figure 3-1 above, Indonesia cannot move from A_1 to D_2 by price policy, although it may in the long run be more economical than the move from A_1 to A_2. But the move to D_2 is simply not an option in the short run, say three to five years, while the move to A_2 is. It still may not be economic, but it is an option.

Three other sets of results are also of interest. Equation P-III is an analysis of covariance speçification where separate intercepts and separate β coefficients are estimated for each country (while holding the area coefficient the same for all countries). The increase in R^2 from 0.9952 to 0.9973 is very small but significant in terms of the nine degrees of freedom cost in achieving it. On the other hand, a number of A_i and F_i coefficients are no longer significant. Although Equation P-III provides statistical evidence that the fertilizer response coefficients are not constant across all nine countries, it does not provide a very satisfactory explanation of what these coefficients are. Neither does the next step, reported as Equation P-V, although in actuality these are nine separate equations, one for each country. Thus the generally low significance attached to one or more of the coefficients for each country is not surprising: each regression is run on only nine observations and the data are relatively unrefined.[h] On the other hand, all the fertilizer coefficients are positive and in a generally reasonable range.

Equation P-IV is an attempt to back off from the disaggregation of Equations P-III and P-V while retaining some of their differences in fertilizer responses. Accordingly, the three temperate countries, Japan, South Korea, and Taiwan, are permitted a fertilizer elasticity modifier. When this is done, the overall fertilizer response coefficient continues to drop to 0.109. The coefficient for the three temperate countries is significantly higher, however. The modifier has a value of 0.181; so the total fertilizer response coefficient for these three countries is 0.290. It should be noted that the higher fertilizer response comes at the expense of the significance of the separate intercept terms for Japan, South Korea, and Taiwan. In terms of total explanatory power, Equation P-IV is not significantly better than the simple analysis of covariance model in Equation

[h]In particular, the fertilizer data relate to total nutrients applied to all crops. No attempt has been made to sort out proportions applied to rice for individual countries or years. Similarly, the production and area data relate to upland as well as wetland rice. Upland rice seldom receives artificial fertilizer in any of the countries in this sample.

P-II. The difference in response elasticities between the three temperate countries and the six more tropical countries has considerable intuitive appeal, however, and these values of β (0.109 for the tropical countries and 0.290 for the temperate countries) are used in the supply function simulations to be presented later.[i]

Although it is probably no longer necessary to defend the proposition that farmers will react appropriately to price changes in their inputs and outputs, a slightly broader methodological issue is at stake. In particular, do farmers in different countries, faced with different relative input/output prices, react as though they were constrained by similar production functions? It is not essential for the argument that they do, but the results portrayed in Figure 3-2 make it easier to argue that prices count.

Figure 3-2 plots the relationship between the relative price of rice to fertilizer in each country in 1970 (taken from Table 3-1) against rough estimates of fertilizer applications per hectare on rice. These latter figures are based on the total fertilizer application data used for the production function analysis, modified by rough judgments of the proportion of the total actually applied to rice. All fertilizer in Burma and Thailand was assumed to be used on rice (although lowering this figure toward zero would marginally improve the results). Two-thirds of the total was assumed to be applied to rice in Japan, South Korea, Taiwan, Ceylon, Indonesia, and the Philippines, which reflects alternative uses on vegetables, sugar, or plantation crops. Data for Taiwan that show approximate applications by crop support the two-thirds assumption. Malaysia is assumed to apply only 20 percent of its total fertilizer to rice. This figure is the high estimate derived from cross-section surveys of paddy farmers where actual fertilizer applications were measured. The remaining 80 percent is used mostly by the very modern rubber and oil palm estates.

The simple plot in Figure 3-2 of the relationship between the relative price of rice to fertilizer and the application of fertilizer per hectare on rice is striking enough, but Table 3-3 presents the almost startling results of estimating the statistical relationship between these two variables. A very simple linear equation, F-1, explains nearly 88 percent of the variation in fertilizer applications per hectare on the basis of relative price. Permitting a separate intercept for the three temperate countries, Japan, South Korea, and Taiwan—in keeping with their separate fertilizer response coefficients from the production function estimations—improves the fit considerably while somewhat lowering the fertilizer response to price.

The response elasticity at mean values of price and fertilizer application is 1.5 for Equation F-I, and it drops to 1.0 in Equation F-II.

[i]The fertilizer response coefficients reported here are in close agreement with more micro-based results reported for a number of countries. See the results of Shih for Taiwan reported by Lee (7), for the Philippines by Barker (2), for South Korea by Moon (8), and for Indonesia by Timmer (12).

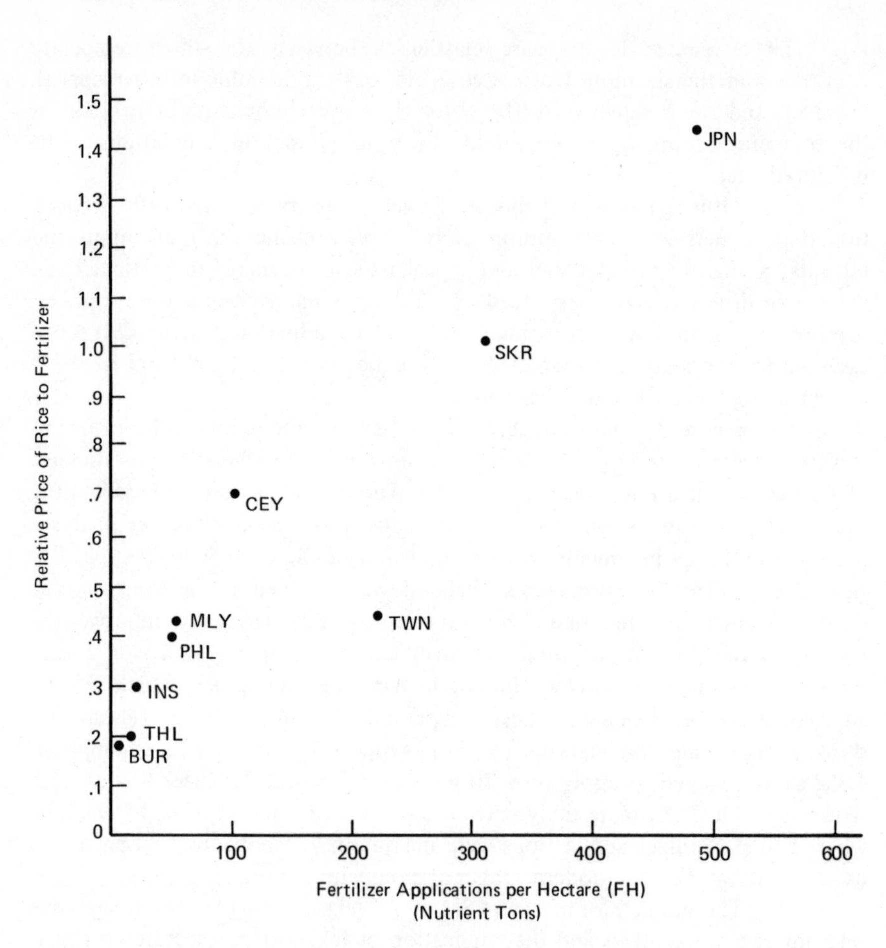

Figure 3-2. Relationship Between the Relative Price of Rice to Fertilizer and Fertilizer Applications per Hectare

Equation F-III and F-IV report the results when both variables are transformed into logs. The simple log function without a separate temperate country intercept fits somewhat better than its linear counterpart since both the overall intercept and the price coefficient have higher *t*-values. But the separate intercept specification is not quite as successful in logs, and Equation F-II provides the best understanding of the underlying relationships. Despite the fact that there are only six degrees of freedom for the price coefficient and only two for the separate temperate intercept, both variables are highly significant.

These results provide a strong rationale for the overall exercise performed here. They argue that the cross-national structure of production does

Table 3-3. Relationship Between Relative Price and Fertilizer Applications on Rice, 1970[a]

Equation Number	R^2	*Dependent*	*Intercept*	*Temperate Dummy*	*Relative Price*	*Log Relative Price*
		Variables and Coefficients				
F-I	0.8793	F/H	−69.580 (−1.9)		373.214 (7.1)	
F-II	0.9853	F/H	−46.480 (−3.3)	154.667 (6.6)	240.427 (8.5)	
F-III	0.8912	Log F/H	5.718 (20.7)			1.972 (7.6)
F-IV	0.9458	Log F/H	5.027 (14.3)	0.970 (2.5)		1.515 (5.6)

[a]There are nine observations, one for each country in the sample. The temperate dummy has a value of one for Japan, South Korea, and Taiwan. Figures in parentheses are *t*-values.

depend to a significant degree on the structure of relative prices of rice to fertilizer via the physical fertilizer response function. In turn, since this relative price ratio depends so critically on governmental policies (not a single country among the nine permits internal prices to be freely determined by c.i.f. international trade prices), it does no violence to reality to imagine that these prices might change. What happens when they do is the question addressed by the trade simulation runs discussed later.

Consumption

Although the results of Table 3-3 are convincing evidence that relative prices do indeed influence fertilizer applications, it was not possible to estimate this relationship directly from the nine-year cross-section sample. The relationship to be used in the trade simulation runs is derived from the technical production function by assuming profit maximization. But the price issue must be faced directly in the consumption estimations, and it was necessary to draw from a wide variety of international and national publications for consumption, retail price, and income data for the same nine countries and the same nine years.

Since the Houthakker-Weisskoff approach has been excluded for present purposes, it was also necessary to collect exchange rates for each of the nine countries for each year from 1962 through 1970. An attempt was made to formulate "realistic" exchange rates by comparing official rates with black market rates reported in *Pick's Currency Yearbook.* Some countries caused more problems than others. For Indonesia and Burma it was necessary to rely on informed estimates from the World Bank and elsewhere to reach benchmark figures for certain years. The overall results are not very satisfactory, especially in terms of year-to-year variations in prices and incomes for particular countries. The only solution will be to get reasonably accurate prices for several competing foodstuffs (and possibly clothing) for each country and then to construct a relative price series—largely neutral with respect to exchange rates—for some typical market basket of goods. But this for the future.

In the meantime, despite significant shortcomings in any particular figure from the data, the overall structure seems not too far from reality. In some ways it is almost immaterial whether the price or income data for Indonesia or Burma are wrong by plus or minus 50 percent. They are such extreme observations that the difference would be minor, relative to countries at the opposite end of the spectrum. Consequently, a number of essentially experimental estimations were made by excluding various countries from the sample to test the sensitivity of the coefficients. The results are reported in Table 3-4.

Both prices and per capita incomes for all countries are constructed by applying the best U.S. dollar exchange rate estimate available to the current value of price and income in domestic currency. The result is a value in U.S. dollars, but the U.S. dollar was not entirely stable during this period (although most countries in the world suffered at least as much inflation as the United States). Consequently, rice prices (but not incomes) were deflated by the U.S. Consumer Price Index for the relevant years to gain some impression of the impact of converting to constant dollar prices. The results are reported in Table 3-4 as equations with a "d" attached to the number. In general the results are not strikingly different. Only those equations with the more dramatic differences are reported. As expected, since rice consumption tended to rise over the period for most countries, deflating the prices magnifies any tendency for a decline in price. Thus the resulting price elasticities tend to be slightly more negative, and more significantly so, than the same elasticities for undeflated prices.

If nothing else, the results in Table 3-4 suggest that some caution should be used in picking *the* price elasticity for this sample of countries—or indeed, even in picking a single equation with a variable price elasticity that adequately represents the entire sample. Equations C-I to C-IV report the more interesting results of the estimations involving the entire sample set. A very simple log double inverse function for price and incomes shows only a marginally significant negative income coefficient, hence declining (as incomes rise) but positive income elasticities, with an insignificant but positive price coefficient, which indicates a negative and decreasing (in absolute terms, as prices rise) price elasticity.[j]

Equations C-II and C-III are far superior to this simple function.

[j]When the functional form is $\log C = \alpha + \beta \log P + \frac{\gamma}{P} + \delta \log Y + \frac{\epsilon}{Y}$, the price elasticity is $\beta - \frac{\gamma}{P}$ and the income elasticity is $\delta - \frac{\epsilon}{Y}$.

Equation C-III in particular has highly significant coefficients attached to both log and inverse of price. The income coefficients are relatively insignificant. This equation also introduces a variable to test for the importance of rice trade in consumption patterns. The variable "trade ratio" is the value of a country's total exports (negative) or total imports (positive) divided by its total consumption. It varies from as much as +0.5 for Burma in occasional years to –0.5 for Ceylon, again occasionally, with a mean value of 0.033, indicating the region as a whole was a net importer over the 1962-70 time period of about 3 percent of its rice. The trade variable is highly significant, with per capita consumption higher in exporting than in importing countries.

Although the evidence is not yet available to test the hypothesis, it seems likely that the trade ratio picks up a number of factors, most important of which is the relative availability of alternative carbohydrates that might compete with rice. Exporting countries have a surplus of rice and do not need to develop alternative carbohydrate sources. Importing countries have probably found it necessary, especially in time of international rice shortage, to develop a nonrice staple as well.

Equation C-III is a relatively satisfactory equation, but its use in the simulations creates a problem. The sign of the inverse price coefficient is negative, which means that the price elasticity increases in algebraic terms as price decreases. At the low price levels of Burma, Indonesia, and Thailand the price elasticity becomes positive. This is contrary to economic logic (and empirical fact in Indonesia). Consequently, equations with negative inverse price coefficients, while revealing something of the structure of consumption among countries, are unsatisfactory as the base of the simulation runs across a very wide range of prices.

It was the dominance and significance of the negative price inverse coefficient that prompted the runs with various countries excluded from the sample. The extreme range of variation in price levels may be distorting the inverse price coefficient so that it reflects something other than relatively short run effects of price changes. It may be picking up taste differences that vary somewhat systematically with price differences (which also vary systematically with income differences). Consequently, the remaining equations, with the exception of C-IV, exclude one or more countries from the regression sample.

The results are quite illuminating. With Japan excluded from the regression, as in Equation C-V, both price and income coefficients become larger and more significant relative to the same coefficients in the same equation for the whole sample, C-II. In addition, the price level at which the price elasticity turns positive decreases in Equation C-V, from \$72.5 per ton to \$69.8 per ton. Japan, therefore, seems to be one of the culprits in the unsatisfactory sign of the price inverse term.

At the other extreme, Indonesia and Burma may be causing problems. With both Japan and Indonesia excluded, a simple log price term

Table 3-4. Rice Consumption Functions, 1962-70[a]

Equation Number	Equation Excludes[b]	R^2	Constant	Rice Price		Per Capita Income		Trade Ratio
				Log	Inverse	Log	Inverse	
C-I	none	.0294	4.899 (78.9)		6.326 (0.6)		−10.622 (−1.2)	
C-I d	none	.0343	4.891 (77.5)		11.004 (0.9)		−12.461 (−1.5)	
C-II	none	0.1668	8.037 (8.4)	−0.456 (−1.9)	−33.051 (−1.4)	−0.075 (−0.6)	−29.594 (−1.8)	
C-III	none	0.4271	7.735 (9.6)	−0.482 (−2.4)	−45.210 (−2.3)	0.007 (0.1)	−14.080 (−1.0)	−0.706 (−5.8)
C-IV	none	0.8976	c	−0.157 (−1.3)	−17,862 (−1.8)			
C-V	J	0.2046	10.838 (6.6)	−0.629 (−2.4)	−43.927 (−1.8)	0.393 (−1.9)	−65.213 (−2.7)	
C-VI	J	0.4200	7.123 (4.4)	−0.451 (−2.0)	−43.958 (−2.1)	0.084 (0.4)	−5.140 (−0.2)	−0.745 (−4.9)
C-VII	J,I	0.0637	5.718 (14.1)	−0.166 (−2.0)				
C-VIII	J,I	0.0646	4.744 (53.3)		19.722 (2.0)			
C-IX	J,I	0.2371	4.916 (2.1)	0.426 (1.0)	104.755 (2.0)	−0.455 (−2.2)	−79.424 (−3.2)	
C-X	J,I,B	0.1479	4.802 (45.8)		44.573 (2.4)		−30.538 (−2.9)	
C-XI	J,SK, TW,M	0.0505	4.998 (31.7)		9.528 (0.6)		−20.908 (1.4)	
C-XI d	J.SK TW,M	0.0592	4.976 (30.9)		17.270 (0.9)		−23.830 (−1.6)	

C-XII	J,SK, TW,M	0.6055	19.872 (4.9)	−2.356 (−3.7)	−157.047 (−3.7)	−0.366 (−0.4)	−71.185 (−1.1)	−0.526 (−3.0)
C-XII d	J,SK TW,M	0.6026	21.466 (5.2)	−2.160 (−3.6)	−175.794 (−3.6)	−0.783 (−1.0)	−99.058 (−1.6)	−0.569 (−3.4)
C-XIII	I,TH,B P,CY	0.4278	6.213 (23.5)	−0.246 (−5.1)				
C-XIV	I,TH,B P,CY	0.4574	4.601 (83.3)		58.676 (5.4)			
C-XIV d	I,TH,B P,CY	0.4904	4.574 (81.3)		75.672 (5.7)			
C-XV	I,TH,B P,CY	0.7296	4.962 (2.9)	0.257 (0.8)	75.277 (1.2)	−0.276 (−3.4)	−49.648 (−3.8)	−0.440 (−3.6)
C-XV d	I,TH,B P,CY	0.7480	1.573 (0.6)	0.811 (1.7)	224.164 (2.0)	−0.326 (−3.8)	−53.256 (−4.0)	−0.308 (−2.1)

[a]Figures in parentheses are *t*-statistics. The sample size is 81 except when countries are excluded from the estimated equation. Each excluded country drops nine observations from the sample. The dependent variable is always log of per capita consumption per year.

[b]The following code indicates countries dropped from the estimation: J = Japan, I = Indonesia, TH = Thailand, B = Burma, SK = South Korea, P = Philippines, TW - Taiwan, CY = Ceylon, and M = Malaysia.

[c]The country specific intercepts are as follows: Japan = 6.012, Indonesia = 5.678, Thailand = 6.451, Burma = 6.245, South Korea = 6.059, Philippines = 5.653, Taiwan = 6.206, Ceylon = 5.757, Malaysia = 5.954. The *t*-statistics exceed 5.8 for all coefficients.

becomes significantly negative for the first time, for an implied constant price elasticity of about –.17. Also, the price inverse term alone is significant, and, for the first time, satisfactorily positive at 19.722. There is little to choose between these two equations (C-VII and C-VIII), and the value of approximately 20 for the price inverse coefficient is one of four used later for simulation runs to calculate implied trade flows at various prices. Lastly, with this sample it is useful to compare Equation C-IX with Equations C-V and C-II, already discussed. The income terms continue to gain in significance. At higher income levels the income elasticity turns negative, which accords well with some empirical variants of Engel's Law. The most pleasing aspect of Equation C-IX, however, is that the price inverse term is now significantly positive and large. It is large to offset a marginally significant positive coefficient attached to the log price term. These two terms taken together imply an increasing price elasticity in algebraic terms as price increases, from highly negative at low prices to positive at prices over $245 per ton. This too accords with the expected direction of change.

The remaining equations report some of the results obtained from other sample variations. The value of about 40 for the price inverse term in Equation C-V, when Japan, Indonesia, and Burma are excluded, is also used for one of the trade flow simulations. The value of nearly 60 in Equation C-XIV, when the sample *includes* only the higher income countries of Japan, South Korea, Taiwan, and Malaysia, is also used for one run. The fourth value used for the trade simulations is zero, suggested perhaps by the coefficient of 6 in Equation C-I, which is not significantly different from zero.

Before moving directly to the trade simulations, one last issue must be discussed. What happens when analysis of covariance consumption functions are estimated? They were very revealing about the nature of specification bias and the difference between short run and long run response in production functions, but what is their impact and role in consumption function estimation? Equation C-IV in Table 3-4 reports the only results worth reporting. First, and obviously, separate intercept terms for each country raise the R^2 dramatically to more than double the level in the next best equation. This says no more than that consumption levels are very significantly different between countries. The marginally significant price coefficients in C-IV indicate that even when the average differences in consumption levels are removed, price continues to have an impact on consumption (with a negative elasticity for prices over $115). The smallness and marginal significance of this impact is due to the rather questionable accuracy of year-to-year changes for any single country's data.

It is tempting to say that the separate intercept terms pick up neutral differences in taste in the consumption function, just as separate intercepts in a production function might pick up neutral shifts due to managerial differences. But dumping all this into the economic wastebasket labeled "tastes" obscures much of the real impact of prices over the longer run.

Both theory and a great deal of evidence support the contention that price response is greater in the long run than in the short run. The analysis of covariance consumption function demonstrates that and no more. The full impact of price, albeit in the slightly longer run of perhaps three to five years, can be measured only by looking at differences among countries as well as within countries. All the equations except C-IV do this.

The results of the consumption function cannot be neatly summarized. No single number emerges; no equation is best. What does stand out from the combination of equations is that prices and incomes are significant determinants of rice consumption across countries, but neither the data nor possibly reality will permit a neat conclusion as to just how. Perhaps this is enough. For the analytical purposes of the trade simulations it is sufficient to test a range of parameters. As indicated above, the consumption function for these simulations takes the form of the log inverse term varying from zero to 20 to 40 to 60. All these numbers have some empirical justification in Table 3-4. None of them should be singled out—at least at this stage—as better than the others with the exceptions that zero and 60 are both less likely than 20 to 40 on statistical grounds. The results have shown some price response but not a lot.

Much remains to be done on the consumption side, just as on the production side. Although further variations could be pursued with the present data, they are unlikely to achieve major improvements over the results presented here. More and better data are needed, and they are being collected. For the moment, however, we have enough evidence to proceed.

TRADE

Before the trade levels at various prices can be calculated, a functional relationship and several calibrating parameters must be determined. This is most easily seen in terms of the equation system needed to generate net trade flows:

$$P = A\,(PRF)^{\frac{\beta}{1-\beta}}$$

$$C^* = B + \frac{\gamma}{(RPR)}$$

$$(RPR) = M + \theta\,(PRF)$$

$$C = (e^{C^*})\,(POP)$$

$$T = P - C - DSTK, \text{ where}$$

P = Production

PRF = Relative price of rice to fertilizer

C^* = Log of per capita consumption

RPR = Retail price of rice

C = Total consumption

POP = Population

T = Net trade in rice

$DSTK$ = Change in stocks in 1970

In addition to the variables, the system contains three estimated parameters (β, γ, and θ) and three calibrating parameters (A, B, and M). For all equations the value of β is 0.109 for the six tropical countries and 0.290 for the three temperate countries. As noted earlier, four values of γ are tried: 0, 20, 40, and 60. The values of A and B for each country are determined directly from the estimated production and consumption functions except that corrections must be made for any errors in estimating the actual 1970 levels from observed levels of 1970 independent variables. This correction has been made so that both production and consumption are calibrated to actual 1970 levels as a base and then are coupled to the estimated response coefficients.

Determining the levels of M and θ requires a determination of the functional relationship between the relative price of rice to fertilizer to the farmer and the retail price to the consumer. The relationship is not simple because: (1) fertilizer prices vary significantly from country to country; (2) the marketing margin between paddy prices to the farmer and retail prices to consumers varies from country to country; (3) some countries attempt to subsidize urban rice prices and/or support farm paddy prices (independently); and (4) the relationship will vary between net importers and net exporters. What is needed here is a full study of rice marketing in these nine countries as it interacts with rice price policy. In the meantime a simple expedient has been taken: the parameter M has been set to zero and θ has been set equal to the simple ratio of the retail rice price to the rice-fertilizer price ratio. When this is done, θ varies widely but around a clear central tendency.[k]

With the system fully calibrated, it is possible to generate some net trade levels as a function of price. These are shown in Tables 3-5 to 3-8 for the four different consumption coefficients starting with zero response of consumption to price and gradually increasing. The price elasticity for each coefficient, at the mean price for the entire sample of $133 per ton, rises in absolute terms from zero to –.15, –.30, and –.45. The elasticity is not, of course, constant for all price levels, although it is always less than or equal to zero.

[k]The values of θ for each country are as follows: Japan, 350; South Korea, 286; Taiwan, 395; Malaysia, 509; Ceylon, 144; Indonesia, 307; Thailand, 650; Philippines, 295; and Burma, 325. Marketing margins are receiving further treatment under the auspices of the Stanford Rice Project.

Table 3-5. Net Trade in Rice at Different Assumed Ratios of Rice to Fertilizer Prices (000 metric tons)

Pi	*Japan*	*South Korea*	*Taiwan*	*Malaysia*	*Ceylon*	*Indonesia*	*Thailand*	*Burma*	*Philippines*	*Total Excluding Burma and Thailand*	*Total*
0.1	–6969	–3136	–1045	–420	–746	–2406	344	184	–547	–15268	–14740
0.2	–5681	–2632	–640	–350	–676	–1514	1063	640	–285	–11778	–10075
0.3	–4390	–2265	–344	–307	–632	–956	1513	925	–121	–9363	–6925
0.4	–3970	–1964	–102	–275	–600	–542	1846	1137	–0	–7453	–4470
0.5	–3308	–1706	107	–249	–574	–211	2113	1306	97.0	–5844	–2425
0.6	–2720	–1476	291	–227	–552	66	2336	1447	178	–4440	–656
0.7	–2188	–1269	459	–209	–553	305	2529	1570	249	–3186	913
0.8	–1699	–1078	613	–192	–517	516	2700	1678	311	–2047	2330
0.9	–1246	–901	755	–177	–502	705	2852	1774	366	–999	3627
1.0	–821	–735	889	–164	–489	877	2990	1862	416	–26	4826
1.1	–420	–578	1015	–152	–476	1034	3117	1942	462	884	5943
1.2	–41	–430	1134	–141	–465	1179	3234	2016	505	1741	6991
1.3	320	–289	1248	–130	–454	1314	3343	2085	545	2553	7980
1.4	665	–154	1356	–120	–445	1439	3444	2149	582	3324	8917
1.5	996	–25	1460	–111	–435	1558	3539	2210	616	4059	9808
1.6	1314	99	1560	–102	–427	1669	3629	2267	649	4763	10659
1.7	1621	219	1657	–94	–418	1775	3715	2321	680	5439	11474
1.8	1916	334	1750	–86	–410	1875	3796	2372	709	6089	12256
1.9	2203	446	1840	–79	–403	1971	3872	2421	737	6715	13009
2.0	2480	554	1927	–72	–396	2062	3946	2468	764	7321	13735
1970 Actual Net Trade	770	–737	5	–266	–534	–950	1064	640	0	–1712	–8

Positive levels are exports; negative levels are imports. The log inverse coefficient used for the consumption function in this table was 0–i.e., no consumption response to price is permitted.

Since production reacts positively to price changes and consumption negatively, the lowest overall response of trade to price is shown in Table 3-5 where the consumption coefficient is zero. Even with what must be taken as the lower bound estimate of short run price response the results are rather dramatic. The weighted average price implied by the total net trade figure of –8,000 tons is 0.64. If all countries had this price ratio, rather than their actual ratio, total net trade for 1970 would have been the same, but the distribution would have been quite different. Japan would have imported nearly two-and-one-half million tons while Indonesia would have moved to a net exporter of nearly one-quarter million tons. The major increased production response would have come from Burma and Thailand, since their actual price ratios of only 0.2 were so much lower than the weighted average. Even with a very low physical response of output to increased fertilizer actual fertilizer applications in these two countries are so low that considerable scope exists for dramatically higher output within the mid range of relative prices existing in Asia in 1970.[1]

Figure 3-3 plots the results of Table 3-5 on a country basis to demonstrate the point that self-sufficiency is a relative concept. Within the range of price ratios actually observed in 1970, from the lows of 0.2 for Burma and Thailand to the high of 1.43 for Japan, nearly all things are possible for all countries. At the top end, only Ceylon, Malaysia, and South Korea remain as net importers at Japan's prices. But below the Philippine price of 0.4 all countries except Burma and Thailand would import. The reactions depicted in Figure 3-3 must be taken as a minimum estimate because no consumption response to price changes is included.

Table 3-6 shows the results of introducing a low estimate of consumption response to price. Especially at the lower price ratios where the price elasticity becomes fairly large—approximately –0.6 for the mid range of marketing coefficients (θ)—the trade values already show some tendency to explode. Thus at the price ratio prevailing in Burma and Thailand in 1970, Japan would import nearly nine million tons, and if all countries paid the same relative price of 0.2, the total region would import 18 million tons. Such numbers are impossible in reality, but so would be the low relative rice to fertilizer prices that generated them. It is thus the price ratios that are impossible rather than the resulting trade flows.

The consumption response to price is dampened as the relative price rises due to the smaller (in absolute terms) implicit price elasticity. At a price ratio of 1.0, for instance, the net trade values by country in Table 3-6 are not nearly as different from the values in Table 3-5 as when the price ratio is 0.2. The major differences that do occur are for Indonesia, Burma, and Thailand, where exports increase by more than three-and-one-half million tons under the influence of the consumption reaction to price. Even with a low consumption

---

[1]This fact has not been lost on knowledgeable observers, as the recent article in the *Far Eastern Economic Review* attests. See Phelan (10).

Figure 3-3. Net Trade in Rice as a Function of Price, by Countries, Assuming Zero Consumption Response

Table 3-6. Net Trade in Rice at Different Assumed Ratios of Rice to Fertilizer Price (000 metric tons)

Relative Price	*Japan*	*South Korea*	*Taiwan*	*Malaysia*	*Ceylon*	*Indonesia*	*Thailand*	*Burma*	*Philippines*	*Total Excluding Burma and Thailand*	*Total*
0.1	–14797	–7231	–2148	–804	–4228	–9016	–935	–1585	–2848	–41073	–43592
0.2	–8789	–4141	–985	–471	–1654	–2907	1064	640	–926	–19874	–18170
0.3	–6551	–3093	–476	–350	–1093	–955	1897	1404	–323	–12843	–9540
0.4	–5179	–2480	–134	–282	–844	100	2417	1837	0	–8820	–4567
0.5	–4168	–2044	132	–235	–700	800	2793	2134	213	–6002	–1076
0.6	–3354	–1699	355	–199	–603	1316	3088	2358	369	–3816	1630
0.7	–2662	–1411	549	–171	–533	1723	3331	2539	492	–2013	3857
0.8	–2055	–1160	722	–147	–480	2058	3539	2689	593	–468	5760
0.9	–1510	–937	880	–126	–436	2343	3721	2819	678	891	7431
1.0	–1013	–734	1026	–109	–401	2590	3883	2933	752	2112	8927
1.1	–554	–548	1162	–93	–370	2809	4028	3035	818	3223	10286
1.2	–126	–376	1289	–78	–344	3005	4161	3128	876	4247	11534
1.3	277	–214	1410	–65	–321	3183	4283	3210	929	5198	12691
1.4	657	–62	1524	–53	–301	3345	4396	3288	978	6088	13772
1.5	1018	83	1634	–42	–282	3495	4501	3359	1022	6927	14788
1.6	1362	220	1738	–32	–266	3635	4600	3426	1064	7721	15747
1.7	1692	351	1838	–22	–250	3765	4693	3488	1102	8476	16657
1.8	2009	478	1935	–12	–236	3887	4780	3547	1138	9197	17524
1.9	2314	599	2028	–4	–223	4001	4863	3603	1172	9886	18352
2.0	2608	715	2118	4	–211	4100	4942	3655	1205	10548	19146
1970 Actual Net Trade	770	–737	5	–266	–534	–950	1064	640	0	–1712	–8

Positive levels are exports; negative levels are imports. The log inverse coefficient used for the consumption function in this table was 20.

response coefficient and within the mid range of price ratios for the sample, changes in consumption due to price changes drastically alter net trade flows for several countries. The results are even more dramatic as the consumption coefficient is increased to 40 and then to 60. The results are seen in Tables 3-7 and 3-8. These tables give some hint of what might be expected over the longer run if relative prices were to be changed and held at new levels for perhaps a decade.

Figures 3-4 and 3-5 illustrate what some of the effects might be. Figure 3-4 shows the net trade in rice for the total sample of nine countries and a subtotal that excludes Burma and Thailand, assuming consumption response coefficients of zero and 40. The most dramatic impact from including the mid range estimate of consumption response is a significant lowering of the implicit price at which self-sufficiency is reached for the seven countries excluding Burma and Thailand. Without a consumption response this subtotal of countries reaches self-sufficiency at a relative price of just over 1.0. But when the consumption coefficient is 40, self-sufficiency is reached much easier at a price ratio of 0.75. Both figures are within the range of actual relative prices in 1970, but the value of 0.75 is only slightly higher than the 1970 average relative price level, weighted by production levels, of 0.62.

A somewhat different perspective is shown in Figure 3-5 where implied trade levels for Ceylon and Indonesia are plotted for several different consumption response coefficients. Ceylon achieves self-sufficiency through short run price policy only by using the highest consumption response coefficient of 60. This is not too unreasonable, for at Ceylon's actual 1970 retail price of $101 per ton the implied price elasticity is –0.6, and it declines (absolutely) to –.27 at the self-sufficiency price ratio of 1.55. It should be noted that this price ratio exceeds any actually observed in 1970. On the other hand, Ceylon announced plans to ban further rice imports after 1974. It will be interesting indeed to see what internal prices rise to after this self-sufficiency is "achieved."

The changes in Indonesian trade levels are rather more dramatic. If the consumption coefficient is 60–implying a price elasticity of –.65 at Indonesia's 1970 retail price–self-sufficiency is reached at a relative price of 0.34, only 13 percent above the actual level in 1970. On the other hand, if there is zero consumption response to price changes, self-sufficiency can be reached only with a relative price of 0.58–nearly double the 1970 level, although still below the weighted average price for the entire sample. Very clearly, the size of the consumption response to rice price changes is an extremely critical parameter for planning Indonesia's rice policy.[m]

AN OVERVIEW

A broader look at the results presented here shows that the consumption response parameter is critical not just for Indonesia but for nearly every country in

[m]The same conclusion was reached earlier from a different starting point. See Afiff and Timmer (1).

Table 3-7. Net Trade in Rice at Different Assumed Ratios of Rice to Fertilizer Price (000 metric tons)

Relative Price	Japan	South Korea	Taiwan	Malaysia	Ceylon	Indonesia	Thailand	Burma	Philippines	Total Excluding Burma and Thailand	Total
0.1	–28106	–14916	–3783	–1324	–15652	–19220	–2426	–3995	–6675	–89675	–96096
0.2	–12763	–6135	–1382	–605	–3258	–4458	1065	638	–1686	–30288	–28584
0.3	–8658	–4067	–616	–396	–1694	–953	2265	1835	–537	–16921	–12821
0.4	–6519	–3055	–167	–289	–1128	710	2946	2436	0	–10446	–5065
0.5	–5095	–2407	158	–221	–836	1728	3412	2820	325	–6347	–114
0.6	–4023	–1932	417	–172	–656	2439	3766	3099	550	–3378	3486
0.7	–3157	–1557	636	–134	–533	2977	4050	3315	718	–1049	6315
0.8	–2423	–1243	827	–103	–443	3406	4287	2492	852	874	8652
0.9	–1782	–973	999	–78	–374	3761	4492	3641	962	2517	10649
1.0	–1209	–734	1156	–56	–318	4063	4671	3770	1056	3958	12399
1.1	–689	–519	1300	–36	–272	4326	4832	3883	1136	5247	13961
1.2	–211	–322	1435	–19	–233	4558	4976	3985	1207	6415	15376
1.3	233	–140	1561	–4	–199	4766	5108	4077	1271	7487	16672
1.4	648	29	1681	10	–170	4954	5230	4161	1328	8480	17871
1.5	1039	188	1794	23	–145	5125	5343	4238	1381	9406	18987
1.6	1410	338	1902	35	–122	5283	5448	4310	1429	10276	20034
1.7	1763	481	2006	46	–101	5430	5546	4377	1473	11097	21021
1.8	2100	616	2105	56	–82	5566	5639	4440	1514	11876	21955
1.9	2423	746	2201	66	–65	5694	5726	4499	1553	12617	22843
2.0	2734	871	2294	75	–49	5814	5809	4555	1589	13326	23690
1970 Actual Net Trade	770	–737	5	–266	–534	–950	1064	640	0	–1712	–8

Positive levels are exports; negative levels are imports. The log inverse coefficient used for the consumption function in this table was 40.

Table 3-8. Net Trade in Rice at Different Assumed Ratios of Rice to Fertilizer Price (000 metric tons)

Relative Price	*Japan*	*South Korea*	*Taiwan*	*Malaysia*	*Ceylon*	*Indonesia*	*Thailand*	*Burma*	*Philippines*	*Total Excluding Burma and Thailand*	*Total*
0.1	–50738	–29334	–6210	–2028	–53132	–35005	–4164	–7265	–13038	–189483	–200913
0.2	–17842	–8773	–1841	–755	–5890	–6197	1066	640	–2586	–43884	–42178
0.3	–11105	–5215	–765	–445	-2476	–958	2613	2226	–763	–21726	–16887
0.4	–8003	–3692	–201	–297	–1457	1282	3435	2952	0	–12368	–5981
0.5	–6093	–2796	182	–208	–983	2574	3977	3394	433	–6891	480
0.6	–4731	–2177	476	–145	–711	3442	4377	3704	720	–3127	4954
0.7	–3672	–1707	718	–99	–533	4080	4693	3940	929	–285	8349
0.8	–2802	–1323	926	–62	–408	4578	4954	4130	1090	1994	11079
0.9	–2059	–1010	1110	–32	–313	4983	5176	4289	1221	3900	13365
1.0	–1408	–734	1276	–6	–240	5324	5369	4425	1330	5542	15336
1.1	–826	–489	1428	16	–180	5617	5540	4545	1423	6988	17073
1.2	–298	–269	1569	36	–130	5873	5693	4651	1503	8284	18629
1.3	188	–67	1700	53	–88	6100	5873	4747	1575	9462	20041
1.4	639	118	1824	69	–52	6305	5961	4834	1639	10543	21337
1.5	1061	291	1941	83	–21	6490	6079	4914	1697	11544	22536
1.6	1458	453	2053	96	7	6661	6189	4987	1750	12478	23654
1.7	1834	606	2159	108	32	6817	6291	5056	1799	13356	24703
1.8	2191	751	2261	120	54	6963	6388	5121	1844	14184	25692
1.9	2532	889	2359	130	75	7099	6478	5181	1886	14969	26628
2.0	2858	1021	2453	140	93	7226	6564	5238	1925	15716	27519
1970 Actual Net Trade	770	–737	5	–266	–534	–950	1064	640	0	–1712	–8

Positive levels are exports; negative levels are imports. The log inverse coefficient used for the consumption function in this table was 60.

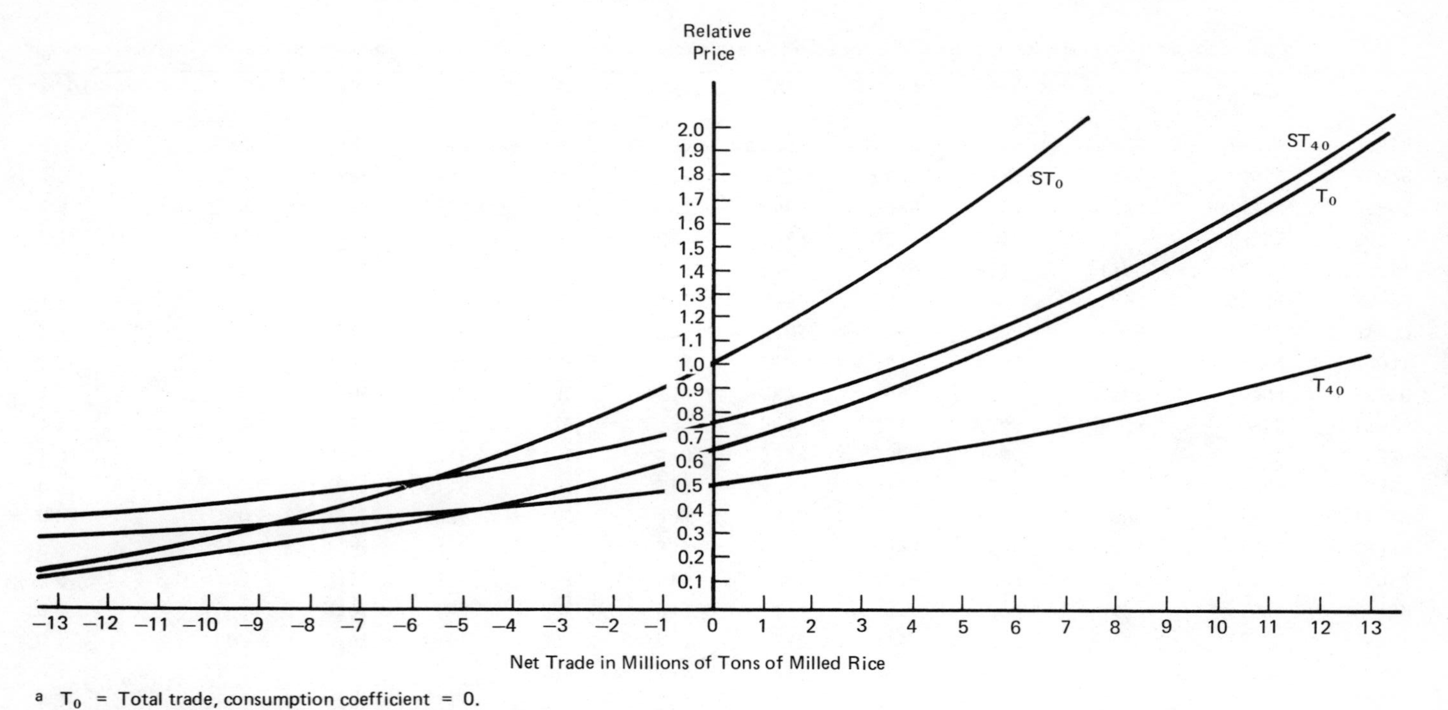

[a] T_0 = Total trade, consumption coefficient = 0.
ST_0 = Total trade, excluding Burma and Thailand, consumption coefficient = 0.
T_{40} = Total trade, consumption coefficient = 40.
ST_{40} = Total trade excluding Burma and Thailand, consumption coefficient = 40.

Figure 3-4. Net Trade in Rice as a Function of Price[a]

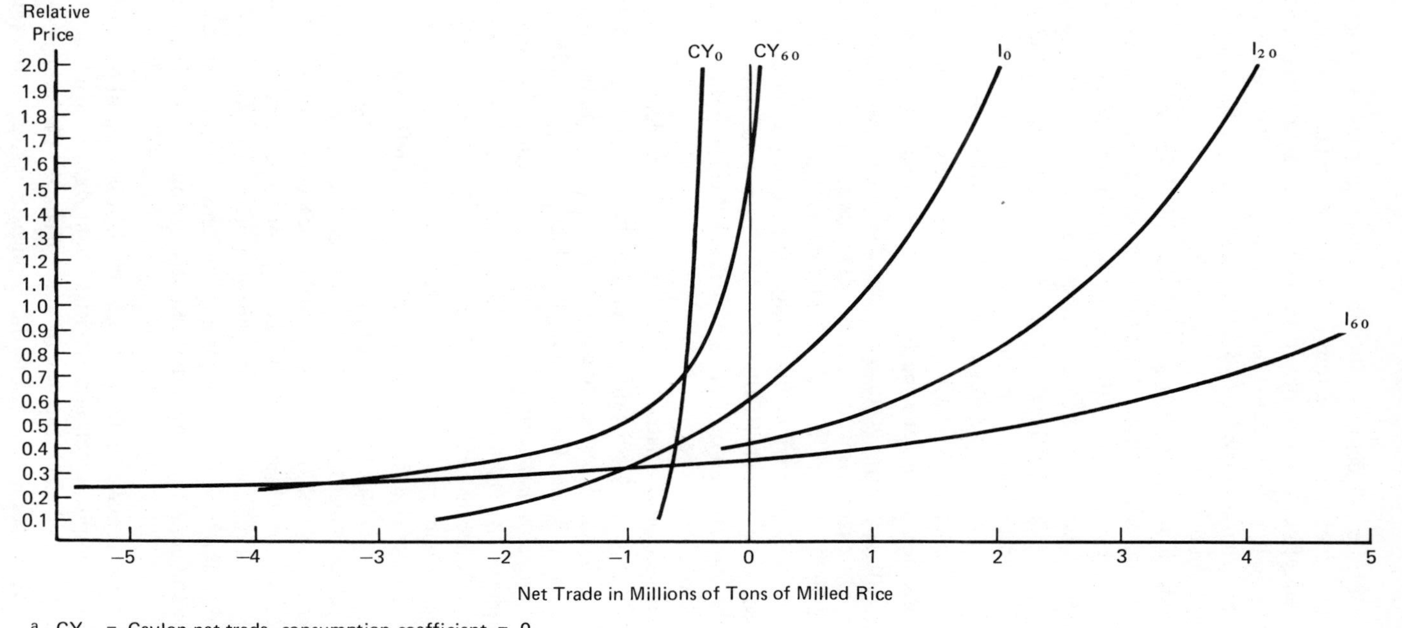

[a] CY_0 = Ceylon net trade, consumption coefficient = 0.
CY_{60} = Ceylon net trade, consumption coefficient = 60.
I_0 = Indonesia net trade, consumption coefficient = 0.
I_{20} = Indonesia net trade, consumption coefficient = 20.
I_{60} = Indonesia net trade, consumption coefficient = 60.

Figure 3-5. Net Trade in Rice as a Function of Price, for Ceylon and Indonesia and Selected Consumption Response Coefficients[a]

Asia. Table 3-5 and Figure 3-3 demonstrated that self-sufficiency is a relative concept with only a production response to price. But even a small consumption response magnifies the effect dramatically. Each country must have good evidence of what its overall price response is and what the welfare effects of changes would be, but the double-edged role of price policy in the drive for self-sufficiency should not be ignored.

The broader look also reveals some of the impact on trade patterns of a regional common market for rice. Although such a market is clearly not remotely possible in the near future, the extent of the implied changes are interesting nonetheless. Assuming the mid range consumption response (a coefficient of 40) and the same 1970 regional net imports of 8,000 tons but at a uniform price for all countries, what happens to the internal pattern of trade in rice? The important changes in sign are for Japan and Indonesia: Japan becomes a net importer of five million tons instead of exporting three-quarters of a million tons; Indonesia becomes a net exporter of one-and-three-quarter million tons instead of importing nearly one million tons. The important magnitude changes, apart from sign changes, involve a three-fold increase in South Korea's import requirements and a more than three-fold increase in exports from Burma and Thailand. The other countries exhibit only minor changes under these assumptions because their actual 1970 rice to fertilizer price ratios were relatively close to the assumed uniform price of 0.503 that leads to the regional net trade that did occur in 1970.

These changes are dramatic, but they are probably understated from the point of view of rice per se. On the production side, no acreage response due to higher relative rice prices with respect to competing crops has been permitted. For Indonesia, Thailand, South Korea, and the Philippines especially, this acreage response is probably larger than the short run yield response due to higher fertilizer applications. On the consumption side no direct substitution effects with respect to other major carbohydrates have been estimated. They are subsumed—but probably only partially so—in a single overall own-price response. Many countries have a more significant substitution effect than reflected here.

It is important not to lose sight of the fact that gains in rice production due to acreage substitution are only marginal in a total output sense. Similarly marginal are the welfare effects of higher rice consumption at the expense of maize, barley, or wheat. But what is happening to rice alone is also important for several reasons, including the heavy weight most Asian policy makers place on rice production and consumption and for the impact of changing production and consumption on the relatively narrow world market for rice.

What are we to make of all this? First, it might be helpful to restate what is now obvious. Despite great uncertainties about exact magnitudes of responses of production and consumption of price changes, the evidence is overwhelming that differences in rice and fertilizer prices across countries (and over time) are an important determinant of levels and patterns of international trade in rice. If nothing else, this has been established. Less certainly, some understanding of the statistical relationships implied by the above statement has been established, and, equally important, several areas of further research have been isolated. Much of this research is currently in progress.

But in the end we have been left holding an empty bag if the ultimate purpose of this chapter has to understand what causes levels and patterns of trade in rice. Prices do, among other things, but what determines prices? Here we are drawn up short. The answer to this question obviously lies beyond the realm of econometric models. It lies with urban masses who take to the streets when prices rise, with sullen peasants who withdraw from the market when prices fall, with relative availability of foreign exchange, with who owns the fertilizer plants—in short, the answer lies within the political economy of each country. If we can understand this—and a group of collaborative scholars in the U.S. and Asia is trying—then the frontiers of understanding of the Asian rice economy will have been pushed outward.

Part II

The Analysis of Development Experience

Chapter Four

The Interaction of Growth Strategy, Agriculture, and Foreign Trade: The Case of India

John W. Mellor and Uma Lele

In the relationship between agriculture and trade in economic development, agriculture is usually depicted as providing exports to earn the foreign exchange requisite to industrial growth.[1] That agricultural exports of low income countries have comprised a major proportion of their total exports and were expected to have poor prospects for growth only reinforced the argument for a pattern of industrial development designed for increasing self-sufficiency. Such a pattern then tends to lead to an increasingly capital intensive industrial structure. In this context, agriculture may have a further related role of displacing agricultural imports to further release the foreign exchange constraint on industrial growth.

In contrast to this passive role for agriculture, we depict a relationship among agriculture, trade, and growth in which development of the agricultural sector plays a basic role as determinant of the strategy of growth, with profound implications to overall growth rates and the pace and pattern of industrial growth, and thereby becomes a major determinant of the volume and composition of foreign trade. In this chapter we briefly contrast strategies of growth with divergent roles for agriculture and trade, and then within that context analyze the pattern of imports and exports for India. The Indian case is particularly relevant to our purpose because of the early emphasis on a capital intensive growth strategy with related slow growth of agriculture and of foreign trade and the current opportunities for a change in that strategy based on the nascent potentials in new agricultural production technologies.

This chapter gives particular emphasis to the close interrelation

Note: This paper is based substantially on a background paper prepared by Uma Lele for the Twentieth Century Fund Study, directed by John W. Mellor, *India and the New Economics of Growth*, forthcoming, 1974.

among policies for agriculture, increased employment growth, the structure of industrial growth, trade, and even the nature of planning. We will of course dwell on the trade aspect, but always within the broader context of which trade strategy is a component. We argue that the capital intensive industrial strategy, so much in the ascendancy in the recent past in India specifically and in the literature of economic development generally, inevitably was associated with slow growth in agriculture, in employment, and in trade.[2] And conversely, an increased rate of employment growth, now of so much policy concern, requires complementary change in agricultural and trade policies and of planning procedures.

THE STRATEGY OF GROWTH

We simplify the presentation by dichotomizing between what we will term a high employment strategy of growth and a capital intensive strategy of growth. Japan, Taiwan, South Korea, Hong Kong, and Singapore represent variants of the high employment strategy. India, particularly by the record of the Second Five Year Plan, epitomizes the capital intensive strategy. In making this simplified classification it should be clear that the objectives of economic development are complex and an employment orientation has not often been in the past (nor for many countries is it now) an overriding objective of growth.[3]

A high employment strategy for economic growth has four major components that differentiate it from the capital intensive strategy.[4]

First. It includes provision for an elastic supply of basic wages goods. Low income laborers spend as much as 60 percent of increments to their income on food grains and 80 percent on all agricultural commodities.[5] Thus as rapid mobilization of labor into more productive employment raises incomes there is sharp increase in demand for agricultural commodities.[6] Money wages rates, social discord, or both are likely to rise with consequent efforts to reduce employment growth unless the increased demand is met by increased supply.

In the case of a few small nations such as Singapore, Hong Kong, and South Korea, all or part of the increase in demand for agricultural commodities may be met by rapid growth in agricultural imports and compensating growth in exports of other labor intensive commodities. Thus trade may play an important direct role in a strategy emphasizing labor mobilization. However, for large countries, and the collectivity of small countries, the volume of agricultural imports to support rapid employment growth may strongly affect international terms of trade and hence require that wages goods demand be met largely by increased domestic production, leaving a less direct role for trade in the strategy.

Second. The employment oriented strategy requires a supply of capital commensurate with the needs for the expanded rate of agricultural growth and to complement the large additions to effective employment made possible by increased supply of wages goods. Vigorous growth in agriculture may assist in meeting the capital need through higher savings rates in that sector.[7] Nevertheless, it seems certain that the employment oriented strategy would require lower capital intensity in the industrial sector than the capital intensive strategy. Such reduction in capital intensity may occur in part through change in the structure of domestic demand towards relatively labor intensive consumer goods, prompted by rising incomes in the more rapidly developing agricultural sector.[8]

Third. Capital intensity of industrial production may also be reduced by foreign trade, becoming the third element of an employment oriented strategy. Increase in labor intensive exports is at once facilitated by relaxation of the wages goods constraint and concurrently allows increased employment with a given stock of capital. The larger and more rapidly growing domestic market for relatively labor intensive consumer goods, incident to rising rural incomes, further encourages economies of scale and efficient production of goods with a potentially competitive position in export markets. Concurrently, increase of capital intensive imports frees domestic capital for more employment oriented, labor intensive production. This need is accentuated as labor intensive production is likely to be materials intensive—with particular demand for capital intensive intermediate products such as steel, aluminum, plastics, and synthetic fibers.[9] Thus both exports and imports serve to reduce the average capital intensity of production through change in industrial structure.

Fourth. Increased agricultural production to relax the wages goods constraint, change in industrial structure, and foreign trade each play a complementary role in an employment oriented strategy of growth. The increased emphasis on agriculture and trade in particular, and the likely greater importance of small scale industry in this strategy, also argue for this fourth element of the strategy—a lesser role for central direction of the economy and hence greater use of the market for allocation of resources. Thus the planning procedures also change with a change from a capital intensive to an employment oriented strategy of growth.[10]

The employment oriented strategy outlined above is in sharp contrast to the strategies implicit in the Indian Second Five Year Plan and generally reflected in the literature of multisectoral consistency and optimizing models.[11] In that strategy, growth is seen as a function of increase in the capital stock. Greater employment is implicitly unfortunate because it tends to increase demand for consumer goods and divert resources away from capital goods and hence from growth. It can be seen that there is little place for investment in a consumer goods sector such as agriculture in such a strategy. And trade tends to be ignored (as by Mahalanobis) or treated simplistically (as by Chakravarty), with the export growth rate given exogenously and imports primarily comprised of machinery for increased capital goods production.[12] The models for this strategy are one factor of production growth models, à la Harrod-Domar, and hence the complex question of resource allocation between capital goods and wages goods does not arise. Three points of importance to this chapter should be noted.

First. Just as the strategy has no significant role in growth for agriculture, so it is an appropriate strategy if it is not known how to increase agricultural production through technological change: for then agriculture will be subject to diminishing returns and increasing costs and hence there will be rising costs of labor. The Mahalanobis strategy, including the small role for foreign trade, then follows inexorably through increasing substitution of capital for increasingly costly labor.

Second. The capital intensity of industrial production increases (a) on theoretical grounds, in order to reduce resource leakage away from capital goods and towards employment and wages or consumer goods; and (b) on practical grounds, in that the strategy tends to be associated with political factors arguing for large scale, public sector industries, which are normally highly capital intensive. Thus in India structural change alone, excluding the effect of change in technology, resulted in a level of industrial employment in 1965 that was half as great as would have occurred if all the increments to industrial investment subsequent to 1952 had been invested proportionately to the initial investment.[13] That structural change was the product of the strategy.

Third. Leading directly from the first and second, the basis for foreign trade is lost. Labor is then not a cheap resource, because of the wages goods constraint, thus eliminating a basis for low income countries to have labor intensive production to trade with high income countries having capital intensive production. Further, since in this strategy growth will then depend solely on mobilizing savings and producing capital goods, there will be little growth in consumer expenditure and so domestic consumer goods markets will stagnate. Thus both the Lindar[14] and Heckser-Ohlin[15] bases for trade are lost. The capital intensive strategy is of course self-fulfilling in that it tends to starve agriculture of resources and structures industry away from commodities with which a low income country has trade advantage. Of course, the practice of development diverges from the theory, and Indian agriculture in particular received attention greater than that suggested in the theory and even the theory was bent to provide greater emphasis on intermediate products, such as fertilizer. But, the strategy follows from a situation of poor agricultural prospects, whether those poor prospects be a function of the natural environment or lack of a positive development effort in the agricultural sector.

It is in this context that we wish to review the Indian record, first in imports and then exports. In the section on imports we wish to emphasize the quite different structure of imports and the higher rate of growth that would follow a shift to an employment oriented strategy. In the section on exports we emphasize that the export potentials are much greater than assumed in justifying the capital intensive strategies and that the capital intensive strategy has served to stifle existing areas of exports and promises to stifle new export possibilities in the same manner. We will use the difficult case of Indian textile exports to underline the argument.

THE CHANGING GROWTH AND STRUCTURE OF INDIA'S IMPORTS

The capital intensive strategy of growth suggests a large increase in import of capital goods as the growth strategy is initiated and then gradual decline as the policy of self-sufficiency is successfully pursued. India's import record was initially consistent with the strategy—imports increasing little from 1950 to 1956, then growing at 12.7 percent per year from 1956 to 1961 as the capital oriented strategy was applied, and then declining to a 7 percent growth rate in the 1961 to 1964 predrought period of rapid industrial growth.[16] Imports then actually declined by one-quarter between 1964 and 1970, but that was due to the industrial recession incident to the great drought of 1965-67 and the concurrent sharp decline in foreign aid.

A useful perspective on the course of Indian import policy is provided by comparison of the Indian record with that of a set of other countries. For example: from 1950 to 1960 India's imports grew at 5.5 percent per year; this was comparable with mature economies such as the United States at 4.6 percent and the United Kingdom at 3.3 percent (Table 4-1). Its growth in that period was much more rapid than Singapore's and was comparable with Taiwan (6.4 percent), the Philippines (4.5 percent), and Hong Kong (5.7 percent) among developing countries. South Korea was an exception, having a greatly higher rate of 14.2 percent.

The sharp contrast between India and the other countries occurs in the 1960s. While every other country in the comparison greatly increased its rate of growth of imports, India actually experienced decline in essentially every major category of imports except agriculture, petroleum products, and chemicals, the latter comprised substantially of fertilizers (Table 4-2). In contrast, other countries experienced rapid growth in nearly all categories of imports and particularly in manufactured commodities. This is particularly true of those countries which were successful in achieving high rates of growth in both exports and national income.

Consistent with the capital intensive strategy, machinery and transport equipment comprised a large and rapidly growing component of India's

Table 4-1. Import Performance of Selected Countries by Commodity Groups, 1950-60

Commodity Groups	*Taiwan*	*India*	*Japan*	*South Korea*	*Philippines*	*Hong Kong*	*Singapore*	*United Kingdom*	*United States*
					(percent per year)				
Food & Live Animals	6.45	1.61	–1.25	– 1.33	2.31	4.13	–0.49	3.30	1.10
Beverages & Tobacco	6.65	–11.19	–1.97	–66.39	–35.63	4.82	–5.42	4.43	7.14
Crude Materials	2.56	– 1.32	7.26	39.96	26.72	1.33	3.69	–1.12	–1.28
Mineral Fuels & Lubricants	18.39	2.00	15.69	51.16	4.60	7.73	–6.28	7.17	11.81
Animal & Vegetable Oils	7.47	18.73	9.73	14.80	9.00	–8.74	4.29	–4.85	–2.28
Chemicals	9.72	10.07	22.58	16.45	7.76	–1.33	2.72	7.44	5.32
Manufactured Goods	–0.68	14.81	20.44	3.58	–1.83	10.10	–0.54	5.20	5.48
Machinery & Transport Equipment	10.41	14.80	19.72	30.39	13.59	14.44	0.77	13.18	22.26
Miscellaneous Manufactured Articles	2.82	9.65	16.87	15.05	–5.21	6.59	1.76	16.53	14.07
Miscellaneous Transactions	–	25.85	7.43	30.93	31.65	3.13	–1.02	2.37	15.22
Total	6.36	5.51	8.61	14.21	4.54	5.72	0.35	3.34	4.62

Source: Computed from data in United Nations, Dept. of Economics & Social Affairs, Statistical Office, *Yearbook of International Trade Statistics*, New York, various issues.

Table 4-2. Import Performance of Selected Countries by Commodity Groups, 1960-69

Commodity Groups	*Taiwan*	*India*	*Japan*	*South Korea*	*Pakistan*	*Philippines*	*Hong Kong*	*Singapore*	*United Kingdom*	*United States*
	(percent per year)									
Food & Live Animals	12.63	6.59	14.52	13.92	6.97	10.60	6.91	2.28	0.41	5.15
Beverages & Tobacco	7.98	–11.62	12.69	43.82	–0.12	27.64	6.91	4.84	1.19	9.32
Crude Materials	18.51	–1.43	9.95	18.56	1.69	4.41	5.76	–5.75	0.23	2.37
Mineral Fuels & Lubricants	12.10	4.43	15.07	13.49	–1.36	10.43	9.21	6.64	5.49	5.88
Animal & Vegetable Oils	3.79	14.87	6.89	10.14	6.18	6.19	–0.32	8.80	4.12	5.89
Chemicals	18.64	7.06	11.60	9.41	10.97	8.41	8.44	8.22	10.55	12.89
Manufactured Goods	23.35	–5.45	21.57	22.35	3.81	9.81	10.69	9.62	11.35	11.52
Machinery & Transport Equipment	30.27	–5.04	8.92	31.45	8.62	12.99	13.63	10.12	14.64	26.24
Miscellaneous Manufactured Articles	22.84	–8.40	19.72	15.06	4.60	9.63	14.89	7.14	9.89	16.52
Miscellaneous Transactions	14.26	31.81	–	–30.93	–	–28.60	–1.86	4.75	23.58	15.49
Total	17.61	–1.18	12.60	18.94	6.08	10.17	9.76	4.46	5.81	11.81

Source: Computed from data in United Nations, Dept. of Economics & Social Affairs, Statistical Office, *Yearbook of International Trade Statistics*, New York, various issues.

imports. However, India's limited resource base required additional large imports of natural resource based commodities; the vagaries of the monsoon and failure to constrain consumer incomes resulted in large food grain imports; and again, somewhat despite the strategy, capital intensive intermediate products such as steel and fertilizer comprised a major portion of imports. It is quite possible that in changing to an employment oriented strategy, growth of imports in each of these categories would accelerate substantially. It is that prospect that lends such urgency to accelerating export growth if the employment oriented strategy is to succeed.

Machinery and transport equipment comprised over one-third of all imports in 1965 and in 1969 still equalled over one-quarter of imports.[17] In the employment oriented strategy, it is likely that a higher proportion of capital goods would be produced domestically to meet the needs of smaller scale, more labor intensive and more consumer goods oriented industries compared to the large scale heavy industry emphasis of the capital intensive approach. Nevertheless the faster overall growth rate could well result in accelerated machinery imports—quite possibly, however, with compensating greater exports of more labor intensive types of machinery. In this context the Japanese example is instructive. Despite development of a broad base of domestic industrial capacity, Japan's imports of machinery and transport equipment grew at a rate of 20 percent per year from 1950 to 1960, and even from 1961-69 such imports grew at a rate of 9 percent per year (Tables 4-1 and 4-2). Japan's machinery exports grew even more rapidly (see Table 4-4).

The future course of food grain imports is a function of the pace of technological change in agriculture: the extent to which a demand increasing, employment oriented strategy is pursued on the one hand, and on the other, the extent to which demand is contained by fiscal policy and the availability of foreign exchange from exports or aid. For individual years, of course, weather is the primary determinant of food grain imports. In the longer term, it is perhaps likely that imports would be least with both slow and fast growth rates of food grain production and fastest for an intermediate level.

For example, a 4 to 5 percent growth rate of production might result in a low level of imports, as a relatively high growth rate of employment could be sustained with domestic production; while a slow rate of food grains production, of say less than 3 percent, would also be accompanied by only slow growth in food grains imports, as political concern for sustainability of a high level of imports of food grains argued for a low employment growth strategy. Yet a moderate rate of growth of food grains production of 3 to 4 percent might provide sufficient confidence for an expansionary employment policy and an economic base for accelerated export growth and hence both the necessity and the means of large food grain imports in years of poor weather and low food grain production. Further complicating estimation—particularly within the context of accelerated food grains production and a high employment strategy—

food grain exporting nations could foster increased Indian imports through bilateral concessionary trade agreements and the reduced risks and uncertainty incident to long term agreements.

It seems virtually certain that an employment oriented strategy would require accelerated growth in imports of nonfood grain agricultural commodities. These commodities, particularly including vegetable oils and cotton, had grown to comprise over one-quarter of India's imports by 1968–and that for commodities for which demand is highly income elastic and in a context of both slow growth of consumer incomes and slow growth of exports such as textiles for which agricultural commodities are raw materials.[18] To avoid accelerated rate of growth of imports would require a substantially more rapid rate of production growth for these commodities than for food grains production, presumably requiring a faster rate of technological change than for food grains, or substantial acreage shift induced by relative decline in food grain prices. Such a configuration seems unlikely in the near term.

In the favorable years of industrial growth, such as 1963 and 1964, the capital intensive intermediate products, iron and steel plus fertilizers, comprised about 15 percent of India's import bill.[19] In a labor intensive strategy of growth, demand for these commodities and others of similar characteristics such as aluminum and synthetic fibers will grow rapidly in response to rising demand from rising national income as well as from growth of labor intensive industries that process such commodities for the export market. Concurrently, the new strategy will allocate capital supplies largely to more labor intensive industries; thus imports of this already large category of commodities must increase rapidly.

Mineral fuels, the most important of the direct resource based imports, have only exceeded 10 percent of imports in one year, 1957, prior to the sharp price increases of 1973-74.[20] For the same reasons as the capital intensive intermediate products, demand for such commodities will grow at an accelerated pace with an employment oriented strategy. Insofar as such natural resource based commodities are not produced domestically or are exploited through highly capital intensive processes for which foreign exchange is not readily and specifically available, then imports will grow rapidly. A general upward shift in relative primary product prices, as for petroleum in 1973-74, serves to reinforce the logic of shift to an employment oriented growth strategy because of the inefficiency with which the capital intensive strategy provides the then much larger requirement of foreign exchange.

The "Approach to the Fifth Plan"[21] is basically at variance with the import expectations set forth here. The "Approach" document is in roughly the same conceptual mould as the Second Plan, is based on an input-output model, assumes a fixed, slow rate of growth of exports at 7 percent, concludes that imports must be constrained to that rate or slower, and argues for doing so in large part by reducing "luxury" consumption and expanding the capital intensive sector to displace imports. Such a plan is probably infeasible, at least at the targeted level, without resumption of large scale net foreign aid on a long term basis. It is certainly inconsistent with an employment oriented strategy.

Further sharpening the contrast between the earlier argument that the capital intensive strategy prejudices exports, the "Approach" document argues that it facilitates exports.[22] This is presumably because imports are considered relatively fixed and so domestic production of intermediate products relaxes that constraint on production of goods for which they are a raw material. Similarly:

> The exercise indicates that progress towards self-reliance will be significantly accelerated if higher levels of production can be achieved in a few sectors such as steel, non-ferrous metals, fertilisers and crude oil. All efforts should be concentrated on expanding production at a fast rate in these sectors.

Likewise . . .

> It may be possible to improve the projected rate of growth of output of fertilisers. Since in the accepted variant, fertilisers continue to be imported in substantial quantities in the terminal year, any increase in production above the estimated level will be desirable from the balance of payments angle.[23]

Again the emphasis falls heavily on these capital intensive sectors. Indeed, so much weight is placed on them that expansion of electric power—clearly nonimportable—seems to have been slowed dangerously even by the standards of the "Approach" document, let alone by the standards of an agriculture and employment oriented strategy as set forth here:[24]

> Rate of growth of electricity (for the Fifth Plan) is appreciably lower compared to the rate postulated by the Fuel Policy Committee. This is partly attributed to the same factors as mentioned for coal (slower than expected economic growth) and partly on account of restriction implied on the rate of growth of domestic demand for electricity as a result of reduced inequality.

This is, of course, not to say that such an allocational policy will follow as the pragmatic and politically influenced process of policy determination and implementation proceeds.

If India follows an employment oriented strategy, with its consequent substantial increase in trade, the related problems of ensuring vital supplies and protecting against large increases in relative prices must be dealt with. Presumably an effective planning mechanism could make estimates of long term needs and use those as a basis for long term contracts with foreign suppliers; such contracts could be dispersed among political and economic blocks to minimize scope for external pressure. It is by no means clear that such a process involves any greater risk to supplies than do reliance on domestic supplies in circumstances of capital constraint, apparently poor ability to estimate future demand, and uncertain management and technology. It must be remembered that the fertilizer crises of 1972-74 was in the context of an effort to achieve substantial self-sufficiency and probably arose in large part through misestimate of future domestic production, based in particular on overly optimistic estimates of capacity utilization.

INDIA'S EXPORT PERFORMANCE AND ITS DETERMINANTS

Exports provide the means of payment for imports and therefore are at the core of a strategy that attempts to spread domestic capital over a larger employment through import of necessary capital intensive commodities. Thus, one of the prime arguments for the capital intensive strategy is a pessimism with respect to export prospects—usually based on expectation of poor prospects for growth in demand for primary commodities and of protectionism against manufactured goods by high income countries. At least ex poste, this argument was also frequently raised in India.[25] However, the evidence, particularly of the 1960s, does not support the pessimistic view of exports either for low income countries generally or for India specifically.

Total exports from less developed countries grew at a rate of 6.9 percent from 1960 to 1969 (Table 4-3). This is more than two-thirds the rate of growth of exports from the developed countries for the same period, and 90 percent as fast as growth in exports from the Eastern Bloc countries. More important, the less developed countries had faster rates of growth in almost every major category of exports to nearly every category of area. In all the categories for which developed countries' exports grew rapidly, less developed countries' exports grew even more rapidly.

Food and raw materials and ores are the two categories of commodities for which world exports increased slowest. With the minor exception of textiles and clothing to Eastern Bloc countries and the "residual" exports, it is only in these two slow growth categories of exports that less developed countries have performed less well than high income countries. It is of course these commodities that have in the past comprised the bulk of less developed countries' exports and it is the heavy weight to these slower growth commodities that accounts for the overall slower growth rate of exports of less developed areas.

It is particularly noteworthy that imports of the various categories of manufactured goods from the developed areas grew much less rapidly than

Table 4-3. Growth Rates of World Exports by Regions and Commodity Groups, 1960-69

Commodity Groups	*Exports of Industrial Areas to:*				*Exports of Developing Areas to:*				*Exports of Eastern Trading Bloc to:*				*World Exports to World*
	Industrial Areas	*Developing Areas*	*Eastern Areas*	*World*	*Industrial Areas*	*Developing Areas*	*Eastern Areas*	*World*	*Industrial Areas*	*Developing Areas*	*Eastern Areas*	*World*	
						(percent per year)							
Food	7.15	4.38	2.45[a]	6.39	3.50	4.27	7.02	4.17	22.33	14.39	3.57	7.11	5.54
Raw Materials & Ores	5.34	5.80	5.05	5.36	2.84	4.10	2.79[b]	2.82	10.31[a]	3.72[a]	1.69[b]	4.92	4.33
Fuels	5.34	0.52[a]	–	5.60	10.19	4.23	–	8.60	8.02	3.75	3.68	5.50	7.43
Basic Metals & Chemicals	11.27	5.12	8.59	9.84	12.52	14.87	12.36	12.33	16.78	7.98	4.63	7.45	10.13
Machinery & Transport Equipment	14.75	9.22	14.08	13.15	32.23	12.67	0.00	19.60	12.56	10.53	10.01	10.27	12.89
Textiles & Clothing	10.12	3.85	24.05	8.55	13.98	5.21	22.15	10.58	15.55	12.18	14.15	13.72	9.34
Other Manufactures	10.52	5.62	16.04	9.46	16.06	10.23	18.77	13.60	12.01	4.39	2.61	4.67	9.14
Residue	15.77	12.09	6.83[a]	13.77	8.49[b]	−6.03	–	8.70	21.50[b]	36.68	9.27	23.37	14.39
Total	10.79	6.81	11.39	9.87	7.41	5.42	6.50	6.89	12.24[a]	10.51	5.77	7.55	8.92

[a]Not significant at 5 percent level.

[b]Not significant at 1 percent level.

Definitions: *Industrial Areas* comprise North America, Western Europe, and Japan; *Developing Areas* consist of Latin America, Southeast Asia, Middle East, Africa, and other parts of the world. *Eastern Trading Areas* include Eastern Europe, U.S.S.R., Mainland China, North Vietnam, Albania, North Korea, and Mongolia.

Source: Computed from data in General Agreement on Trade and Tariff, *International Trade*, various issues.

exports of the same categories of commodities from the developing areas to the developed areas. Most striking, exports of machinery and transport equipment from developing to developed areas grew at 32 percent per year during this period while their imports of these commodities from developed areas grew at only 9 percent per year.

Thus the efforts of less developed countries to industrialize seem to have paid off in the form of rapid growth of exports in those export categories experiencing most rapid growth in overall world trade. Presumably manufactures have been found in which less developed countries can quickly become competitive with the more developed nations. As the fast growth sectors expand, the size of the sectors relative to the slow growth sectors increases and overall rates of export growth increase.

Relatively slow growth in the food, raw materials, and ores sectors may be in part due to rapid growth in domestic demand for these commodities as manufacturing increases and to rigidities of supply due to natural resource constraints. The emphasis on developing manufacturing may also have resulted in some perhaps temporary neglect of the primary commodity areas and consequent loss of productive output and export potentials. This neglect has probably been most substantial in agriculture and has taken the form of underinvestment in the means of cost reducing technological change.

India's export performance has been an exaggerated version of the less developed country pattern. Exports of the various manufactured goods categories, except for textiles and clothing, have grown more rapidly than those of the collectivity of less developed countries. The fastest export growth category for less developed countries was machinery and transport machinery—for which India's rate of export growth in the period 1960 to 1969 was nearly 50 percent faster than that of all less developed countries (Tables 4-3 and 4-4). India's generally good export performance in the general category manufacturing was depressed by the poor performance in the subcategory textiles, as shown in a succeeding section. In contrast, for each of the primary commodity areas, India's export performance was considerably worse than that of all less developed countries.

Compounding India's problem of initially unfavorable commodity composition of exports was an unfavorable country composition of export markets, which can be traced from the colonial period. This problem reinforced the pessimistic view of export prospects and thereby strengthened the argument for the capital intensive strategy and its consequent neglect of agriculture and foreign trade.

Thus in 1953, the United Kingdom received 29 percent of India's exports, a share which had declined to 15 percent by 1968.[26] The value of India's exports to the United Kingdom declined 15 percent in this period. The record is similar for other ex-colonies, as the uneconomic aspect of colonial trading relationships disappears with the loss of imperial power. Thus from 1952

Table 4-4. Export Performance of Selected Countries by Commodity Groups, 1960-69

Commodity Groups	*Taiwan*	*India*	*Japan*	*South Korea*	*Pakistan*	*Philippines*	*Hong Kong*	*Singapore*	*United Kingdom*	*United States*
	(percent per year)									
Food & Live Animals	11.6	−0.5[a]	7.5	19.7	3.0	2.3[a]	−3.7[a]	0.5[a]	19.6[b]	3.3[a]
Beverages & Tobacco	7.3[a]	1.9[a]	6.7	69.0	65.5[b]	6.9[a]	−4.1[a]	−1.6[a]	7.8	4.9
Crude Materials	26.0	2.0[b]	8.4	17.7	2.0[b]	8.1	−1.8[a]	1.1[a]	1.0[a]	5.0
Mineral Fuels & Lubricants	12.2[b]	−1.6	11.3	−4.5[a]	13.9[a]	51.9	21.9	13.1	−0.4[a]	4.4
Animal & Vegetable Oils	−9.7[a]	−17.0[a]	−11.4[a]	4.0[a]	–	19.8	−15.8	10.7	−0.3[a]	−0.4[a]
Chemicals	−11.5[b]	10.3	20.4	18.2[a]	10.8[a]	17.8	−0.9[a]	3.6	6.5	8.5
Manufactured Goods	23.2	4.2	13.2	50.9	18.9	15.7	7.3[b]	0.4	6.6	6.6
Machinery & Transport Equipment	55.0	28.4	22.2	45.4	38.7	–	25.0	−0.2[a]	−4.6[a]	10.1
Miscellaneous Manufactured Articles	42.1	14.7	16.0	76.9	19.9	26.1[a]	16.6	7.4	9.4	7.0
Miscellaneous Transactions	107.8	−5.0	52.7	16.5[b]	14.6[b]	23.5[b]	−5.2	−1.3[a]	1.1[a]	11.5
Total	20.2	2.8	16.5	35.3	9.4	8.1	12.4	3.3	5.4	7.5

[a]Not significant at 5 percent level.

[b]Not significant at 1 percent level.

Source: Computed from data in United Nations, Dept. of Economic & Social Affairs, Statistical Office, *Yearbook of International Trade Statistics*, New York, various issues.

to 1969, Japan's share of South Korea's and Taiwan's exports declined from 54 and 53 percent to 22 and 15 percent respectively, while the United States increased its share from 33 to 56 percent for South Korea and from 6 to 43 percent for Taiwan.[27] In the case of India, however, there was the double liability of reducing a tie with a relatively stagnant trading partner. Thus from 1961 to 1969, United Kingdom imports increased by 5.8 percent per year—in sharp contrast to world imports, which increased by 8.9 percent per year, United States imports, which increased by 11.8 percent per year, and Japanese imports, which increased by 12.6 percent per year.[28]

The major offset to decline of the United Kingdom market was increased trade with the Eastern Bloc countries. Exports to that region were less than 1 percent of India's exports in 1957. From 1960-61 to 1969-70 they had quadrupled, increasing from 7.5 percent to 21 percent of all exports. The increase was facilitated by Eastern Bloc emphasis on repayment of aid through trade and perhaps by the facility of Eastern Bloc countries and India to manage large trade agreements through state trading agencies.[29] The only other area with which India's exports have increased rapidly during this period is Japan, to which exports grew at over 10 percent per year from 1950 to 1969. The high growth rate was largely due to rapid growth in iron ore exports.

INDIA'S POLICY CONSTRAINTS ON EXPORT PERFORMANCE

India's failure to realize the export potentials nascent in the past two decades of development trace primarily from the capital intensive growth strategy and secondarily from the bureaucratic restraints that were, at least initially, themselves a product of the growth strategy. The strategy reflected in compromise of the two principal areas of trade advantage upon which India might have capitalized. The one was use of low cost labor to compete in producing labor intensive commodities for export to high wage countries, and the other, closely interacting with the first, was to use a large, growing domestic market to foster efficient manufacture of relatively labor intensive consumer goods. The consequences for exports that rose from the theory of growth applied in the Second and Third Plans were reinforced by the simplifying assumptions in the planning models developed to guide decision making and the bureaucratic administrative procedures under which they were executed.

Trade between countries with unlike factor proportions is one of the more plausible theories of trade.[30] In this view India would produce labor intensive commodities; and as a variant on that theme, India, with its relatively large expenditure on higher education, might give particular emphasis to commodities low in capital intensity but high in requirements of both skilled and unskilled manpower. In practice, however, India's pattern of industrial growth has been highly capital intensive. Thus for the period 1951 to 1965, out of nineteen major industry groups, the four most capital intensive groups increased their proportion of capital investment, value added in production, and employment; while with one exception the four industry groups with lowest capital intensity decreased their share by each of the three measures. All four of the low capital intensity groups are producers of final consumer goods and none of the four most capital intensive industries falls in that category.[31]

Even if the structure of capital investment had been more labor intensive, the slow growth in agriculture would have created a wages goods constraint. Further, the lack of foreign exchange for capital intensive machinery and intermediate product imports required to produce a labor intensive value added, reinforced the underlying problem. Reflecting the increased capital intensity of production, the capital intensity of exports increased 18 percent from 1964 to 1969.[32] In four of eight industrial trade categories the weighted average capital intensity of exports increased during the period.[33] There is also a statistically significant tendency for the industries with greater capital intensity to have had the faster growth in exports,[34] although the weighted average increase in capital intensity of exports was somewhat less than that for the economy as a whole.[35]

The capital intensive strategy in practice removed an alternate but related basis for trade. India could have produced inexpensive, low quality consumer goods and capital goods for the home market, thereby achieving efficiency in production, and thus provided competitive exports to similar markets elsewhere, particularly in other poor countries.[36] This theory is somewhat complementary to the resource endowment theory in that poor countries would in practice consume lower quality goods that were labor intensive in production and maintenance, and similarly for capital goods.

The Indian growth strategy militated against this approach to exports on two grounds. Most important, consumer income—particularly of low income people—was stagnant, and without such growth in income there is little potential for the aggregate of consumer goods industries to expand and increase in efficiency. Thus while particular segments may expand from a small base, the rate of expansion must slow rapidly as they attain significant aggregate size. In this respect, the experience of India is in sharp contrast to Taiwan, which effectively used a rapidly growing domestic market to develop industries that later seized on the export potential.[37]

It is sometimes argued that Indian export performance is poor because the large domestic market draws off all production for domestic use. While the argument is clearly specious, its refutation clarifies the problem of export performance. Under the capital intensive strategy, there was of course little expansion of consumer goods industries. Nevertheless some increased income payments leaked into consumption demand and thus raised domestic prices of the small quantity of consumer goods. Thus, given the strategy, exports could occur only if domestic income was closely contained. In the alternative strategy, incomes may rise, and with resources available to consumer goods industries they will be stimulated to grow, with higher prices providing the basis for investment in capital goods, as necessary.

The deleterious implications to trade of the theoretical model behind the Second and Third Plans was reinforced by the simplifying assumptions of the planning models; those simplifying assumptions in turn appearing reasonable in the context of the theory. With the rate of growth of exports set at a fixed percentage of domestic production, the level of imports was then determined by the low level of exports and by foreign aid. Capital goods had a strong priority for the available foreign exchange. This was consistent with a strategy that concentrated resources on provision of capital goods and contained a particularly large requirement of foreign exchange for the capital intensive industries. Application of such models left little foreign exchange for imports necessary to efficient exports.

It is within this context of a theory of growth and a set of planning models—both inimical to export growth—that a bureaucracy ill equipped for its tasks is able to further prejudice the export effort. Bhagwati and Desai[38] detail the bureaucratic deficiency and inefficiency that has characterized and inhibited the Indian export record. For improved performance the strategy of growth must be changed. Then, in the context of a new strategy, the bureaucracy must perform a new set of tasks with increased efficiency. It is perhaps fair to say that under the old strategy, export performance could not have been impressive even with the best administration; under a new strategy export performance will certainly improve, but could be greatly enhanced by positive public administration.

Export markets tend by nature to be residual markets and therefore more competitive and volatile than domestic markets, thus bureaucratic delays and ineptitude particularly inhibit exports. The importance of the strategy becomes clear in this context because facilitation of exports requires removal of controls on capital intensive imports as both components and raw materials for exports. It seems unlikely that such imports could be isolated from the domestic market, and in any case growth in the domestic market may be necessary to facilitate economic growth of export industries.

The public sector can, however, also play a vital positive role in facilitating exports, first by taking risks to develop markets, and second by taking risks to ensure adequate supplies of raw materials through execution of long term buying agreements. To fulfill this positive role undoubtedly requires technical specialization which is contrary to the generalist philosophy of the Indian civil service. It also requires a change in emphasis away from regulation to compress growth into a plan framework and to prevent leakages of foreign exchange and towards positive facilitation of exports.

In these circumstances the role of the State Trading Corporation might well expand in two directions. First, with expanding volume of imports of easily graded raw materials and capital intensive intermediate products a case can be made for careful estimate of future needs as a basis for use of market power in large scale forward buying. Second, a case can be made for a public investment in market analysis, development, and promotion, including risk absorption, to foster exports in new, promising lines.

Finally, it must be recognized that although they may have been ineffective in achieving export growth, the regulatory bureaucracy is powerfully entrenched and can be expected to fight vigorously and effectively to maintain its power. In doing so it may ally itself with politicians who themselves have much to gain from the distribution of the patronage and windfall profit innate to such a system of regulation. Thus the greatest harm from the bureaucracy may be not so much its poor performance under the old strategy as the role it might play in preventing change to a new strategy.

LESSONS FROM THE TEXTILE CASE

India's performance in textile exports epitomizes the relationship between growth strategy and exports. In 1953, subsequent to the Korean war boom, exports of all textiles and clothing (excluding jute) totalled \$179 million or 17 percent of total Indian exports (Table 4-5). India then provided 58 percent of all less developed countries' exports of these commodities. By 1968 India's exports of the textile group had increased by only \$4 *million*; while total less developed countries' exports of textiles had increased by \$1.9 *billion.* Pakistan had increased from zero to exports two-thirds as large as India's; South Korea from zero to an amount 25 percent larger than India's; and Taiwan from zero to an amount nearly 50 percent larger than India's. India's share of less developed countries' exports of textiles declined from 58 percent to 8 percent between 1953 and 1969. If India had maintained her share of less developed countries' exports of textiles, they would in 1969 have totalled \$1.3 billion–a net addition of over 60 percent to total exports and a sum comparable in size to the largest annual net aid received by India. If India's share of less developed countries' exports of textiles had dropped by half in this period, exports would still have been larger by \$470 million.

It may be argued that India so dominated world textile trade in 1953 that it could not expect a dynamic future performance. Suffice it to say that in 1953 Japan's textile exports were 75 percent larger than India's and then nearly tripled by 1969 for an addition to textile exports of \$1.8 billion–almost exactly equal to India's total exports of all commodities in 1968. Similarly, the sum of the increase in textile exports from Taiwan and South Korea in the two years, 1967 to 1969, was over one-third larger than India's total textile exports in 1969.

India's problem was not market dominance or lack of foreign markets but failure to produce, which in turn was due to lack of market

Table 4-5. Exports of Textiles and Clothing (Excluding Jute Textiles) from Selected Countries, 1953-1964

Year	*India*	*Pakistan*	*Korea*	*Taiwan*	*L.D.C. Total*[a]	*India's Share of L.D.C. Total (percent)*	*Japan*
				(million U.S. dollars)			
1953	179	–	–	–	309	58	311
1955	156	–	–	–	332	47	545
1957	184	18	–	–	460	40	957
1959	180	31	1	9	532	34	964
1960	174	40	2	13	615	28	1,142
1961	181	14	1	18	738	25	1,069
1962	166	11	3	33	775	21	1,143
1963	221	18	4	36	1,004	22	1,126
1964	194	49	26	61	1,108	18	1,290
1965	199	53	47	66	1,215	16	1,427
1966	182	60	68	87	1,388	13	1,611
1967	156	67	108	130	1,562	10	1,565
1968	225	101	174	179	1,926	12	1,822
1969	183	122	227	263	2,183	8	2,097

[a]L.D.C. total is estimated by deducting Indian and Pakistani exports of jute textiles from the total value of exports of textiles and clothing shown in the General Agreement on Trade and Tariff, *International Trade.* Figures for 1953 to 1960 for the L.D.C. total are estimated from the sources below.

Sources: Computed from data in United Nations, Dept. of Economic and Social Affairs, Statistical Office, *Yearbook of International Trade Statistics*, New York, various issues; General Agreement on Trade and Tariff, *International Trade*, various issues; United Nations, Dept. of Economic & Social Affairs, Statistical Office, *Monthly Bulletin of Statistics*, New York, various issues.

orientation, failure to modernize, and failure to import raw materials. These in turn traced from the development strategy and its implementation and suggests the basis for future failure in other export lines if that strategy does not change.

While India maintained traditional product composition of its textile exports, other countries were making dynamic adaptations to changing market conditions.[39] From 1953 to 1968, Japan's exports of cotton fabrics increased by only 30 percent and $60 million.[40] Fabrics of other materials, dominated by synthetics, increased over seven times and added $560 million to exports. Even more spectacular, clothing exports increased ten-fold, by $350 million. For India, clothing exports only increased to $20 million in 1968; regenerated and synthetic fabric exports were actually lower in 1968 than in 1953.[41] Clothing also dominated South Korean export growth, rising from $7 million in 1964 to $112 million in 1968. Taiwan too experienced rapid growth of clothing exports, accounting for nearly half of textile exports in 1968; but Taiwan also experienced rapid growth in cotton fabric exports, rising from $9 million in 1959 to $43 million in 1968.[42]

Pakistan is an exception to this pattern but one that further emphasizes the loss to India of not adapting to new market potentials. Textile exports (excluding jute) grew from essentially nothing in 1953 to $122 million in 1969. Over 80 percent was comprised of cotton yarn and fabrics–almost exactly the same percentage in these two categories as India. Thus, Pakistan textile export growth, which accounted for about a third of its total export growth from 1953 to 1968 was largely of the traditional type and probably significantly in competition with India. India did not take advantage of its early start to move on to more promising areas, staying instead to compete with latecomers who may have had few alternatives.

India's textile industry has also tended to stagnate technologically, resulting in high cost production and consequent poor competitive position. The relatively stagnant domestic demand required little expansion of the industry and hence the average age of equipment increased as new capacity comprised only a small proportion of the total. In addition, the capital intensive policies in the capital goods sector left little capital or foreign exchange available for the textile industry. Thus import of special machinery to facilitate exploitation of new markets was not possible.[43]

This natural result of the chosen development path was reinforced by explicit decision to emphasize the small scale sector of the textile industry.[44] As a result, from 1951 to 1969 the mill sector stagnated while the small scale sector nearly quadrupled its output. During that period, the physical volume of cotton fabric exports declined 30 percent. Favoring the small scale sector was recognition of the generally deleterious welfare effects of the capital intensive approach to development. The result may well have been the worst of both worlds: inefficient production in the favored sectors by emphasis on overly capital intensive production, and inefficient production in other sectors (such as textiles) by emphasis on excessively labor intensive methods.

The technological problems of the textile industry also illustrate some of the genuine dilemmas of development. Efforts at import substitution in the textile machinery industry may well have been a sensible policy, for India may only require a short period of time to develop the essential skills for competitive position in textile machinery production. During the period of protection the domestic textile industry suffers from high cost machinery and probably from technological backwardness as well. In the vigorous expansion incident to an employment oriented strategy, this interim period would be passed quickly. Under India's capital intensive strategy it has continued for a long period.

An additional difficulty of India's textile industry is high cost and unreliable supply of basic fibers, which comprise over 50 percent of the total cost of the industry.[45] Again, we illustrate that exports require imports. Cotton production has grown slowly in India and hence even with slowly rising demand, cotton prices have risen relative to other prices. Thus in the last half of the 1950s, while the United States subsidized cotton exports to the benefit of Japan and many other textile exporters, Indian producers encountered rising cotton prices. India's potential comparative advantage in providing value added in the textile industry was, in effect, sacrificed to her then comparative disadvantage in cotton production.

Similarly, the plan effort to restrict imports to capital goods prevented imports of synthetic fibers—themselves the product of a highly capital intensive industry. And, as synthetics became more acceptable in the plan framework, the emphasis has shifted to domestic production, with further concentration of capital in a few industries and firms and on a few employees, thereby starving other users of capital, including the more labor intensive textile industry.

CONCLUSIONS

The detail with respect to India's textile exports was presented not to make a general case for textile exports from low income countries, but rather to illustrate that export growth is related to the overall growth strategy affecting (1) the supply of wages goods and the extent to which labor can be mobilized; (2) the structure of domestic demand and hence the commodity composition of increasing production efficiency; (3) the basis for allocation of capital and foreign exchange and its further affect on commodity composition of output; and (4) the planning procedures themselves.

It is implied that the rapid growth rate in a few relatively labor intensive exports, such as engineering goods, is in risk of being truncated as expansion becomes sufficient to meet the aggregate constraints faced by textiles. Conversely, these and many other commodities could expand rapidly to major aggregate proportions with change to a facilitative overall strategy.

It is argued further that India's strategy of growth illustrates how either the fact or the expectation of poor prospects in domestic agricultural production may confirm a strategy inimicable to export performance, and conversely, how expectation of poor export performance may confirm a capital intensive strategy that is in turn inimicable to providing resources or demand for rapid growth of agriculture. It follows that to be successful, attempted changes in trade policy, agricultural policy, or employment policy must be accompanied by appropriate changes in policy in the other complementary areas.

Chapter Five

Agricultural Trade in the Economic Development of Taiwan

Anthony M. Tang and Kuo-shu Liang

INTRODUCTION

The postwar economic development of Taiwan falls into two stages. The first, from the end of World War II through the 1950s, was characterized by efforts to promote growth incentive in the agricultural sector coupled with import substituting industrialization. During this early industrialization period, agriculture was given a dual role: to generate sufficient growth in output and surplus to permit both balanced growth à la Ranis-Fei (i.e., stable relative wages-goods price), hence a perfectly elastic labor supply facing industry, and to increase exports of agricultural staples in accommodation of the rising import requirements (capital goods and raw materials) of industrialization. As we shall see, Taiwan's agriculture was singularly successful in meeting these exacting demands.

Thus the way was paved for the second stage of Taiwan's postwar economic development, which since 1960, following a major policy shift, became characterized by a new thrust in the direction of what may be appropriately called export substituting industrialization. The transition to an outward looking program of industrialization was also highly successful. As industrial exports displaced agricultural staples as the centerpiece of Taiwan's foreign trade, the unenviable circle of staple-export-for-capital-goods-import was broken. Thus, in a remarkable span of a little more than a decade, Taiwan managed to meet the ultimate Hicksian test of a successful program of industrialization.

The final preparation of the paper was done at the Institute of Economic Research (Instituto de Pesquisas Economicas) of the University of São Paulo, Brazil, where Professor Tang was Visiting Professor in 1973. Assistance from the Institute is gratefully acknowledged.

During the second phase it can also be said that, although analytically less exact, Taiwan passed the Ranis-Fei "takeoff" point in the sense that the exacting demands placed on agriculture within the context of the two-sector model ceased to apply and industrialization became self-sustained. The purpose of this chapter is to examine the role played by agriculture, particularly in a trade context, in the economic development of Taiwan in the postwar years–a process that is being looked upon with increasing frequency as representing an "ideal" model.

The reconstruction of the Taiwan economy began in earnest in 1949, a year that witnessed the fall of the Chinese mainland to the Communist insurgents and the relocation of the Nationalist government on the island. The first major government economic measure was land reform (earlier conceived for the whole of China), which was carried out in Taiwan in three steps during 1949-53. The first step brought about a rent reduction in 1949, which limited land rent to a maximum of 37.5 percent of the total yield of the principal crop. The second step, taken in 1951, was the sale of public land acquired from Japanese nationals at the conclusion of World War II to the tillers. The final step, taken in 1953, instituted the broad land-to-the-tiller program, under which landlords were required to sell (at prices calculated from a capitalization formula based on normal yields) all land in excess of the maximum allowable holding of three hectares. The main features and contributions of the land reform program to postwar economic development can be summarized as follows.

1. Perhaps the most important aspect of land reform has to do with its positive effect on growth incentive. Well developed technology was transmitted to Taiwan's farmers mainly through the Joint Commission of Rural Reconstruction. The successful development of new practices and inputs, articulated by a high rate of economic adoption on the part of an educated and suitably motivated farm population, ensured an adequate supply of foodstuffs over time, thus contributing to price stability even as Taiwan continued to be saddled with one of the world's highest natural rates of population increase (at about 3.5 percent per year). Furthermore, agricultural and processed agricultural exports retained their dominant position in the island's growing total exports throughout the 1950s. Thus, during its critical stage of economic development, Taiwan's policy makers skillfully implemented agricultural development programs that met the essential conditions of the well known two-sector model for industrialization and modernization.

2. Landlords were duly compensated. Of the total compensation based on the capitalization formula mentioned earlier, 70 percent was paid in land bonds redeemable in kind over a ten-year period and carrying a 4 percent interest. The other 30 percent was paid in stocks of several public enterprises, thus converting land holdings into industrial holdings and broadening the

economic interests of the landed class.[a] Both forms of payments also served to minimize the consumption (and other possible countergrowth) consequences that would otherwise obtain had payment been made in cash.

3. Land reform and the consequent expansion of agricultural output (at about 5 percent per year in real terms) contributed to Taiwan's industrial development in many ways. Increased demand for inputs and consumer goods under a rising and more equally distributed income provided a powerful stimulus to industrial expansion at a time when industry was inward oriented. Taiwan also enjoyed continuous net capital contributions from agriculture through government taxes and other direct and hidden levies.[1] A significant part of the agricultural surplus, thus siphoned off for financing economic development, took the form of installment payments by the tillers to the government for the land redistributed to them.

4. Through land reform, farmers developed a strong vested interest in the economy, which was instrumental in creating a condition conducive to social and political stability.

5. By removing distortions inherent in certain tenancy contracts, land reform stimulates the demand for and formation of human capital. This follows from the internalization of returns to the cultivator that it permits. Increased income made possible by land reform further removes or lessens cost barriers to education. Furthermore, land reform, by placing scarce land in the hands of the cultivators, helps prevent transfer of benefits from education and adoption of innovations from the cultivators to the owner of scarce resource—a transfer which might take place under conditions of an imperfect land market. A broad base for economic development was thus laid by land reform. The positive role played by the agricultural sector in Taiwan offers a sharp contrast to the experiences of many other less developed countries, where lack of agricultural development acted as a drag on industrial and general economic development.

The principal focus of our study is to examine how agricultural trade contributed to Taiwan's successful economic development and to review the process and the changes in the pattern of agricultural trade in Taiwan's postwar economic development. The principal questions of concern that we attempt to answer are as follows:

[a]Public enterprises formed a very large segment of the industrial sector at the end of World War II as the government took over all the enterprises of the Japanese nationals. Of these, the Taiwan Cement Corporation, the Taiwan Paper and Pulp Corporation, and the Taiwan Agricultural and Forestry Development Corporation were transferred to private ownership in 1954 as part of a compensation scheme for landowners on land compulsorily redistributed under the land-to-the-tiller program.

1. How did agriculture contribute to the development process in terms of foreign exchange earnings within the context of a two-gap constraint growth model?
2. How did the pattern of agricultural trade tend to change over time under the progress of industrialization?
3. In what ways did the pattern and the strategy of agricultural development assist the transition of industrialization from inward oriented import substitution to outward oriented export expansion?
4. How did domestic marketing of agricultural products develop in Taiwan, and what price policies were taken by the government regarding key farm commodities?

FOREIGN AID, AGRICULTURAL TRADE, AND CONSTRAINTS ON TAIWAN'S GROWTH

In this section we investigate the nature of the constraints limiting Taiwan's postwar growth and the role played by U.S. aid and agricultural trade. There is a substantial literature on the process of development under conditions of two scarce factors: foreign exchange and capital.[2-8] In the short run, a more or less strict complementarity can be said to exist between these two resources. Their availabilities thus place separate limits on growth. Under a given demand and production structure, each level of future output entails a set of minimum import requirements, and the available foreign exchange determines the feasible future output. Similarly, a given output growth requires capital formation, and the economy's capacity to save places a separate limit on growth. If the limit set by foreign exchange is the higher of the two, growth is savings constrained. If the limit given by savings is higher, growth is exchange-constrained. It is convenient for our purposes to adopt formally a constraint model of the Harrod-Domar type constructed by R.I. McKinnon.[9,10]

The Model

Let b be the incremental ratio of output to imported capital goods which are essential to growth, given its structure and the Leontief type of production processes, and for which there are no domestic substitutes; f, foreign exchange availability (i.e., the ratio to GDP of foreign exchange earned that is maximally available for capital goods import); r, the incremental output-capital ratio; and s, the savings ratio. Then, under the assumptions to be made more specific later:

(1) when $bf < rs$, a foreign exchange bottleneck exists and bf is the maximum feasible rate of growth

(2) when $bf > rs$, a savings constraint exists, and rs is the maximum feasible rate of growth

Capital transfers from abroad increase the feasible growth rate in both cases, acting as a supplement to earned foreign exchange and to domestic savings, respectively. However, since imported capital goods constitute only a fraction of domestic capital formation, transfers will have a proportionately greater effect upon the growth rate where an exchange bottleneck is operative than if a savings constraint holds. In other words, b is greater than r. Therefore, letting F^* be the ratio of foreign capital transfers to domestic product, $bf < rs$ need not imply that $b(f + F^*) < r(s + F^*)$. The feasible growth rate of the economy after capital transfers is determined by:

(3) $b(f + F^*)$ when $b(f + F^*) < r(s + F^*)$
(4) $r(s + F^*)$ when $b(f + F^*) > r(s + F^*)$

The main difficulties in applying this highly simplified aggregate model are rather obvious. The model entails several restrictive assumptions for its validity.[b] There is the further problem about the lack of data bearing on past ex ante parameters of the model. Observed data reflect adjustments made by the policy maker in light of ex ante bottleneck conditions that obtained and for that reason are not really suitable. To this problem we now turn our attention.

The constraint model at hand is popularly known as a two-gap model. To achieve some desired rate of growth, one may find that the required investment exceeds the maximum feasible savings (gap I) and/or that the required imports exceed the maximum foreign exchange available (gap II). If gap I is greater than gap II, growth is savings constrained; otherwise it is exchange constrained. Ex post, however, the two gaps are always equal.

McKinnon sees the equality being brought about in the following way:[9-11] If gap I is seen by the planner to be the larger of the two, then he simply curtails exports to a level below that originally projected (or increases imports to include "nonessential" consumer goods). If gap II is governing, he causes less savings to be realized. This view about how the adjustment process works is shared by Chenery and Eckstein.[c]

The closing of the larger gap can take place under conditions of equilibrium or disequilibrium. If it takes place under disequilibrium, accommodating foreign finance is necessary. Suppose the trade gap (II) is binding, then ex ante $(X - M)$ is larger than $(S - I)$, the savings gap (I), in absolute terms. Yet, ex

[b]The following major assumptions are required in a strict sense:

1. Imported capital goods are not reproducible domestically.
2. Only one technology with fixed proportions of domestic and imported inputs is employed in each industry.
3. Demand structure (and production structure) is fixed.
4. Exports and savings cannot exceed some maximum at any current output level.
5. Only capital and foreign exchange are scarce.
6. Output and growth are consistent with full capacity.

[c]See Note 12, especially p. 968.

post, the foreign transfer needed to close the trade gap simultaneously closes the savings gap—i.e., the two gaps are always equal. This can be seen clearly in the following way: from the income identity we have $Y = C + I + (X - M)$ or $Y = C + S$; therefore, $S - I = X - M$. The latter identity comes about because foreign transfers needed to close the larger $(X - M)$ gap serve to raise C and lower S, thus widening the $(S - I)$ gap. That is the view expressed by McKinnon and others.

Chenery states the argument in more economic terms.[d] Since in this case the trade gap is binding (exchange being the scarce factor of production) and since transfers supplement both exchanges and savings, they tend to make saving redundant and displace it on a one-to-one basis until its redundancy is eliminated. More explicitly, redundancy occurs because although savings supplemented by transfers could finance more investment, this is not possible during the redundancy phase. Savings are redundant due to lack of complementary foreign capital goods whose total availability as augmented by transfers is already fully committed under the initial level of investment.

The closing of the gaps can also take place under equilibrium. This is done by lowering the rate of growth to be realized until the larger of the two gaps is eliminated. This is equivalent to producing under-full-employment equilibrium in the Keynesian system. Here, too, the ex post equalization of the two ex ante unequal gaps takes place in the manner shown in the preceding paragraph. In both cases, whether the economy is in or out of equilibrium, the ex post equality of the gaps is reminiscent of the familiar savings-investment identity.

For further explanatory details, let us this time take the savings gap as governing. The economy gets on a lower growth path to close the gap by reducing investment. A slack now develops in the trade sector in the sense that export permits capital goods import in a quantity that can support a larger investment. But a larger investment would once again outstrip savings capacity. Meanwhile, the adjustment mentioned earlier, through either export reduction or (consumer goods) import expansion, is clearly needed to "flesh out" the implied consumption requirements at the equilibrium savings-investment level. (In this sense, Chenery's use of the term "nonessential" consumer goods import is inappropriate). These remarks make it clear why historical data bearing on the parameters in inequalities (1)-(4), unless suitably manipulated or defined and taken from appropriate empirical settings, are not suitable for identifying the binding constraint on an economy's growth. The question of definition and setting is taken up in the next section.

A superior approach would be to deduce from the constraint model a series of empirically testable behavioral predictions pertaining to actions by the policy maker, and then subject them to the data. Thus, ex ante, if the economy is savings constrained, the prediction is that actions, say, A, B, and C will follow.

[d]See Note 12, especially pp. 972-975.

If the economy is foreign exchange constrained, the predicted actions by the policy maker are, say, D, E, and F. These illustrative actions can then be checked against simple ex post observations. Such procedure eliminates the need for data on the ex ante parameters of the constraint model itself.[e] The indirect inference approach just suggested is not attempted in this chapter, however. At any rate, given the rather unambiguous results (presented later), we are inclined to take them as indicative of the location of the binding constraint and the shift that has occurred in Taiwan's postwar development.

Empirical Results: Constraints in the Absence of Transfers

To identify the effective constraints and shifts in their location, the period 1953-1970 will be divided into four subperiods: the early aid period, 1953-55; the middle aid period, 1956-60; the late aid period, 1961-65; and the post aid period, 1966-70.

The incremental capital-output ratio, r, is estimated by relating real capital formation of each year to the increase in real domestic product one year later. This and other parameters are averaged for each period. The savings ratio, s, is the average annual domestic savings rate out of the annual domestic product. The incremental ratio of output to imported capital goods, b, is estimated from r/I^*_m, where I^*_m is the average import component of domestic investment. To estimate b, it is assumed that actual imports of capital goods reflected the requirements of the Taiwan economy. The assumption plausibly implies that the imported goods could not have been produced domestically within reasonable cost limits.

Foreign exchange availability, f, is based on the maximum amount of foreign exchange, earned through commodity exports and net receipts from services, which could be used to import capital goods. The amount is taken to be net of materials imports (assumed to be nonsubstitutable) needed for current production. Capital transfers from abroad are excluded (being considered for the time being as accommodating finance) but will be introduced later. Thus f is defined as $(X - M_m)/Y$, where X is the sum total of foreign exchange receipts from commodity exports and net receipts from services, M_m is the amount of nonsubstitutable raw material imports, and Y is gross domestic product.

The estimation of parameters r, s, and b is given in Table 5-1 while Table 5-2 shows the critical values of foreign exchange needed for importing capital goods for each period. The critical value of foreign exchange shown in Table 5-2 for each time period is that minimum amount, for the purpose of capital goods import, that is necessary if growth is to take place at the maximum rate set by domestic savings. Therefore, if maximum available foreign exchange

[e]For an application of the indirect inference approach to a two-gap constraint model, though used in an entirely different context, see A.M. Tang's comparative study of China and the USSR (Note 13).

Table 5-1. Estimated Values of Parameters, *r*, *s*, and *b*, 1953-1970

	1953-55	*1956-60*	*1961-65*	*1966-70*	*1953-1970*
Incremental output/ capital ratio (r)	0.498	0.482	0.517	0.384	0.472
Savings rate (s)	0.084	0.101	0.162	0.233	0.152
Import component of gross domestic investment (I_m^*)	0.223	0.301	0.279	0.374	0.302
$r/I_m^* = b$	2.233	1.601	1.853	1.027	1.563

Source: Directorate-General of Budgets, Accounts and Statistics, Executive Yuan, *National Income of the Republic of China* (October 1971), pp. 112-3, Table XIII; pp. 96-7, Table VI; pp. 110-1, Table XII; pp. 84-5, Table I. Chinese Maritime Customs, *The Trade of China, 1953-1971.*

Note: Capital good imports are estimated from the values under SITC 7.

Table 5-2. Constraints on the Taiwan Economy Without Foreign Capital Transfers, 1953-1970 (in NT$ million at 1966 prices)

	1953-55	*1956-60*	*1961-65*	*1966-70*	*1953-1970*
Critical value of foreign exchange, $X-M_m$ needed for importing capital goods ($X-M_m = \frac{1}{b} rsY$)	933	1,964	4,296	13,311	4,365
Commodity exports plus receipts from services (X)	3,682	5,689	13,180	35,605	15,745
Raw material imports (M_m)	5,048	6,647	10,767	19,858	11,195
Available foreign exchanges ($fY = X-M_m$)	–1,366	–958	2,413	15,747	4,550

Source: Derived from Table 5-1 and DGBAS, *op. cit.*

Note: Raw material imports are estimated from the values under SITC 2-6.

falls short of the critical minimum, growth is constrained by foreign exchange. Conversely, if available foreign exchange exceeds the critical minimum, growth is savings constrained.

As Table 5-2 shows, the Taiwan economy was subject to a serious foreign exchange bottleneck during the entire 1950s, i.e., during the early and middle aid periods. During these periods, when Taiwan relied heavily on U.S. economic aid, foreign exchange earnings did not even cover materials import (presumably essential for maintaining current output), leaving negative balances for exchanges available for capital goods import. That growth was subject to the exchange bottleneck (in the absence of foreign transfers) appears to be an unambiguous inference despite the ex post character of the parameters shown in Table 5-1.

Let us elaborate on this statement as a supplement to the discussion in the preceding section. Just as the concepts of "full employment surplus" popular in the pump priming literature of the 1930s, or of "fundamental disequilibrium" of the IMF, or of the full Keynesian equilibrium, require full employment as the necessary frame of reference, so does the concept of exchange bottleneck in our context. The full employment or capacity output requirement in discussing ex ante or prospective conditions takes on substance once one recalls that critical variables such as imports and savings are all functions of domestic output in these systems. It can happen, for instance, that for an economy to operate at capacity it must incur current materials imports in excess of exports. To illustrate the point, let us take Taiwan. The island received some one million mainlanders (or about 15 percent of total population) between the end of World War II and the fall of the mainland to the communists in 1949. Much of this manpower embodied a high level of skills and education. Not unlike Western European countries and Japan, Taiwan was faced with excess capacity in the postwar years. Without U.S. aid, which more than anything else filled the materials requirements of these countries, none of these countries could have operated at an output level consistent with the existing plant of physical and human capital.

It is true that, as Chenery and Eckstein put it, "The amount of foreign capital actually supplied fills both gaps simultaneously, so that in retrospect the two are necessarily equal."[f] Yet the only way to observe ex post what the ex ante materials bottleneck was like is to have the economy run at capacity with the aid of foreign transfers; then one can measure the imbalance between exports and imports. Otherwise output adjustment (equilibrium adjustment), along with the other forms discussed earlier, would take place and render the historical parameters useless for ex ante inferences.

The import of these paragraphs is to clear up some confusion and ambiguities in the literature on the matter and to stress that for purposes of ex ante inferences from historical data it is necessary to have gap closing under disequilibrium (with the help of transfers) without downward adjustment in output or the desired rate of growth.

To recapitulate, certain conditions are required in order to draw ex ante inferences from the historical data. These conditions are: (1) the economy operates at full capacity within limits imposed by structural and institutional givens; (2) there are no significant "slacks" in the historical parameters—i.e., the planner had not been forced to make ad hoc adjustments by prospective or ex ante bottlenecks; and (3) it is necessary to manipulate or define certain parameters in a way that helps eliminate ambiguity in inferences.

A few brief comments are in order. Condition (1) is clear from the preceding discussions. Condition (2) requires in practical terms that if the economy is faced with an exchange bottleneck, foreign transfers are available to

---

[f]See Note 12, p. 968. This case corresponds to our gap closing under disequilibrium discussed in the preceding section.

close the trade gap obviating any need for retrenchment. This condition, apart from preventing distortions in the historical savings rate, *s*, also ensures that there would be no alterations in the output-capital ratio, *r*, and the output-imported capital goods ratio, *b*, as would take place if the planner had been required to change the incremental output mix to reduce imported capital goods requirements in light of an exchange bottleneck.

Condition (3) relates to the definition of foreign exchange availability, *f*. In this chapter, *f* is defined as the difference between total exchange earnings and the value of current materials import. By treating all consumer goods import as expendable, the definition deliberately overstates the amount of exchange available for capital goods import needed for growth. Thus, if the inference of an exchange bottleneck (available exchange insufficient to meet required capital goods import) is warranted by the historical data, the statement would be unambiguous.

Regarding the above conditions we believe that Taiwan came close to meeting them. By relieving the current materials import bottleneck, U.S. aid permitted the economy to operate at a level consistent with capacity utilization restricted only by internal structural and institutional limitations. There are no apparent signs of "slacks" in any of the crucial parameters as measured in Table 5-1. The incremental output-capital ratio of just under 0.5 is about as high as they come anywhere. So appears to be the domestic savings ratio of approximately 10 percent, considering Taiwan's meager per capita income at that time (not much over $100 in the early 1950s).

The import content of domestic investment is less easy to gauge but it is reassuringly low as compared with, say, the Latin American rates, which are placed at 1/3 by Chenery and Eckstein.[g]

At any rate, it is not crucial to our inference reached earlier that Taiwan *in a prospective sense* was faced with a foreign exchange bottleneck. This follows, since the island's exports did not even cover current materials import, not to mention foreign capital goods requirements whatever they may be. Thus, what foreign transfers (mainly U.S. aid) did in Taiwan's case was to allow us to see what the materials import requirements were like under capacity production and what the parameters of the model are like when there are no ad hoc adjustments to distort them. Armed with these magnitudes one can then see what sort of bottleneck the economy would have run into if it had had to stand on its own. It is in this context that the bottleneck inference in the case of Taiwan is to be understood.

In the late aid period, 1961-65, the economy is seen to be constrained by foreign exchange still. However, it is clear that the bottleneck had weakened noticeably as a large positive balance of available foreign exchange (earned) emerged, although the latter was still short of the critical minimum needed for capital goods import. Available foreign exchange (earned) exceeded

[g]See Note 12, p. 975, fn. 13.

the critical minimum in the post aid period, 1966-70, shifting the constraint from foreign exchange to domestic savings. Although foreign transfers will be introduced in a later section, it is instructive to note the phasing of U.S. economic aid as is made implicit in the designation of our four subperiods. Recall also that the growth impact of aid is much greater when the economy is exchange constrained.

Although for the entire 1953-1970 period (given its length) the average annual relationship between available foreign exchange and the critical minimum is of little analytical significance, we note for the sake of description that, as annual averages, the available quantities had been just sufficient to cover the critical minimum requirements.

Turning to further descriptions, it is interesting to note that Taiwan's incremental output-capital ratios have tended to remain stable during the entire period, at about 0.47. Its domestic savings ratio showed a noticeable rising trend from 8 percent in 1953-55 to 23 percent in 1966-70, while the import component of domestic investment displayed a similar, though milder, rising trend (from 22 percent to 37 percent). At the same time, unlike the incremental output-capital ratio, the incremental ratio of output to imported capital goods followed a strong descending trend, falling from 2.23 to 1.03 during the eighteen-year period (see Table 5-1). The increasing import content of Taiwan's investment and the falling ratio of output to imported capital goods reflect mainly the structural changes in the economy away from agriculture in favor of manufacturing. The latter sector, given Taiwan's resource-poor posture, entails large imports of raw materials, not to mention capital goods, as compared with the modest requirements of agriculture.

The above parameters together determine the critical minimum value of foreign exchange, as defined earlier, which in relation to available foreign exchange serves to locate the effective constraint. For further descriptive perspective, therefore, we turn to a summary of the several value trends shown in Table 5-2. The critical annual minimum foreign exchange requirements displayed a strong upward trend rising from (constant 1966 New Taiwan dollars) NT$933 million a year during 1953-55 to NT$13,311 million during 1966-70, or US$23.3 and 332.5 million, respectively. In relative terms, this represents a thirteen-fold increase.

Export earnings rose less rapidly, from NT$3,682 to NT$35,605 million, or almost a nine-fold increase. Materials imports grew even less rapidly, from NT$5,048 to NT$19,858 million, or about a three-fold rise. Available foreign exchanges–the difference between exports and materials imports–thus rose from a *deficit* of NT$1,306 million to a positive balance of NT$15,747 million–a sum more than enough to cover the critical requirements. For added perspective in testimony of Taiwan's incredible export performance, we note that exports in 1972 stood at approximately NT$120,000 million or US$3,000 million, in current prices.

Foreign Transfers and Easing of Bottleneck

In this section we highlight the significance of U.S. economic aid to Taiwan. As shown in Table 5-3, net foreign transfers, consisting almost entirely of U.S. aid, amounted to NT$3,560 million per year during 1953-55 and to NT$3,140 million during 1956-60. These injections easily turned Taiwan's negative foreign exchange availability (shown in Table 5-2) into positive sums large enough to meet the critical requirements needed to relax the foreign exchange bottleneck (Table 5-3). The transfers were also supplemented by borrowings from abroad, which, starting from a relatively insignificant level in the early 1950s, quickly rose to about half the magnitude represented by aid in the latter part of the decade. Thereafter, borrowings tended to remain fairly stable while aid transfers dropped sharply as U.S. aid officials correctly concluded that with Taiwan's successful transition from import substituting to export substituting industrialization in the early 1960s, the island no longer depended on foreign aid for growth at a high and acceptable rate. Moreover, with the easing of the exchange bottleneck through export expansion by 1965, aid to Taiwan was no longer as productive. U.S. economic aid terminated in the mid 1960s with later minor transfers representing disbursements of funds committed earlier.

During its early industrialization phase Taiwan was thus able to achieve a remarkable rate of growth (about 8 percent a year in real terms), having passed, thanks to U.S. aid, from a phase of foreign exchange constrained

Table 5-3. Constraints on the Taiwan Economy after Foreign Capital Transfers, 1953-1970 (in NT$ million at 1966 prices)

	1953-55	*1956-60*	*1961-65*	*1966-70*	*1953-1970*
Critical value of exchange needed for importing capital goods ($\frac{1}{b}rsY$)	933	1,964	4,296	13,311	4,365
Commodity exports plus receipts from services (X)	3,682	5,689	13,180	35,605	15,745
Net foreign transfers (F_a)	3,560	3,140	2,060	759	2,290
Net borrowing from abroad (F_b)	110	1,564	1,107	1,711	1,236
Net material imports (M_m)	5,048	6,647	10,767	19,858	11,195
Available foreign exchange ($fY = X + F_a + F_b - M_m$)	2,304	3,746	5,580	18,217	8,076

Source: Derived from Table 5-3, and DGBAS, *op. cit.*

Note: In estimating net foreign transfers and net borrowing from abroad at 1966 prices, the implicit price deflator of commodity imports is applied as deflator.

growth to one of a higher rate of savings constrained growth.[h] In fact, the realized rate of growth can be said to have exceeded the maximum rate feasible under domestic savings, since foreign transfers supplemented savings while filling the exchange gap. This is clear from the determination of the growth rate by $r(s + F^*)$.

A Disaggregated Constraint Model

For additional insights, it may be useful to present a graphical representation of a two-sector constraint model, as shown in Figure 5-1. The assumptions embedded in the earlier aggregate model (as stated in footnote b above) reduce, in a two-commodity, two-scarce-factor world, to a linear programming scheme where the constant *incremental* output mix vector desired by the planner is QA. Let X_i and X_a be *incremental* output of two composite goods—agricultural and industrial—whose internal compositions are also fixed. Given the saving that the economy (at capacity output) can mobilize for growth, its resource content consists of (1) foreign resource (imported capital goods), R_f,

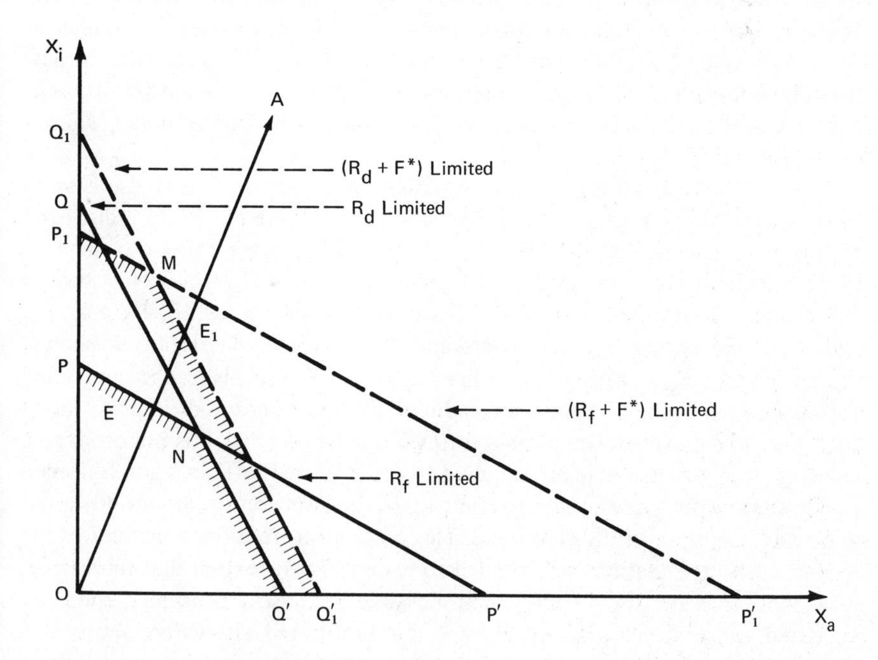

Figure 5-1. The Two-Sector Constraint Model

[h]For instance, during 1956-60, $r = 0.482$, $s = 0.101$, $b = 1.601$, and $F^* = 0.073$. It is clear that $rs > bf$, but $r(s + F^*) < b(f + F^*)$.

independently determined by available foreign exchange as defined earlier and (2) domestic resources for capital formation, R_d. The latter is residually obtained and is thus a surrogate for savings capacity. Under the fixed coefficient linear production systems, PP' represents the production possibilities under the assumption that R_f alone is limited and QQ' is the feasible boundary when R_d alone is limited. To restate, R_f and R_d represent resources available for investment and output growth feasible under the given savings. The relative gradients of the two lines are consistent with the empirical generalization that agricultural output is domestic resource intensive and industrial output is foreign resource intensive. PNQ' then constitutes the feasible maximum *incremental* output locus.

During the early postwar development, Taiwan's growth was limited by foreign exchange or foreign resource, R_f, in the absence of transfers. This is shown by the point E on PNQ'. Introduction of foreign transfers shifts PP' out by enlarging the amount of foreign resources available. The shift is proportional to F^*/R_f where F^* is the amount of transfers. QQ' also shifts out since transfers supplement domestic savings and free domestic resources for augmented investment. The latter shift is proportional to F^*/R_d. Note that R_d is usually several times as large as R_f (about two-and-one-half times in Taiwan). The graph as drawn is roughly consistent with these requirements. P_1MQ_1' represents the new maximum feasible incremental output locus. At point E_1 the constraint passes from R_f to R_d after transfers. This is what happened in Taiwan under U.S. aid during the 1950s.

Aside from the ex ante situations just portrayed, it is also easy to show what the ex post picture is like after adjustment of the sort discussed earlier. At E Taiwan was R_f constrained. Accordingly, were Taiwan to stand on its own without aid, it would have to remove redundant R_d by lowering savings and raising consumption until QQ' shifts down to pass through E. Ex post, R_d and R_f would appear as joint constraints. After aid of the magnitude shown, Taiwan became R_d or savings constrained as at E_1. Now, R_f is seen as containing redundancy and either exports are reduced or consumer goods imports raised such that PP' moves down to pass through E_1. Notice that this import-export adjustment alternative is really required in order to free sufficient goods needed to allow domestic consumption to come up to the level consistent with the given domestic output and savings at hand. This point clear from the viewpoint of the income identity equations was alluded to earlier. To the extent that this is true, it is inappropriate for Chenery and Eckstein to regard consumer goods so imported as "nonessential" or to view the adjustment alternative above as a simple matter of assumption (see Note 12, p. 968). Once again, ex post R_d and R_f as supplemented by F^* become joint constraint.

In returning formally to the McKinnon model, the adjustment after aid is handled by substituting f' for f in $b(f + F^*) > r(s + F^*)$, where f' stands for the amount of available foreign exchange after raising import of consumer goods or diminishing export. When so substituted, equality automatically obtains between the two sides.

General Remarks on the Model

It is a well known characteristic of the Harrod-Domar construct, which underpins the constraint model used in this chapter, that even for the long run the economy is balanced precariously on the knife edge of equilibrium growth. There is no built-in stabilizer in the system to pull the economy back the moment it wanders away from the natural rate of growth. Slight deviations from the equilibrium growth path send it into growing unemployment or prolonged inflation. The culprit is the assumption of fixed factor proportions. Disenchantment with the properties of the construct has led to an alternative growth model formulation in which all rigidities are assumed away.[14] This is known as the "neoclassical" growth model, whose centerpiece is a production system with variable proportions and constant returns to scale. Both models deal with the one-product economy which entails the same restrictions on adjustment possibilities as our assumption of fixed production structure in the multiproduct case being considered.

Sato has shown, however, that even with the neoclassical system under a wide variety of assumed conditions, simulations indicate adjustments taking place at "an extremely slow rate."[15] There is a fairly general agreement that in the short run, at least, factor proportion adjustment offers limited scope. The real adjustment possibilities lie in output mix changes by introducing the multiproduct case. In modern market economies, where consumer sovereignty asserts itself, this no doubt constitutes the more important reason why such economies do not behave in accordance with the properties of the Harrod-Domar model or, for that matter, with the adjustment implications of the neoclassical model. However, in economies where the primacy of planner sovereignty is paramount and where either both demand and output structures are rigidly specified, or specification of one largely determines the other due to limited trade possibilities, the assumed rigidities, technical and structural, take on much more substance.

Adjustments are still possible (to which we have devoted much earlier discussion), but they are clearly of the accommodating variety—a forced departure from what is narrowly preferred by the planner, and thus unlike consumer responses to price changes. In short, our constraint model is best addressed to growth-conscious LDCs endowed with limited production and trade possibilities and characterized by planner imposed rigidities in output and demand structures consistent with his aspirations for industrialization and modernization.

Contributions of Agriculture via Trade

Within the context of intersectoral relations between agriculture and industry, with trade acting as an intermediary, the graphic scheme offers the advantage of bringing out explicitly the implications of a restructuring of the incremental output. If the incremental output mix vector OA sweeps upward—changing the mix in favor of X_i (industrial goods), as indeed happened in Taiwan with astonishing speed—the critical amount of foreign transfers needed to relax the exchange bottleneck gets larger. This can easily be seen from Figure 5-1. Thus, if OA pivots in such a manner as to intersect the transformation frontier P_1MQ_1' within the segment P_1M, growth would remain exchange constrained. As we have seen earlier, the same transfers were able to relax the bottleneck when OA remained as drawn.

Now, for any given output structure chosen, whether or not a given foreign transfer will in effect allow the economy to pass onto the higher savings constrained growth path depends upon the base of its own current account export earnings. Had Taiwan's agricultural exports done less of a yeoman's job—especially during the vulnerable foreign material intensive phase of import substituting industrialization (where the classic extreme is the negative value added case)—the massive U.S. aid would not have sufficed to put the economy on the higher savings constrained growth path. And this is to be understood against the background, where planner directed output mix changes were constantly raising the exchange requirements needed for staying on the higher path. That Taiwan managed to stay on that path even during its early postwar development period is an extraordinary testimony to agriculture's successful discharge of its role in the context of the familiar two-sector model. To Taiwan's almost singular agricultural performance we now turn our attention.

During the 1950s, real agricultural output rose at an average rate of almost 5 percent per year—a rate that more or less held during the 1960s as well.[i] Such increases in agricultural production made it possible for Taiwan not only to meet the food requirements of a rapidly expanding population (at 3.5 percent a year), further reinforced by the income effect of rising real earning levels and of a better income distribution, but also to leave substantial surplus for exports and otherwise financing industrialization. It is also clear that all this implies expanding demand from the sector for industry's output. Agricultural exports, raw and processed, accounted for an astonishing 92.4 percent of all exports in 1953-55, 80.9 percent in 1956-60, and did not dip below 50 percent until after 1961-65 (Table 5-4). During the critical import substituting decade of the 1950s—when industrialization was vulnerable and could easily turn into a

[i]These rates are high as compared with those shown below in Table 5-6. They represent the most recent revisions of Taiwan's historical agricultural data series, as taken from a preliminary paper by T.H. Lee and his associates, presented at a Conference on Agricultural Development of Japan, Taiwan, Korea, and the Philippines, held in Honolulu on February 5-9, 1973.

Table 5-4. Composition of Taiwan's Exports, 1953-1970 (percentage distribution)

	1953-55	*1956-60*	*1961-65*	*1966-1970*
Agricultural products	19.7	17.9	16.4	12.7
Processed agricultural products	72.7	63.0	38.5	18.1
Industrial products	7.6	19.1	45.1	69.2

Source: Council for International Economic Cooperation and Development, *Taiwan Statistical Data Book 1972*, p. 166, Table 10-6.

Note: The percentage distribution is compiled by the Bank of Taiwan and the Central Bank of China from the data of export exchange settlement rather than from the customs data.

blind alley for lack of essential resource support–agricultural exports financed well over 50 percent of total imports (Table 5-5). Even in the early export substituting industrialization period of 1961-65, the amount so financed remained at 50.3 percent.

The striking changes in the role of agriculture from 1965 on signify completion of the early development phase whose analytical attributes are aptly described by the two-sector model. Whether the dethroning of the two-sector model means the beginning of a takeoff into sustained growth, as Ranis and Fei argued, or a prelude to uncertain growth as Kindleberger believed, is another story.[j] What is clear is that it is a milestone marking the start of a process of industrialization that is export oriented and self-sustainable without strict impositions upon the agricultural sector. It is also a new phase in which prices assert themselves at the expense of controls and economic activities of a

Table 5-5. Percentage of Total Imports Financed by Agricultural Exports, 1953-1970

Year	*Percentage of total imports financed by agricultural exports*
1953-55	57.0
1956-60	53.7
1961-65	50.3
1966-70	28.2

Source: CIECD, *Taiwan Statistical Data Book 1972*, p. 166, Table 10-6, and p. 167, Table 10-7.

Note: Agricultural exports include agricultural and processed agricultural products.

[j]For details of their arguments, see Gustav Ranis and John C.H. Fei, "A Theory of Economic Development," *American Economic Review* (September 1961); and Charles P. Kindleberger, *Europe's Postwar Growth* (Cambridge, Mass.: Harvard University Press, 1967), Chapter 1.

hothouse variety, whose burdens too often fall on the rural sector, become less tempting. The remarkable time span and the equally remarkable stable price path that characterized the transition have prompted some students of economic development to regard Taiwan's model as an "ideal." No doubt U.S. economic aid played an important and timely role; equally, so did the agricultural sector of Taiwan. To return to the sector's changed role in the 1960s, we note that its share of exports fell from about 80 percent at the start of the decade to 30 percent at the end. Accordingly, the sector's role in financing imports declined, with the proportion financed by agricultural exports dropping from about 54 percent to less than 30 percent. These ratios should be viewed against the backdrop of a strong rising trend in the value of exports, representing a nine-fold increase in real terms during the eighteen-year period and still accelerating since 1970.

Input-Output Relations in Agriculture

Some insight into Taiwan's agricultural performance can be gained by examining changes in the sector's input-output relations. Table 5-6 shows average annual rates of changes in output, inputs, and certain partial measures of productivity. Examination of annual statistics suggests that it is meaningful to divide the period into two subperiods: 1952-64 and 1965-68. It can be observed from Table 5-6 that in the first subperiod output expansion (averaging 4.19 percent per year) was achieved by relatively moderate increases in total inputs (1.74 percent). The substantial total factor productivity increases in the

Table 5-6. Average Annual Rates of Changes in Output, Inputs, and Land Productivity of Taiwan's Agriculture, 1952-1968

Item	*1952-64*	*1965-68*
Total output	4.19	3.01
Total input	1.74	4.18
Crop area	0.80	0.19
Labor input	1.25	0.55
Chemical fertilizer	5.84	9.70
Feed input	4.83	15.68
Implement and depreciation on farm equipment and building	2.31	8.16
Multiple cropping index	0.71	–0.20
Crop yield index	3.33	1.40
Land productivity per ha.	4.15	2.62

Source: Compiled by T.H. Lee, Rural Economic Division, the Joint Commission of Rural Reconstruction.

Note: Agricultural output includes only crop and livestock production.

subperiod is to be contrasted against moderate declines in the second subperiod. In the latter subperiod, output grew at an annual average rate of 3.01 percent, while total inputs increased at 4.18 percent. Also noteworthy is the difference in the composition of incremental inputs. Increases in chemical fertilizers and feed and capital inputs bulked much larger in the second subperiod. Such compositional alterations are not unexpected in light of the transitional threshold which Taiwan passed in the early 1960s and of the rising affluence of the population. The tripling of the rate of increase of feed input (mostly imported) is in response to increased demand for meats. The doubling of the rate of increase of fertilizer input and the near quadrupling of that of capital inputs resulted partly from changes in factor price structure in line with altered scarcity relations and partly from government relaxation of earlier squeeze policies imposed on agriculture through manipulated prices paid and received by farmers. The extractive, government set rice-fertilizer barter ratio is a particular case in point.

It seems clear that during 1952-64, increases in the multiple cropping index resulted in substantial increases in land productivity. With chief reliance on a labor intensive, land saving type of technical improvement rather than large capital investments during this period, agriculture provided increasing job opportunities to absorb "surplus" labor in the rural areas. As a result, the release of agricultural workers appeared to have borne an appropriate relationship with expansion of employment opportunities in the nonagricultural sector. Much of the rural-urban migration has probably occurred from urban "pull" factors rather than from "push" factors within agriculture.

Estimates of agricultural labor force and outflow rates are given in Table 5-7. Outflow rates were moderate in the early 1950s and increased gradually as industrialization and shifts in relative sector weights took place. The absolute size of the agricultural labor force began to decline in 1969 as outflow rates accelerated in the late 1960s.

In spite of its success in the past, Taiwan's agriculture began to face transitional problems. The dynamics of growth dictated less reliance on labor and crop area and more on capital and other purchased inputs. In this connection, it is noteworthy that the multiple cropping index began to decline in the second subperiod. Taiwan has reached a new phase requiring reorganization of agriculture and increasing dependence on capital using, labor saving, and purchased input intensive techniques. In this phase, the central farm policy consideration, once accorded agricultural output and growth, shifts to intersectoral adjustment, factor flows, and comparative incomes.

Output originating in agriculture, forestry, hunting, and fishing (as calculated from the data on net domestic product at factor cost) fell from 38 percent of the net domestic output in 1952 to 19.1 percent in 1970, while industrial production, including manufacturing, mining, public utilities, and construction increased from 17.6 percent to 32.5 percent during the same period. At the same time, labor force in agriculture declined from 61 percent of

Table 5-7. Agricultural Labor Force and Outflow Rate of Agricultural Labor, 1952-70

Year	*Agricultural Labor Force (Person)*	*Outflow Rate of Agricultural Labor (%)*
1952	1,528,265	–
1953	1,569,273	0.49
1954	1,594,404	0.86
1955	1,609,675	1.50
1956	1,618,379	1.93
1957	1,591,758	3.56
1958	1,605,646	1.73
1959	1,627,990	1.71
1960	1,641,070	2.18
1961	1,653,378	2.15
1962	1,659,062	2.30
1963	1,675,452	1.78
1964	1,683,764	2.24
1965	1,687,843	3.41
1966	1,708,807	2.82
1967	1,732,676	2.72
1968	1,738,564	3.87
1969	1,732,479	4.74
1970	1,691,603	6.81

Source: Agricultural labor force is compiled by Manpower Development Committee, CIECD, and outflow rate by T.H. Lee, Rural Economic Division, JCRR.

Note: The outflow rate of agricultural labor (d) is estimated by the following formula:

$$d = \frac{P_a V - \Delta P_a}{P_a}$$

where P_a = agricultural labor force,

V = natural growth rate of agricultural labor force,

ΔP_a = actual increase in agricultural labor force.

the total in 1952 to 38 percent in 1970. The transformation, notable as it was, had a direct bearing on Taiwan's trade pattern, as is discussed in some detail in the following section.

POSTWAR DEVELOPMENT IN TAIWAN'S AGRICULTURAL EXPORTS

Foreign trade has been the leading moving force in Taiwan's postwar economic development. Table 5-8 shows the ratios of exports and imports to gross domestic product at current prices. The ratio of exports to GDP increased dramatically from 10 to 31 percent between 1951 and 1970. On the import side, the ratio rose from 15 to 31 percent. Taiwan is clearly a trade oriented economy. These figures also show that beginning with sizeable import surpluses Taiwan by 1970 had reached external current account balance. The trend is still continuing, yielding increasing export surpluses in the last several years. Real exports grew at a cumulative annual rate of 15.4 percent, and real imports at a rate of 13.9 percent during the period. With exports and imports growing rapidly, the commodity composition concurrently underwent marked changes during the period under review.

Role of Agricultural Exports

The breakdown of export by major commodities is presented in Table 5-9. Agricultural exports from Taiwan reflected the preeminence of the staples sugar and rice during the 1950s. Together these two crops accounted for over 70 percent of total exports in 1953-55, falling dramatically to less than 4 percent by 1970. Transformation of economic structure and export substituting industrialization brought in their wake dramatic offsetting increases in exports of manufactured goods. The leading manufactured exports were clothing, textiles, electrical machinery and appliances (mainly telecommunications equipment), plywood, and plastic articles. Manufactured exports rose from under 2 percent in 1953 to 54 percent of the total in 1970. Total exports in 1970 were valued at just under US$1.5 billion.

Accompanying the declines of traditional agricultural exports, there was the emergence of new export oriented products of which canned mushrooms and asparagus spears were the most notable examples. These enterprises, started in the mid 1960s, had by 1970 reached an export value of about US$30 million each. Ascendancy of these new export crops was due not so much to sudden shifts in relative world prices (although new legislation in the U.S. restricting seasonal Mexican farm laborers in California conditioned expectations) as it was to government initiative in Taiwan in recognizing the opportunities in providing overseas market information, and in instituting technical, supervisory, and marketing arrangements conducive to rapid adoption by the

Table 5-8. Exports and Imports as Percentage of GDP: 1951-1970 (at current prices)

Year	*Exports as Percentage of GDP*	*Imports as Percentage of GDP*
1951	10.2	14.9
1955	8.2	12.5
1960	11.2	18.7
1965	18.4	21.6
1970	30.6	30.7

Source: DGBAS, *op. cit.*, pp. 84-85, Table 1.

Table 5-9. Major Export Commodities, 1953-70

	1953	1955	1960	1965	1970
			(percent)		
Agricultural products					
Rice and paddy	10.6	23.3	3.1	9.1	0.1
Banana	2.4	3.1	3.7	10.8	2.2
Processed agricultural products					
Sugar	67.2	49.9	44.0	13.1	3.2
Tea	5.3	4.4	3.7	2.0	0.9
Canned pineapple	1.9	4.2	4.8	3.8	1.4
Canned mushrooms	–	–	–	4.3	2.2
Canned asparagus spears	–	–	–	2.3	2.3
Manufactured products					
Plywood	–	0.1	1.5	5.9	5.5
Textiles	0.1	0.9	11.6	10.3	13.8
Cement	0.7	–	0.7	1.9	0.7
Clothing and footwear	0.8	1.4	2.6	4.9	16.8
Plastic articles	–	–	–	2.6	5.1
Electrical machinery and appliances	–	–	–	0.4	12.4
Total exports	100.0	100.0	100.0	100.0	100.0

Source: Chinese Maritime Customs, *op. cit.*, various years.

farmers. The details on the government's role appear in the next section on domestic marketing and price policy.

The relative decline of total agricultural exports shown in Table 5-9 is to an extent misleading since their contribution to *net* foreign exchange earnings is more than proportional to their export value because of their lower import content. Average rates of net foreign earnings, after making allowance for imported inputs, by groups of export commodities, as estimated by the Foreign Exchange and Trade Commission for 1965-67, are: 91.5 percent for agricultural products, 79.0 percent for processed agricultural products, and 55.5 percent for manufactured products.

Food Balance Sheet and Capital Flows

As shown in Table 5-10, Taiwan's agriculture was able to supply enough food to meet the needs of both increased population and expanded agricultural exports up to the early 1960s. Such success, characterized by stable wages and prices, was particularly important in the period of inward oriented

Table 5-10. Food Balance Sheet of Taiwan (at 1935-37 Constant Price: NT$ thousand)

Period	*Total Supply of Food (1)*	*Domestic Food Consumption (2)*	*Net Exports of Food*	*(2)/(1)*
1946-50	290,716	268,754	21,962	92.45%
1951-55	429,985	404,536	25,448	94.08
1956-60	534,119	505,396	28,723	94.62
1961-65	738,065	726,123	11,942	98.38
1966-70	1,066,313	1,074,731	–8,417	100.78

Source: Estimated by T.H. Lee, Rural Economic Division, JCRR.

industrialization with the rate of population growth far exceeding 3 percent per annum, income elasticity of demand for food at 0.5-0.6, and the increase in real per capita income averaging about 3.5 percent annually. As a result of this balanced growth of agricultural and nonagricultural sectors, Taiwan becomes one of the few LDCs which have achieved an impressive growth record under price stability. Food balance sheet data show Taiwan's supply exceeding consumption by a steady margin of more than 5 percent during 1946-1960. The margin dipped to under 2 percent in the early 1960s and became negative thereafter, when the island easily managed the food deficit with its fast expanding industrial exports. The stable internal price level has undoubtedly contributed to improvement in Taiwan's international competitive position and made the transition from its initial import substituting industrialization to one oriented toward exports relatively easy.

As pointed out in the previous section, it was agriculture, together with U.S. economic aid, that financed industrialization in the early stage of economic development. T.H. Lee estimated the flows of resources and fund out of agriculture to nonagricultural sectors for the period 1895-1960. His study shows that the sectoral net real capital outflow was all positive for agriculture throughout the entire period. The major factors determining the capital outflow from agriculture during the period 1950-60 can be summarized as follows:

(a) Total output of agriculture increased rapidly at more than 4.0 percent per annum, with technological change contributing as much as 2.4 percent. In addition to increasing the rate of per capita consumption, this growth rate far exceeded the population growth rate;

(b) during the rapid industrialization at more than 17 percent per annum in this period, the wage rate in industry was two times higher than that in agriculture. The large food requirements of the industrial sector, combined with export demand, provided a major demand potential for agricultural products;

(c) the capital-output ratio in agriculture increased to some extent in this period but was still less than the capital-output ratio in the nonagricultural sector;
(d) investment in agriculture in this period was accompanied by a large multiplier effect, although the ratio of capital goods allocated to agriculture was only about 5 percent;
(e) taxes, forced savings on agriculture, and farmers' autonomous savings constituted a large squeeze on agriculture. However, invisible capital transfer occupied more than 50 percent of the total net capital transfer from agriculture throughout the period.[k]

Invisible capital outflow refers to the amount of capital outflow caused by manipulations of the sectoral terms of trade between agriculture and nonagriculture. Effective protection for rice was negative in Taiwan, attributable to the system of compulsory bartering of rice for high-priced chemical fertilizers. The import price of chemical fertilizer was only a little more than 50 percent of domestic price in 1964.[16]

Economic Policy Change

The squeeze applied through direct and hidden methods on agriculture has resulted in depressed incomes and per capita consumption of farmers. It is estimated that farmers' consumption expenditures reached only 66.1 percent of nonfarmers in 1964, and 64.6 percent in 1966.[17] The infant industry argument aside, the modest demand support from the rural areas appeared to be one of the important factors that caused the allegedly "simple and relatively easy phase of import substitution" to reach its apparent limit in a relatively short period.[l] As shown in Table 5-11, the industrial survey for 1959 indicates that many plants producing simple manufactures such as rubber canvas shoes, electric fans, soap, insulated wire, plywood, synthetic fabrics, woolen yarn, sewing machines, iron rods and bars, and paper, were operating at only 23 percent to 67 percent of capacity.

It was recognized that only an outward looking or export oriented industrialization policy could sustain a high rate of economic growth in such a small island economy as Taiwan, and a series of major policy reforms were undertaken during 1958-61. Overvalued currency was devalued, and the complicated exchange rate structure was simplified and finally unified in June 1961. Laws and regulations governing investment and imports were liberalized. The emphasis of trade policy was shifted from strict import controls to export promotion.

---

[k]See Note 2, p. 139.

[l]In addition to the narrow domestic market, the preferential allocation of undervalued foreign exchange for imported raw materials and capital equipment created incentive to expand capacity even when there was underutilization of existing capacity.

Table 5-11. Rates of Capacity Utilization of Selected Manufactures, 1959 and 1970

	1959	*1970*
Rubber canvas shoes	23.3%	70.9%
Electric fan	38.1	65.3
Soap	39.2	82.1
Insulated wire	40.0	64.6
Plywood	46.9	86.2
Synthetic fabrics	49.7	85.4
Woolen yarn	52.6	100.0
Sewing machine	64.3	51.2
Iron rod and bar	65.4	98.7
Paper	67.4	90.2

Source: Ministry of Economic Affairs and Council for International Economic Cooperation and Development, Executive Yuan, *Industry Surveys in Taiwan* (various years).

With a favorable investment climate created by constructive government policies, industry underwent startling changes, aided as before by abundant and efficient labor. Industrial exports rapidly expanded, especially after 1963,[m] and by the mid 1960s the somewhat pessimistic views of the late 1950s had been replaced by a popular sense of confidence and prosperity. It can be seen from Table 5-11 that, with the exception of sewing machines, the rates of capacity utilization of simple manufactures had improved significantly in 1970 compared with those in 1959.

Other performance indicators bearing on growth rates of real expenditures on GDP are shown in Table 5-12. They indicate striking improvements in economic performance after the policy switch. Growth of GDP went up from 7.7 percent per year to 11 percent, of capital from 12 to 16, of exports from 9 to 22, and of private consumption from 7 to 8 percent. Perhaps more astounding still is the accompanying deceleration of the growth of government expenditures, down from 6.6 to 6.1 percent per year. Outward orientation was clearly the more desirable strategy. Exports contribute not only to foreign exchange earnings, but also to efficient industrialization while contributing to socioeconomic changes pertinent to the initiation of a self-sustaining growth process.

With export oriented industrialization having asserted itself firmly in the late 1960s, the altered role of agriculture in foreign trade became unmistakable. As export processing and livestock production expanded rapidly, Taiwan had become by 1970 a sizeable and growing market for agricultural raw materials and foodstuffs. Export and import values of the unprocessed products of agriculture, forestry, hunting, and fishery for 1970 are shown in Table 5-13.

[m]An exceptionally high export price of sugar in 1963 and 1964 helped to build up exchange reserves and stabilize the exchange rate.

Table 5-12. Average Annual Growth Rates of Real Expenditures on GDP, 1951-1970

	1951-60	*1961-70*
Gross domestic product	7.7%	11.0%
Private consumption expenditures	7.4	8.0
Government consumption expenditures	6.6	6.1
Gross capital formation	12.0	15.9
Fixed capital formation	12.8	16.6
Increase in stocks	9.2	12.0
Exports of goods and services	9.2	22.0
Imports of goods and services	8.8	17.6

Source: GDBAS, *op. cit.*, p. 112, Table 13.

Table 5-13. Export and Import Values of Agriculture, Forestry, Hunting, and Fishery Products, 1970 (Unit: US$ million)

	Exports	*Imports*	*Trade Balance*
Crop products	50.8	188.4	–137.6
Forestry products	9.2	60.7	–51.5
Livestock products	6.3	19.5	–13.2
Fishery products	21.4	0.6	20.8
Hunting products	0.7	0.2	0.5
Total	88.5	269.4	–180.9

Source: Department of Statistics, Ministry of Finance, *Monthly Statistics of Foreign Trade Commodities, The Republic of China*, No. 45 (October 1972), Table 12.

Considerable trade deficits were recorded for crop, forestry, and livestock products. Total trade in terms of agricultural commodities proper also showed a large import surplus of US$150 million, or nearly three times the value of total agricultural exports. It is obvious that manufactured exports have substituted for traditional agricultural exports, and the trade for agricultural products had turned into deficits in the late 1960s. The strategic role played by the agricultural sector in earning foreign exchange and financing industrialization ceased in this period.

DOMESTIC MARKETING AND PRICE POLICY FOR AGRICULTURAL PRODUCTS

As shown in Table 5-14, total output value of agriculture, forestry, and fishery was NT$57 billion in 1969. Rice remained the most important crop, accounting

Table 5-14. Domestic Production, Imports, Exports, Home Demand, Commercial Margin, and Transport Margin of Agricultural, Forestry, and Fishery Products, 1969 (Unit: NT$ million)

Industry	*Domestic Production*	*Imports*	*Exports*	*Home Demand*	*Commercial Margin*	*Transport Margin*
Rice	15,172	113	267	15,018	816	189
Other common crops	4,622	4,838	2	9,458	825	132
Sugar cane	2,294	0	0	2,294	2	54
Crops for processing	4,507	2,246	149	6,604	291	56
Misc. horticultural crops	6,732	153	1,898	4,987	2,667	190
Hogs	9,065	99	339	8,825	1,784	31
Other livestock	5,658	728	215	6,171	467	37
Forestry	2,949	1,575	322	4,202	348	191
Fisheries	6,021	229	2,306	3,944	1,616	98
Total	57,020	9,981	5,498	61,503	8,816	978

Source: CIECD. *Taiwan's Interindustry Transactions Table for 1969.* Tables 1 and 2.

Notes: "Other common crops" include wheat, sweet potatoes, corn, soybeans, and others.

"Crops for processing" include tea, tobacco leaves, peanuts, cassava, miscellaneous food crops for processing, raw cotton, miscellaneous fiber crops, pineapple, mushrooms, asparagus, water-chestnut, peppermint, citronella, and miscellaneous special crops.

"Misc. horticultural crops" include bananas, citrus fruits, other fruits, vegetables, and flowers.

"Other livestock" includes cattle, hides, wool and hair (not treated), milk, meat, eggs, chickens and ducks, other poultry and feathers thereof, and others.

"Forestry" includes timber, fire wood, bamboos, natural rubber, and by-products and others.

for 26.6 percent of the total. Miscellaneous horticultural crops accounted for 11.8 percent, other common crops 8.1 percent, crops for processing 7.9 percent, and sugar cane 4.0 percent. Livestock production amounting to 25.8 percent of the total was mainly made up of hogs. Forestry products accounted for 5.2 percent and fishery products for 10.6 percent of the total. Fishery output has been expanding very rapidly in recent years as the tonnage of powered fishing vessels in operation rose from 26,806 tons in 1952 to 249,444 tons in 1970.

Rice was produced primarily for domestic consumption. Its net export surplus was only US$3.6 million in 1969. Considerable amounts of other common crops, crops for processing, and forestry products were imported. The import ratios were 51.2 percent for other common crops, 34.0 percent for crops for processing, and 37.5 percent for forestry products. On the other hand, fishery products and miscellaneous horticultural crops were major exports with export ratios standing at 38.3 percent and 28.2 percent, respectively. Although the export ratio of crops for processing was only 3.3 percent, mushrooms, asparagus spears, and pineapples are being canned and produced mainly for export. This is also true in the case of sugar cane.

Commercial and transport margins were relatively high for such farm products as miscellaneous horticultural crops, other common crops, and hogs. Perishability and too many small retailers and peddlers appear to be the primary reasons for high marketing costs. In addition to commercial and transport margins, a slaughter tax is imposed on hogs that is now NT$303 per head, or almost 10 percent of the retail value. The slaughter tax is one of the principal tax revenues for the prefectural and municipal governments: it accounted for 28.6 percent of total tax revenues of these governments in fiscal 1972.[18]

Agricultural prices are basically settled by the interaction of the forces of market demand and supply. However, government intervention of varying degrees is applied to stabilize the markets for some agricultural products. In the case of rice, for example, the food authority determines the official price every season, which is mainly based on production costs and is applied to compulsory government purchase of paddy from cultivators. The market price, however, has never fallen below the official price in the past. If the market price rises sharply, the government sells rice in the market to force the price down or to prevent it from increasing further. The government is able to do so because the total government collection of rice through land taxes and rice-fertilizer barter takes up more than 50 percent of total supply.[19]

The government prohibits exports of vegetables and frozen pork when supply is insufficient to meet the market demand at existing prices. To protect the growers of mushrooms, asparagus, jute, tobacco, and pineapples, forward contract prices are determined by collective bargaining between the farmers and the processors, subject to approval by the government. No canner is allowed to collect mushrooms from noncontract growers or at prices lower than the forward contract price. The right to export canned mushrooms is suspended in case the contract agreement is violated. The scheme reduces price uncertainty and through production control maintains prices above their competitive levels. Output and export expansion is geared to overseas market development whose expansion is sought through export promotion efforts. The government also provides technical assistance for the growers and market information, export inspection, and quality control for the processors. Production of mushroom and asparagus is recognized as consistent with Taiwan's agricultural resource posture, given its labor intensive and land saving characteristics.

In the case of sugar cane, the price is guaranteed by the Taiwan Sugar Corporation, a state enterprise that monopolizes the manufacturing of refined sugar. The guaranteed price is announced before the planting season, and is a floor price rather than a fixed price. If the price in the international market goes up, then a higher price is paid to the sugar cane growers.

It is generally felt that marketing needs more emphasis and strengthening. Promotion of cooperative marketing, enlargement of the scale of the small marketing outlets, and revision of outdated laws and regulations will narrow the differences between producers' and consumers' prices. Given the new economic realities of Taiwan, there is also a need to reexamine the government's agricultural price and income policy and to place it in the larger context of a total program aimed at promoting resource mobility and reorganization of agriculture consistent with efficiency and welfare.

Finally, for information purposes, composition of per capita food consumption in 1970 is shown in Table 5-15. Although rice still loomed large (20.5 percent) in the consumer's budget, it was outweighed by pork (21.2 percent) and closely pushed by fish (16.7 percent). Poultry and eggs come next at 14 percent. The average food budget per person was US$110 a year. These data show that the traditional concept of rice as the preeminent staple food has been changing. The rapid increases in the production of livestock and fishery products in recent years, as noted earlier, reflect the changing pattern of consumption of food under the influence of rising real per capita income, which since the mid 1960s has averaged on the order of 8-10 percent per year.

SUMMARY AND CONCLUSIONS

On conventional a priori grounds, the prospects for economic development are poor for small island economies. They are too densely populated to hope for further significant expansion of their traditional primary exports, and their domestic markets are too small to accommodate economic industrialization programs applicable to large economies.[20] Even so, the recent rapid growth of the Taiwan economy, with the expansion of manufactured exports providing the main thrust, has made it one of the relatively few developing countries that have successfully reached the phase of "self-sustained" growth.

It is hoped that this study will contribute to a better understanding

Table 5-15. Composition of Per Capita Food Consumption, 1970 (Home Consumption Only)

Item	*Value (NT$)*	*Percentage Share in Total Consumption*
Rice (polished)	901.60	20.45
Wheat flour	70.38	1.60
Sweet potatoes	12.73	0.29
Beans	100.14	2.27
Corn	6.90	0.16
Pork	935.85	21.23
Beef	31.68	0.72
Poultry	394.26	8.94
Eggs	224.09	5.08
Fats and oils	239.99	5.44
Milk products	139.06	3.15
Fruits	244.63	5.55
Vegetables	283.63	6.43
Sugar	89.32	2.03
Fishes	734.72	16.66
Total	4,408.98	100.00

Source: Hsu and Chen, *op cit.*, p. 3, Table 3.

of Taiwan's postwar growth process, which is being increasingly thought of as embodying a set of experiences and policy lessons perhaps rich in transfer value. The principal focus of the study is to examine how agriculture, in general, and its export trade, in particular, have contributed to Taiwan's singular success story. A related purpose is to review the changing role of agriculture and evolutions in its trade and internal structure as industrialization and modernization proceeded apace. The major findings and conclusions are summarized as follows:

1. A broader base for economic development was laid by land reform. The positive role played by the agricultural sector in Taiwan offers a sharp contrast to the situation in a number of other less developed countries, where chronic shortage of foodstuffs and failure to develop agricultural exports served as a drag on industrial and general economic development.

2. Despite the limitation imposed by inadequate data and restrictive assumptions of the model employed, the findings offer the suggestion that foreign exchange rather than domestic savings constituted the constraint on

Taiwan's growth until the early 1960s. Assisted by timely U.S. economic aid, the economy passed, however, from a phase of foreign exchange constrained growth to one of a higher growth limited by savings. During the aid period, when the development focus was on import substituting industrialization, agricultural products retained their dominant position in the island's total exports, with a share ranging around 90 percent. The significant increase (nearly 5 percent per year) in agricultural production made it possible for Taiwan not only to meet the domestic food requirements of a fast growing (3.5 percent per year) population, but also to leave a substantial surplus (about 5 percent of output) for export. As a result, balanced growth à la Ranis and Fei, conducive to industrialization, prevailed. And Taiwan reached the "takeoff" into self-sustained growth in a remarkably short span of time. Agriculture financed more than half of total imports during the crucial period when the effective constraint upon Taiwan's development was the amount of available foreign exchange. The importance of agricultural exports declined dramatically since the mid 1960s as growth ceased to be restricted by the exchange bottleneck and as surging industrial exports brought current trade account into balance.

3. With chief reliance on labor intensive, land saving technical advances rather than large capital investments during 1952-1968, the release of agricultural workers appeared to be moderate and to have borne an appropriate relationship with employment growth in the nonagricultural sector. The adoption of labor using, land saving, multiple cropping farming resulted in a rapid increase in land productivity. Economic development in Taiwan is a successful demonstration of a comparative advantage approach as development strategy. Import substituting industrialization was seen not as an end but as an infant industry phase, to give way in time to export oriented, competitive industrialization. It makes it possible to achieve the twin objectives of output growth and employment growth with little conflict even in the short run.

4. The transformation of economic structure and assertion of export substituting industrialization in the late 1960s had a direct bearing on Taiwan's trade pattern. Manufactured exports displaced traditional agricultural exports, and the trade for agricultural products turned into deficit. With that, the Lewis two-sector model was dethroned and its strict impositions on agriculture ceased to apply.

5. It was agriculture together with U.S. economic aid that financed industrialization in the early stage of Taiwan's postwar economic development. However, the harsh squeeze on agriculture, through direct and hidden methods, has resulted in a slow increase in per capita consumption of farmers. Together with the infant industry considerations, this appeared to be one of the important factors that caused the allegedly simple and relatively easy phase of import

substitution to reach its limits in a relatively short period. With low capacity utilization rates in industry acting as a signal, the government soon began to introduce a series of major policy reforms during 1958-61. By the mid 1960s the somewhat pessimistic views of the late 1950s had been replaced by confidence and prosperity as industrialization, now reoriented, accelerated apace. Competitive export promotion contributed not only to foreign exchange earnings but also to efficient industrialization, while laying the groundwork for socioeconomic changes conducive to the process of self-sustaining growth.

6. As rising affluence brings into operation differential income elasticities, the traditional concept of rice as the only staple food loses its substance. The rapid increase in the production of livestock and fishery products in recent years reflects the changing pattern of demand as well as the sector's surprising supply response. Agricultural prices in the domestic market are basically settled by the interaction of the forces of demand and supply. However, government interventions of varying forms and degrees are applied to stabilize the markets for some agricultural products. Attention is centered on rice (still a key wage good) and the new export crops such as asparagus and mushrooms, which by 1970 had displaced traditional sugar and rice (once accounting for nearly 80 percent of *all* exports) as the leading agricultural export commodities.

Since the late 1960s a new era has dawned upon Taiwan's agriculture. With the farm labor force declining absolutely for the first time, a rapidly shifting food consumption bundle, and relaxation of the old squeeze policy implicit in the classic two-sector model, the need for a new agricultural policy is now evident.

Food production per se is now anachronistic as a basic policy consideration. Present and future policy focus should be to facilitate the economic reorganization of agriculture in a way that can best accommodate needed farm readjustment, to insure proper price relations between agriculture and the rest of the economy, to speed up the outflow of agricultural resources (mainly labor) compatible with equilibrium resource earnings between sectors, and to reorient public research and development programs for agriculture in light of the new emerging economic conditions.

The income gap between sectors is wide and threatens to grow wider. It is hoped that public policy will not seek the expedient of price intervention for remedy but instead follow the lines of inquiry suggested above.

Chapter Six

Growth, Capital Import, and Agriculture in Korea

George S. Tolley

The success stories in development have received less attention than they deserve. Analysis of development has centered on high income countries such as the United States and on the relatively slow growing lower income countries such as India. Korea is among a group of rapid growth countries sharing features not found in the two prototypes. Real income doubles in less than a decade. There is heavy international involvement, with growth of commodity trade and international funds flows. The international involvement has monetary repercussions contributing to inflation. While a literature exists on international trade and growth, that literature is primarily theoretical and is more concerned with balance of payments adjustments and trade policy than with understanding the rate of economic development as such. Thus, in spite of concerns with development from several points of view, understanding of the rapid growth cases from which the most might be learned remains limited.

The dramatic action in the Korean economy has been outside of agriculture. Yet, with half the economically active population still employed in agriculture, agriculture importantly affects and is affected by the rest of the economy. Underlying this chapter is the belief that attention to overall growth and monetary processes is a prerequisite to fully assessing the effects of agricultural policies.

TYPICAL NEAR TERM ANALYSIS

Much overall analysis of the Korean economy has been oriented to the five-year plans. The widely used models are variants featuring demands for outputs of sectors, with domestic savings and foreign exchange availability introduced as constraints. Rates of growth in export industries and real per capita income have typically been assumed to continue near recent rates. After examining the outlook appropriate to a five-year planning effort, our discussion considers determinants of growth for longer horizons. An approach is presented for explaining growth as movement toward a significantly higher long run equilibrium, the rate of approach being determined by the costs of rapid expansion of capital.

Several demand factors might slow down growth in the next one to five years. The decline of the Viet Nam war reduces remittances to homeland by Koreans in Viet Nam, reduces U.S. procurement of war materiel in Korea, and has indirect effects on demands for Korea's exports by nations which are also affected by the war slowdown. Another demand factor unfavorable to growth is reduction in outlays in Korea by U.S. Armed Forces and AID. Still other demand factors, also unfavorable to growth, center on U.S. trade, with dollar devaluation and quotas having direct effects on Korea's exports and indirect effects particularly via Japan. Higher energy prices also deserve mention.

While the recent slowdowns in Korea might be due to the onset of these unfavorable demand factors, an alternate hypothesis is that the economy has been slowed by tight money policies initiated by the Bank of Korea. Facts in support of the alternate hypothesis are the facts that exports have continued strong, there have been retardations in growth in the money supply, and the construction industry has noticeably lagged.

There appears to be a significant connection between investment and changes in the money supply. This is consistent with the view that investment bears the brunt of changes in the money supply. Lending responses of commercial banks, the largest of which are owned by the government, might well lead to this result. Commercial bank lending rates are below curb interest rates so that rationing is required. The rationing may take the form of choosing among the investment desires of prominent Korean businessmen. The hypothesis then is that the extent to which investment desires are met ebbs and flows with the total assets of the commercial banks. These assets are governed by the money liabilities these banks are permitted to create. Analysis of monetary assets and liability changes to test this view is discussed with the causes of inflation.

If the current recession were unambiguously being caused by the unfavorable external demand factors, a slowdown in growth in the next five years might be indicated. The third five-year plan projections were on the conservative side, and the unfavorable factors could, if persistent, improve their accuracy. On the other hand, if the recession is due to tight money, the slowdown may be a more passing phenomenon.

For an intermediate run—as relevant to, say, 1980—foreign debt repayment considerations enter. Investor skepticism about future foreign currency repayment ability could slow foreign investment. As another possibility, the Korean government's fears about repayment abilities may result in restrictions being put in the way of expansions of foreign debt. The ratio of debt repayment obligations to repayment ability from export earnings is high compared to other countries, such as Taiwan, and some feel that a further rise in this ratio might make Korea vulnerable to a temporary balance of payments reversal. Debt repayment obligations and export earnings are both rising rapidly, and so there is room for continued growth of foreign debt without raising the ratio of obligations to repayment ability.

An increase in foreign debt obligations, if used to import capital to expand export industries, will create some ability to repay the obligations. However, many loans are used to expand domestic infrastructure and domestic final goods industries. The total product is presumably greater than the amount of the loan to be repaid, but the increased output may take the form of domestic production whereas the loan repayment is to be made in foreign currency. A possible mechanism for repaying the loan is for the demand and supply of foreign exchange to encourage shifts in resource uses within the country, increasing exports and reducing imports. That is, while the proceeds of the loan are generated in the form of domestic production, there can be a concommitant increase in exports or reduction in imports generating the foreign currency to repay the loan.

If the total product from the loan is greater than the amount of the loan, the sum of the value of increased exports and decreased imports will be less than the increase in domestic production due to the loan—i.e., there will still be a net gain in amount of production available for consumption or other uses in Korea. If the export industries are constant cost industries, there need be no effect on the equilibrium exchange rate (or on Korean price level movement required for balance of payments equilibrium if the exchange rate is fixed). The export industries are then an activity that can be used to expand foreign exchange earnings to repay loans as needed with no diminishing returns.

To consider the case where export industries are not constant cost industries, let the supply function for exports be $E = s(R_E;c)$ where R_E is price in won received for exports and c is elasticity of supply with respect to price. Let the demand function for imports be $I = d(R_I;b)$ where R_I is won price of imports and b is price elasticity of demand. Won prices are related to world prices by $R_E = rP_E$ and $R_I = rP_I$ where r is the exchange rate expressed as won per dollar and P_E and P_I are world prices. Assume that Korean supply and demand constitute a small enough part of world trade so that P_E and P_I can be taken as given. The condition for equilibrium in the demand and supply for foreign exchange is $P_I I + T = P_E E$ where T is net foreign repayments. To find the effect on exchange rate of an increase in net foreign repayments, differentiate the five equations just given with respect to T obtaining five linear equations in the derivatives of E, I, R_E, R_I and r. Solve for dr/dT and multiply by V_E/r where V_E is dollar value of exports. One then finds that the percentage change in the exchange rate resulting from a change in net foreign repayments equal to 1 percent of export value, $(dr/dT)(V_E/r)$, is $.01/(c - bV_I/V_E)$ where V_I is the dollar value of imports. This expression shows how the elasticity of supply c and the elasticity of demand b (a negative number) act to dampen the effect on exchange rate that is likely to ensue from future increases in repayments.

The expression indicates the relation between foreign repayments and the equilibrium exchange rate. While policy does not always keep the exchange rate close to equilibrium, problems of control are likely to be increased the farther from equilibrium the exchange rate is. These problems give incentives not to go indefinitely far from the equilibrium exchange rate. Deliberately, or as a result of control problems, one way of meeting foreign repayment may thus be through resource adjustments generating required foreign currency through exchange rate rise. Without implying that this route alone would automatically take care of repayments without problems of its own, the conclusion seems warranted that exploration of resource and exchange rate adjustments is part of predicting the effect of future foreign repayment on growth. Planning for some adjustments along these lines might help provide for future repayment, thus reducing fear of indebtedness as a constraint on growth.

With an overvalued won—e.g., with an exchange ratio of 375 won per dollar instead of 450 as several observers have indicated would more nearly reflect the market clearing value of foreign exchange—borrowers in Korea incur a liability to repay 375 won for every dollar borrowed. There is a question whether borrowers are receiving a signal to value the repayments at their real resource cost. A consequence of overvaluing a country's currency may thus be to attract future repayment obligations whose real burden is greater than the additional income made possible by the loans. Controls limiting foreign borrowing may be in part a response to this incentive. As is discussed later, controls may make the real position of the Korean economy close to what it would be if the won were valued at its market clearing price.

CONCEPT OF MOVING LONG TERM EQUILIBRIUM

While growth to, say, 1980 may be influenced by the condition alluded to so far, looking beyond that calls for longer run models based on the underlying reasons for Korea's growth. Special factors often mentioned as underlying Korea's growth are expenditures by the U.S. government in Korea, raising the demand for services produced in Korea; and foreign capital gifts, again mainly from the United States. These special factors explain neither the growth of commodity exports (where the most dramatic growth in output is occurring), nor the related inflow of private capital from the rest of the world, which is providing a significant part of the resources necessary to expand production in Korea.

More cogent than the special factors is the idea that Korean growth has been aided by economic reforms carried out in the early sixties, at which time the current output growth began. The export boom appears to be due to the competitive position provided by the low cost of labor in Korea. The economic reforms reduced business reluctance to employ this labor in export production. The competitive position of Korea was enhanced by the rising cost of labor in Japan. Capital began rushing in as a response to differences in factor rewards between Korea and the rest of the world. The rapid rise in returns to labor in Korea may be viewed as a movement to a new equilibrium level of returns vis-à-vis the rest of the world. Factor price equalization reasoning suggests the equilibrium might be one where factor returns become equal to those in the rest of the world. Yet differences in returns to comparable labor appear to have existed more or less permanently even among high income countries, as witness differences between Europe and the United States.

Let national income Y in Korea be interpreted to be the result of inputs of man-hours, L, and a total stock, K, of reproducible human and nonhuman capital in a relationship which is approximately Cobb-Douglas, i.e., $Y = cL^{\alpha}K^{\beta}$. An estimate can be made of the c value for Korea and compared to c's for other countries to obtain an idea of reasons for income differences other than amounts of labor and reproducible capital. This is similar to what Anne Krueger did in her attempts to find out how much of international income differences can be attributed to education. Larry Westphal and I carried out some preliminary measurements of changes in L and K in Korea for the 1960s. The Korean Development Institute is currently undertaking a growth source analysis. While such measurements concentrate on changes over time, they would provide a start in estimating L and K for a particular time as is needed to estimate the c value for Korea.

Rearranging the production function, the estimate of c is $Y/L^{\alpha}k^{\beta}$. Thus c can be calculated using observed national income Y, the estimates of L and K just discussed, and α and β estimated as observed proportions of national income paid to L and K. Thus α is man-hours times wage rate of unskilled labor, as a fraction of national income. Education, along with physical capital, increases the measure of K, and the returns to education should, therefore, be included as the return to K in estimating β.

How could the c value be used to judge where the Korean economy is going? The c value can be used in conjunction with an estimate of the degree to which capital flows equalize marginal product of capital between countries. Using the production function with a particular c value, one can estimate the amount of capital needed to bring about equilibrium marginal product of capital, and the production function can then also be used to estimate the income resulting from that amount of capital. Taking the partial of the production function with respect to K gives the marginal product of capital $\beta cL^{\alpha}K^{\beta-1}$. If, to keep the present discussion simple, linear homogeneity is assumed ($\alpha + \beta = 1$), the marginal product is $\beta c(K/L)^{\beta-1}$ or $\beta ck^{\beta-1}$ where k is capital stock per man-hour. For subscripts, let 1 refer to Korea and 2 to some other country. Capital flows that achieve equality in marginal product of capital imply $\beta c_1 k_1{}^{\beta-1} = \beta c_2 k_2{}^{\beta-1}$ or, rearranging,

$$k_1/k_2 = (c_1/c_2)^{1/(1-\beta)}$$

Let $y\ (= Y/L)$ refer to income per man-hour. Dividing both sides of the production function by L gives $y = ck^\beta$. Thus $y_1/y_2 = (c_1/c_2)(k_1/k_2)^\beta$. Substituting in the result for k_1/k_2 just derived gives the equilibrium income per man-hour ratio

$$y_1/y_2 = (c_1/c_2)^{1/(1-\beta)}.$$

If man-hours were unaffected by differences over time and among countries in dependency rates or other employment-to-population considerations, the income ratio just derived would also be a ratio between per capita incomes.

The ratio just derived is a theory of equilibrium relation of incomes among countries with international capital flows. The basic cause of nonequality of incomes is differences in aggregate output per unit, as reflected in c_1/c_2. The difference in incomes is greater than indicated by the productivity ratio c_1/c_2 alone because differences in productivity affect the profitability of having capital in a country, which further affects income. A country with high output per unit of input would have a higher marginal product of capital, if capital per worker were the same as in a lower productivity country.

It is profitable for the high productivity country to carry investments to a further margin relative to number of workers. The effect of capital accumulation induced by productivity differences is reflected in the exponent $1/(1-\beta)$ in the centered expression just given for the income ratio. Suppose that c_1/c_2, the ratio of output per unit of input for two countries, is 2/3 and that the share of income accruing to capital is 1/2 giving the estimate of $\beta = 1/2$. Then the equilibrium income ratio is $(2/3)^2 = 4/9$, or less than half, instead of the simple productivity ratio between the two countries of 2/3.

The discussion suggests the following two-step procedure for making a long run projection of real income for Korea: first, project future aggregate productivity in Korea and in other countries (i.e., project c_1 as productivity for Korea and a number of c_2's as productivity in other countries such as the United States and Japan), and second, estimate the ratio of Korean per capita income to that projected for other countries by raising projected productivity ratio c_1/c_2 to the $1/(1-\beta)$ power to allow for the magnified effect that productivity differences exert on the profitability of having capital in a country.

As a refinement, one might wish to allow for the possibility that investment is not carried to the same marginal return in all countries. Due to expectational considerations and other impediments to international equalization of interest rates, a distinction could be needed between interest rate in the country in question r_1 and interest rate in other country r_2 instead of assuming the r's are equal. In the formulation above, the conditions for the amount of capital in each country would become $r_1 = c_1 k_1{}^{\beta-1}$ and $r_2 = c_2 k_2{}^{\beta-1}$ which on combining gives

$$\frac{k_1}{k_2} = \left[\left(\frac{c_1}{c_2}\right) \Big/ \left(\frac{r_1}{r_2}\right)\right]^{\frac{1}{1-\beta}}$$

and using the production functions leads to equilibrium income ratio

$$\frac{y_1}{y_2} = \left[\left(\frac{c_1}{c_2}\right) \Big/ \left(\frac{r_1}{r_2}\right)\right]^{\frac{1}{1-\beta}}$$

The original formulation is modified only in that the ratio of c values needs to be divided by the ratio of interest rates.

Quick extrapolations of c values could be used for projections. Ultimately, more serious studies of reasons for differences in c values among countries appear called for. Some of the reasons why c values might not be the same for all nations were listed in Samuelson's original discussion of factor price equalization. In the case of Korea, institutional considerations affecting the profitability of investment come to mind first as affecting c values, since institutional changes constituted the economic reforms which apparently set off the recent growth surge.

The c for a country is a weighted average of output per unit of input for the goods produced in the country. For a country heavily involved in international trade, transportation costs of traded goods provide an impediment to complete equalization of c values. Even if production functions within Korea were the same as elsewhere, the cost of getting the produced goods to markets would have to be subtracted and could make the effective c value lower for Korea. In the case of Korea, relying so heavily on processing imported raw materials for export, the transport costs of getting the raw materials to Korea lead to a further subtraction reducing effective c value. Tariffs, quotas and related measures of other countries affecting international trade further reduce effective c value for Korea. In view of rapidly changing relative factor prices in Korea, comparative advantage in international trade can be expected to change over time, affecting the influence of trade considerations on c values.

Goods and services not exported comprise an extremely large part of national income, which can affect c value for the country. Differences in natural endowments, perhaps the most frequently mentioned reason for differences in production functions, most importantly affect agriculture. Increases in agricultural productivity would shift national aggregate c value up by approximately the percentage increase in productivity times the weight of agriculture in national production. Conversely, a lack of productivity increase in agriculture means a zero change times the weight of agricultural production.

In addition to including almost all agricultural production as well as traditional manufacturing, nonexport goods are produced by retailing and service industries. While the latter are far from immune to the international transfer of technology, they do not appear to have attracted as large amounts of management attention as have the export industries, where through foreign personnel and other means the latest techniques available anywhere in the world have been adopted in Korea.

Economies of scale could affect production functions for both traded and nontraded goods and services. The effect of economies of scale would appear as differences in c values among nations and would lead to an increase in c value for Korea as the economy grows.

What shows up as the effect of capital and the effect of c value depends on the definition of capital. Perhaps the simplest approach is to use the national income accounting definition of net investment. Among broader approaches, it has become common to expand the definition of capital to include human capital and thus count education as part of investment. The approach conceivably could be broadened further to include other human capital investments, such as health measures, raising more difficult conceptual and measurement problems. Research and development expenditures, giving indications of investments in knowledge, could lead to including the value of the stock of knowledge from these investments in the definition of capital.

At an extreme, perhaps any change increasing income could be counted as reflecting capital accumulation due to investment except attitudinal changes not deliberately induced by expenditure and pure learning by doing not influenced by expenditures to increase the learning. Practically, not all activity that is investment from a conceptual point of view is likely to be so counted. Thus some continued increases over time in c values as actually measured can be expected because of an inevitably narrow definition of capital. A major requirement for the analysis at hand is consistency in the definition of capital between nations and over time. For instance, if research and development expenditures are not included in the definition of investment, allowance should be made for increases in c values over time due to these expenditures.

Suppose the true production function is

$$y = ck_1^{\beta_1} k_2^{\beta_2}.$$

If an approximation is to be used in which there is one capital aggregate, a first possible procedure is to exclude k_1 from measured capital. Then the approximated production function is

$$y = c'k_2^{\beta_2},$$

where

$$c' = ck_1^{\beta_1}.$$

As long as the c value used in the approximation is raised in a consistent manner to allow for the effects of the nonmeasured capital, the approximated production function will predict income just as well as the true production function. In the absence of explicit measurement, recognizing the existence of excluded capital might enable informed judgments about how much c values should be raised.

A second possible procedure is to include k_1 as part of the measured capital stock. In this case the approximated production function can be written as $y = ck$. The conditions for income to be correctly predicted by the approximated production function are that the measured capital stock be the geometrically weighted average of the two component kinds of capital

$$(k = k_1^{\beta_1/\beta} k_2^{\beta_2/\beta})$$

and that $\beta = \beta_1 + \beta_2$. Under this procedure there is no problem of allowing for effects of nonmeasured capital on c values, but there is a problem of making predictions of measured aggregate capital consistent with correct predictions of the component kinds of capital. As will emerge later in this analysis, the problem under this second procedure is so serious that a recognition of at least two different component kinds of capital appears needed. For the moment, however, the assumption will be that all measured capital can without error be considered to be homogeneous. Granted this assumption, either of the two alternative capital measurement procedures can lead to correct predictions of future equilibrium income.

THE PATH OF INCOME AS DETERMINED BY SHORT RUN DIMINISHING RETURNS TO CAPITAL FORMATION

For most countries, observed income is probably close to equilibrium income as explained above by c values and equilibrium of capital returns. However, for countries in rapid transition, such as Korea, the rate of growth of income is too great to be explained solely in terms of equilibrium values. The growth appears to be movement toward a new equilibrium, which is not immediately reached. The theory of equilibrium income then gives a target toward which the economy is aiming. As has been suggested, this target can be used in making long run projections.

For the rapidly growing economies, the theory of equilibrium income leads almost inevitably to asking, What determines the time path of approach to equilibrium? To begin to go toward an explanation of short run income consistent with the long run, one could assume continuation of recent rates of growth until the equilibrium is reached.

As a simple example, suppose the ratio of equilibrium to present per capita income is determined to be R and the recent growth rate is g. Then the time t required to reach equilibrium income if this growth rate continues is determined by $R = e^{gt}$ or $t = lnR/g$. Suppose the recent growth rate g is .10, then for $R = 2$, $t = 6.9$; for $R = 5$, $t = 16.1$; for $R = 10$, $t = 23.0$. These values of t give the time required to reach the equilibrium income. The delay in reaching equilibrium income could be interpreted as being due to a limit at which a country can increase its capital stock.

To continue the simple example, if the production function is $y = ck^{\beta}$, then the percentage yearly growth of income $\dot{y}$ is $\beta\dot{k}$ where $\dot{k}$ is percentage yearly growth in capital stock. The g value of 10 percent per year increase in income is then interpreted as being due to a 20 percent per year increase in capital stock, which is supposed to continue until equilibrium income is reached. This approach does not explain why the capital stock is constantly to grow at 20 percent per year. Yet the idea that there would be considerations taken to prevent instantaneous adjustment of the capital stock as would be required to jump immediately to new equilibrium is appealing.

In seeking an economic explanation of the change in capital, one might be tempted to give a role to higher marginal product of capital as reflected in the higher real interest rate observed in Korea than in most other countries. The real interest rate in fairly nonrisky investments in Korea might, in view of the extremely high interest rates there, be judged to be at least 15 or 20 percent, compared with, say, 10 percent in the United States. However, one may question the use of observed interest rates in a short run disequilibrium situation to estimate long run differences. Suppose the exchange rate were flexible or in any case set to equate demand and supply for foreign exchange. Then foreign capital would tend to flow in to eliminate any differences in real interest rates between Korea and the rest of the world.

The higher real interest rate in Korea thus appears to be due either to higher riskiness or controls preventing the inflow of foreign capital. This does not, however, imply that by equalizing interest rates between Korea and the rest of the world one would immediately jump to the long run equilibrium level of capital stock and real income. Short run cost curves, being more steeply sloped than long run curves, would reduce current real interest rates to world levels before the long run equilibrium capital stock was reached. Then capital would continue to flow in at amounts determined by the resource redeployments profitable at the world interest rate. That the long run equilibrium would not be reached instantaneously is suggested by contemplating the large amounts of public infrastructure, migration, training, and acquisitions of management know-how entailed in a country's adjustment to a capital stock of a fundamentally different order of magnitude.

Most explanations of economic growth assume that a unit of income devoted to adding to the capital stock adds a unit to capital. This assumption is not consistent with the existence, suggested in the previous paragraph, of rising marginal cost as large increases in the capital stock are made in a sample period.

In Figure 6-1, the 45° line relating investment and the increase in capital corresponds to the traditional assumption. The schedule *OC* depicts a situation where at zero investment there is a one-for-one contribution of investment to capital, but due to rising marginal costs, the marginal contribution of investment to capital becomes less and less. For gradual growth traditionally discussed, where yearly additions to the capital are relatively small, observed points are near the origin where a one-for-one correspondence between investment and increments to capital stock is closely approximated.

In contrast, the schedule in Figure 6-1 is of interest for analyzing

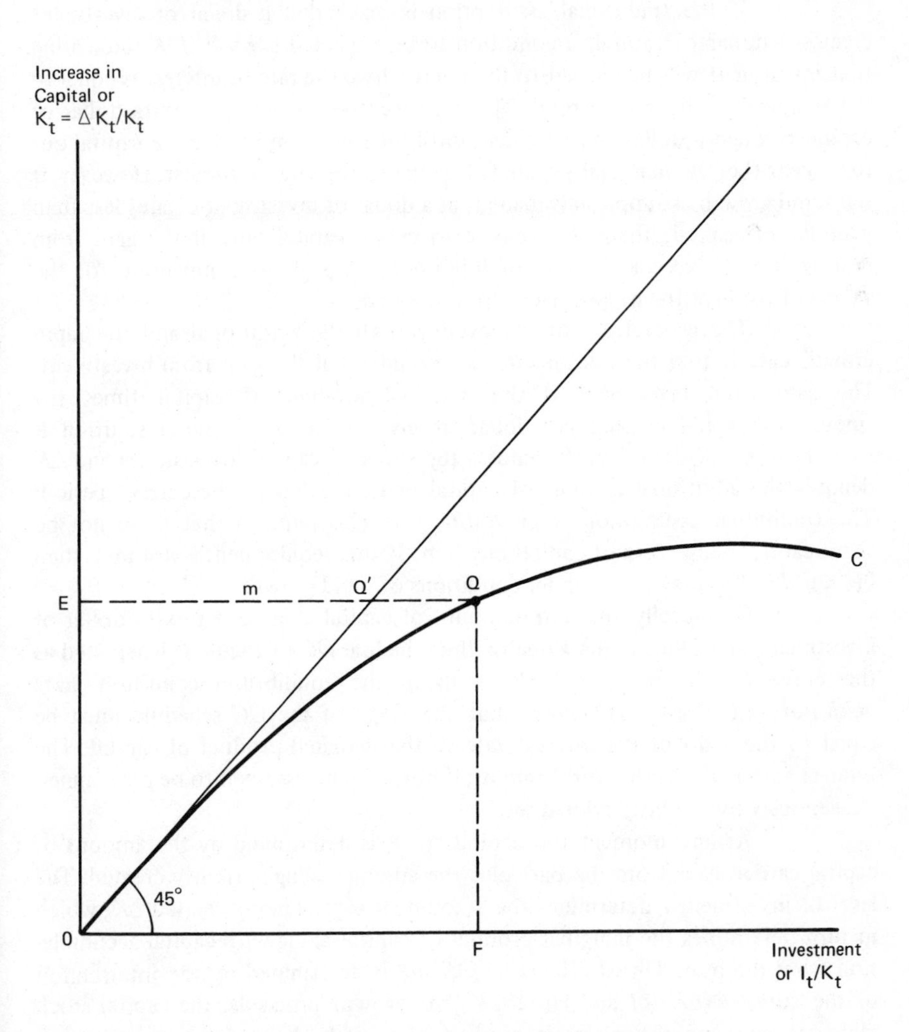

Figure 6-1. The Investment Curve

rapid growth. At an observed point Q far removed from the origin, there is large investment OF resulting in the large addition to capital stock OE. OE is less than OF because of the rising marginal costs of creating in any one year. The explanation of additions to capital in terms of the smooth schedule OC in Figure 6-1 is more reasonable than assuming a kinked schedule such as $OQ'Q$ where there are no diminishing returns to investment up to Q' and zero returns thereafter. An unreasonable kinked situation has to be hypothesized to explain the simple numerical example discussed above of a constant percentage addition to the capital stock regardless of incentives to add to the stock.

If the traditional assumption is made that a dollar of investment creates a dollar of capital, a condition to be expected is $r = \partial Y/\partial K$, indicating that investment will be carried to the point where the rate of interest is equal to the marginal product of capital. There is incentive to create an extra dollar of capital through a dollar of investment until the gain from renting the capital out for a year (i.e., its marginal product) is equal to the rate of interest. However, if the rapid growth assumption is made that a dollar of investment creates less than a dollar of capital, there is incentive to create capital only if the gain from renting it out exceeds the rate of interest by enough to compensate for the excess of the investment cost over capital created.

The general condition covering both the traditional and the rapid growth case is that the rate of interest should equal the gain from investment. The gain from investment is the marginal product of capital times the amount of capital created per dollar of investment. The general solution is $r = (\partial Y/\partial K)(\partial \Delta K/\partial I)$ where K denotes the stock of capital in existence and ΔK denotes the additional amount of capital being created in the current period. The traditional assumption is $\partial(\Delta K)/\partial I = 1$. This requires that there not be significantly rising costs of capital creation. If this requirement is not met, then $\partial(\Delta K)/\partial I < 1$ as may occur under conditions of rapid growth.

Graphically the extra amount of capital created per extra dollar of investment, $\partial(\Delta K)/\partial I$, is the slope of the schedule OC of Figure 6-1 depicted as the curve PS in Figure 6-2. Rearranging the equilibrium condition gives $\partial(\Delta K)/\partial I = r/(\partial Y/\partial K)$, indicating that the slope of the OC schedule must be equal to the ratio of the interest rate to the marginal product of capital. The interest rate is the given world rate or, if not, may be assumed to be determined exogenously by the institutional setting.

At any moment the capital stock is determined by the amount of capital carried over from the past plus the amount being currently created. The level of investment I determines the amount of capital being created ΔK, which in turn determines the marginal product of capital along with capital accumulation from the past. Thus I affects $\partial Y/\partial K$ and is determined by the intersection of the curves $\partial(\Delta K)/\partial I$ and $r/(\partial Y/\partial K)$. As growth proceeds, the capital stock increases lowering the marginal product of capital $\partial Y/\partial K$ for any level of I. Because $\partial Y/\partial K$ is positively related to I and $\partial(\Delta K)/\partial I$ is negatively related to I

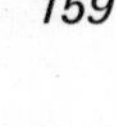

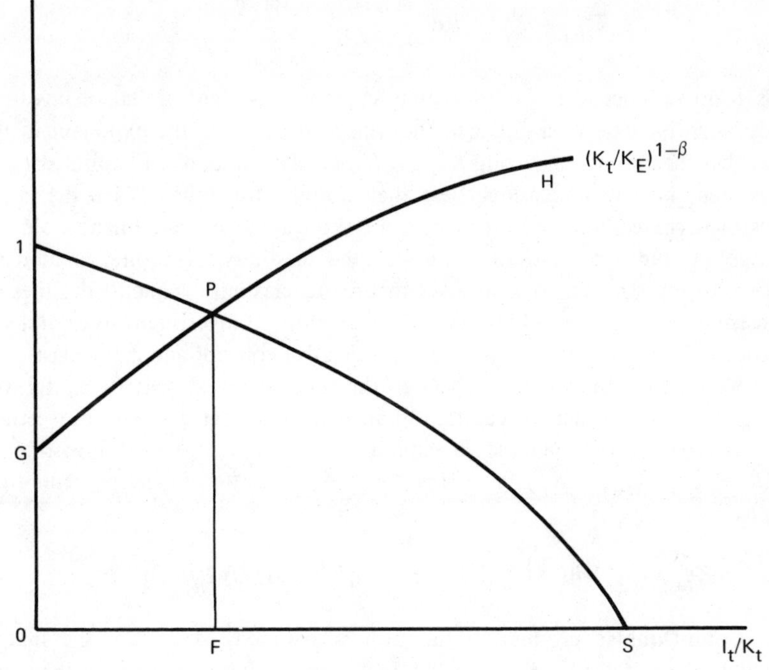

Figure 6-2. Ratio of Interest Rate to Marginal Product of Capital and Slope of Investment Curve

the equilibrium I_t/K_t falls as growth proceeds. With lower marginal productivity of capital, there is less incentive to push far up on the marginal cost curves for creating capital. Investment gradually declines as the economy approaches long run equilibrium–i.e., equilibrium is approached asymptotically.

The determination of investment is depicted more directly in Figure 6-2 where the curve *PS* plots the slope of the *OC* schedule and *GH* plots $r/(\partial Y/\partial K)$. The general condition $\partial(\Delta K)/\partial I = r/(\partial Y/\partial K)$ holds when I_t/K_t is at the level *OF* implied by the intersection of the curves *GH* and *PS* at point *P*. In the following year, with the capital stock having increased because of investment, the marginal product of capital at any I_t/K_t is lower, thereby uniformly raising the curve *GH*, while by assumption *PS* remains invariant. The steady upward shifting of *GH* over time due to capital accumulation leads to successively smaller amounts of investment until long run equilibrium is reached when *GH* and *PS* intersect on the vertical axis.

A possible functional form for the *OC* schedule in the top part of Figure 6-1 is

$$K_{t+1} - K_t = I_t e^{-[(1/s)(I_t/K_t)]^b/b}.$$

This form satisfies the condition that at zero investment, dollar of investment leads to an increase of a dollar in the capital stock since the exponent in the e term then becomes zero giving $K_{t+1} - K_t = I$. The amount of capital rises with investment but by increasingly less than a dollar for dollar. When the ratio of investment to capital stock reaches s, an extra dollar of investment yields zero increase in the capital stock. Consider the elasticity of capital created with respect to investment. At zero investment, this elasticity is one. It declines with increasing investment reaching zero when the ratio of investment to capital stock reaches s. The parameter b is a second derivative concept and is the elasticity of the foregoing elasticity with respect to the ratio of investment to capital stock.

The amount of capital obtained from an extra dollar of investment, or derivative of the increase in capital stock with respect to investment, is $\partial(\Delta K)/\partial I = \partial(K_{t+1} - K_t)/\partial I$. Using the form suggested in the preceding paragraph,

$$\partial(K_{t+1} - K_t)/\partial I = \left\{1 - [(1/s)(I_t/K_t)]^b\right\} e^{-[(1/s)(I_t/K_t)]^b/b}.$$

If a Cobb-Doublas production function is assumed, as before, the marginal product of capital $\partial Y/\partial K$ is $\beta c k^{\beta-1}$. Insertion of these results into the general investment condition $r = (\partial Y/\partial K)(\partial K/\partial I)$ gives

$$r = \beta c K_t^{\beta-1} \left\{1 - [(1/s)(I_t/K_t)]^b\right\} e^{-[(1/s)(I_t/K_t)]^b/b}.$$

Now consider the concept of the equilibrium capital stock. It is the capital stock that would prevail after a number of years of investment gradually reducing the marginal product of capital until I_t/K_t is at or near the origin in Figure 6-2 where the traditional assumption is fulfilled that the interest rate equals the marginal product of capital, i.e. $r = \partial Y/\partial K_E$. With the assumed production function, $r = c\beta K_E^{\beta-1}$. Making this substitution for r in the investment condition and re-arranging leads to the following expression determining investment in any year:

$$(K_t/K_E)^{1-\beta} = \left\{1 - [(1/s)(I_t/K_t)]^b\right\} e^{-[(1/s)(I_t/K_t)]^b/b}.$$

The right-hand side is the capital created per dollar of extra investment, and the left-hand side is the ratio of interest rate to marginal product of capital. The right-hand side is the curve *PS* plotted in Figure 6-2 and the left-hand side gives the position of the curve *GH* which intersects *PS* to determine investment level *OF*.

Given the actual and the equilibrium capital stock, the centered equation just presented can be used to find I_t/K_t or investment as a percent of the capital stock in a particular year. To find the growth of the capital stock resulting from this investment, divide both sides of the equation for schedule *OC* given earlier by K_t:

$$\dot{K}_t = (I_t/K_t)\, e^{-[(1/s)(I_t/K_t)]^b/b}$$

where $\dot{K}_t$ is $(K_{t+1} - K_t)/K_t$. Plugging I_t/K_t into this expression gives the percentage growth in the capital stock determining K_{t+1}, which is then used on the left side of the investment condition in order to determine I_{t+1}/K_{t+1}, which is plugged into the expression for K to find K_{t+2} and so forth. Thus, the two equations just given jointly determine the growth of capital over time. Differentiating the production function with respect to time and expressing derivatives as percentage rates of change, the subsidiary condition giving percentage rate of growth of income is $\dot{Y}_t = \beta\dot{K}_t$.

The exposition of determination of growth of capital so far has assumed no change in production function c values over time. Earlier, it was brought out that c values may be expected to change and that the extent of change will depend on the broadness or narrowness of the definition of capital. An increase in c value increases the equilibrium capital stock K_E. As can be seen from the expression determining investment, the increase in K_E will tend to offset the effect of the increase in the actual capital stock K_t. The upward shift in *GH* in Figure 6-2 could be diminished or even reversed, slowing down the diminution in rate of growth of capital over time or even leading to an increase in the rate of growth.

With a change in c value, the differentiation of the production function gives $\dot{Y} = \dot{c} + \beta\dot{K}$. The change in c value makes a direct contribution to the rate of growth of income, and it makes an indirect contribution by making the rate of growth of capital greater than it would otherwise be. This is a manifestation in the case of the rate of growth of income of the double effect of the c value on income that was discussed at length above in considering effect of the c value on the equilibrium level of income.

From the expression determining investment, the condition determining whether the percentage rates of growth of capital stock and income slow down or rise over time depends on whether the relative growth in actual capital stock exceeds the growth in the equilibrium stock–i.e., it depends on what happens to K_t/K_E. The condition for a stable percentage rate of growth is $\dot{K}_t = \dot{K}_E$. Since K_E is the capital stock where the rate of interest equals the marginal productivity of capital, $K_E = (\beta c_t/r)^{1/(1-\beta)}$. If changes in interest rate can be neglected as is reasonable if determined by world conditions, differentiation of K_E with respect to time indicates $\dot{K}_t = (\frac{1}{1-\beta})\dot{c}_t$. This result can be compared with the centered expression for $\dot{K}_t$ given above to find whether growth slows down or speeds up.

Suppose one wished to use the model as developed so far to predict future rate of growth. A first task would be to interpret the present position of the economy in terms of the parameters of the model. Into the percentage growth rate from the production function $\dot{Y}_t = \dot{c}_t + \beta \dot{K}_t$ substitute the last centered condition for $\dot{K}_t$, and eliminate the e term and K terms by using the following substitutions. K_t can be eliminated by using the solution of the production function $Y_t = c_t K_t^{\beta}$ for K_t. K_E can be eliminated by solving the condition $r = \beta c_t K_E^{\beta-1}$ for K_E. The resulting expression for percentage rate of growth of income is

$$\dot{Y}_t = \dot{c}_t + r(I_t/Y_t)/(1-\epsilon)$$

where ϵ is $[(1/s)(I_t/K_t)]^b$, the elasticity of capital created per dollar of investment with respect to the ratio of investment to capital stock.

As a case of very rapid growth due entirely to increase in measured capital, assume that the observed yearly rate of growth of real income is 10 percent. Suppose the interest rate r is .15 and investment is observed to be 20 percent of income. For this first example, assuming no other growth sources than measured capital, $\dot{c}_t = o$. The numbers in the above equation become $.10 = (.15)(.20)/(1 - \epsilon)$, implying $\epsilon = .7$. Suppose one assumes that, in spite of movements out the *OC* schedule, the amount of capital created per dollar of investment remains high—say at least .9. The reason for this assumption is that low amounts of capital created per dollar of investment would lead to observing very different amounts of capital created per unit of resources used in investment projects, as between rapid growth countries and other countries. Let the amount of capital created per dollar of investment be denoted p. If p were as low as one-half, the amount of physical capital in the form of a factory, hotel, road, or dam obtained per unit of resources invested in Korea would be only half what it is in the United States. There appears to be no such anomalous difference.

Dividing the equation given earlier for the *OC* schedule by I indicates $p = e^{-1/b\,[(1/s)(I_t/K_t)]^b}$. The condition determining investment can now be rewritten $(K_t/K_E)^{1-\beta} = (1-\epsilon)p$. Dividing the production function conditions $Y_t = cK_t^{\beta}$ and $Y_E = cK_E^{\beta}$ and rearranging gives $K_t/K_E = (Y_t/Y_E)^{1/\beta}$. When this result is substituted into the investment condition, one obtains $Y_t/Y_E = [(1 - \epsilon)p]^{\beta/(1-\beta)}$. With a fairly broad definition of capital, β might be .5. The numbers in this paragraph then give $Y_t/Y_E = .27$, implying that the equilibrium income is 1/.27 or 3.7 times as large as current income.

With yearly income in Korea in the vicinity of \$200 per capita, the implication is that the equilibrium income is in the vicinity of \$750 per capita. A priori this figure is not unreasonable and might be much higher or lower in view of the lack of knowledge about what the equilibrium level of income is. The result is not terribly sensitive to changes in the observed magnitudes from which ϵ is deduced, but it is sensitive to assumptions about β. If $\beta = .4$, $Y_t/Y_E = .42$; if $\beta = .6$, $Y_t/Y_E = .14$.

The other parameters may be identified using the expression for p given in the preceding paragraph together with the facts that ϵ appears in the exponent of the expression for p and that numerical values are available for ϵ and p. Thus $p = e^{-\epsilon/b}$ or in this example $.9 = e^{-.7/b}$. The solution for b is 6.4. By definition the amount of capital created per dollar of investment p is $\dot{K}_t/(I_t/K_t)$, or rearranging $(I_t/K_t) = \dot{K}_t/p$. But from the production function $\dot{K}_t = (1/\beta)\dot{Y}_t$, implying yearly capital growth of (1/.5).1 or 20 percent per year. Thus $(I_t/K_t) = (1/\beta)\dot{Y}_t/p$ or using the numbers of this example $(I_t/K_t) = .20/.9 = .22$. Since $\epsilon = [(1/s)(I_t/K_t)]^b$, $.7 = [(1/s)(.22)]^{6.4}$. The implied value of s is .23. The implied value of s, which is the level of investment as a fraction of the capital stock at which marginal capital created is zero, seems somewhat low on intuitive grounds.

To find out what is happening to the growth rate, first differentiate the earlier centered investment condition with respect to time, divide through by absolute values to express changes as percentage rates of change and rearrange so that the percentage rate of change of the ratio of investment to capital stock is on the left hand side: $(I_t/\dot{K}_t) = -[(1-\beta)(1-\epsilon)/\epsilon(1-\epsilon+b)]\ (\dot{K}_t - \dot{K}_E)$. In terms of the lower part of Figure 6-1 this expression shows the percentage movement along the x-axis resulting from yearly shift in the horizontal line as determined by percentage changes $\dot{K}_t$ and $\dot{K}_E$.

Differentiating the earlier centered expression determining $\dot{K}_t$ and dividing by $\dot{K}_t$ gives as the percentage rate of change of the growth of the capital stock $\ddot{K}_t = (1-\epsilon)(I_t/\dot{K}_t)$. Substituting in the percentage change in I_t/K_t just obtained from the investment condition gives

$$\ddot{K}_t = -[(1-\beta)(1-\epsilon)^2/\epsilon(1-\epsilon+b)]\,(\dot{K}_t - \dot{K}_E).$$

In this example, the equilibrium capital stock is not changing ($\dot{K}_E = 0$), and the values for all the other symbols have been presented above. They give $\ddot{K}_t = -.014$. This slow rate of damping implies that the growth rate of the capital stock will fall from 20 percent to 19.7 percent in one year. Since measured capital is the only source of growth in this example, $\dot{Y}_t = \beta\dot{K}_t$, which implies $\ddot{Y}_t = \ddot{K}_t$. The yearly growth of income would slow from 10 percent to 9.9 percent in one year.

Except for the somewhat low value of s, the results for the example presented so far seem reasonable. However, consider that existing capital will tend to be priced to reflect rental on capital and that the rental will be determined by marginal product. A high marginal product of capital thus implies high rental and capital values. The ratio of marginal product of capital in year t to equilibrium marginal product is $\beta c K_t^{\beta-1}/\beta c K_E^{\beta-1}$. Cancelling βc and using the condition previously derived that $K_t/K_E = (Y_t/Y_E)^{1/\beta}$ gives ratio of marginal product to equilibrium marginal product $(Y_E/Y_t)^{(1-\beta)/\beta}$ or, in this example, 3.7. The implication is that capital rental per unit is 3.7 times as high in the economy in question as in economies not growing rapidly. Furthermore, since the capital stock is growing at 20 percent per year and the elasticity of marginal product with respect to capital stock is $-(1-\beta)$, rentals per unit on existing capital are falling at the rate of 10 percent per year. The implications of the model for the level and for the time path of capital rental do not seem reasonable. Such extreme phenomena would be of wide interest if they occurred, and they are not reported.

As another numerical example where growth is not quite as fast and is due partly to c value, assume yearly rate of growth of per capita income is 8 percent and that 3 percent growth is due to c value–i.e., $\dot{c}_t = .03$. Retaining the assumptions that interest rate r is .15 and that investment is 20 percent of income, the condition $\dot{Y}_t = \dot{c}_t + r(I_t/Y_t)/(1-\epsilon)$ implies that a value of ϵ of .4. Using the earlier result $Y_t/Y_E = [(1-\epsilon)p]^{\beta/(1-\beta)}$ with the previous assumptions $p = .9$ and $\beta = .5$ gives $Y_t/Y_E = .54$. The equilibrium income is 1/.54 or a little less than double present income. When c is changing, Y_E is also changing over time instead of being stationary as in the previous example. Y_E is income attained when capital stock K_E is such that $r = \beta c_t K_E^{\beta-1}$. As derived earlier, $Y_E = c_t^{1/(1-\beta)}(\beta/r)^{\beta/(1-\beta)}$, giving an elasticity of $1/(1-\beta)$ of Y_E with respect to c_t.

The other parameters may be identified as before. The condition $p = e^{-\epsilon/b}$ becomes $.9 = e^{-.4/b}$ giving a value of b of 3.6. The condition $I_t/K_t = \dot{K}_t/p$ requires $\dot{K}_t$. The production function with changing c value implies $\dot{Y}_t = \dot{c}_t + \beta\dot{K}_t$, or $\dot{K}_t = (1/\beta)(\dot{Y}_t - \dot{c}_t) = (1/.5)(.08 - .03) = .1$. Thus $I_t/K_t = .1/.9$ or .11. The condition $\epsilon = [(1/s)(I_t/K_t)]^b$ becomes $.4 = [(1/s)(.11)]^{3.6}$ giving an implied value of s of .14, which is even lower than in the previous example.

The change in the growth rate over time is affected in this example by the fact that equilibrium capital stock and income are changing. Since the production function implies $\dot{K}_E = (1/\beta)(\dot{Y}_E - \dot{c}_t)$ and it was shown above that $\dot{Y}_E = .06$, the value of $\dot{K}_E$ is .06. Substituting this value along with indicated values of magnitudes from the previous paragraphs into the earlier centered expression for $\ddot{K}_t$ gives a value of $\ddot{K}_t$ of $-.0064$, a small but somewhat greater slowing down of capital growth than in the first example. Differentiating $\dot{Y}_t = \dot{c}_t + \beta\dot{K}_t$ with respect to time, dividing through by $\dot{Y}_t$ and assuming $\ddot{c}_t = 0$ gives as the percentage rate of change of the income growth rate $\ddot{Y}_t = (\beta\dot{K}_t/\dot{Y}_t)\ddot{K}_t$ or $-.0125$ which is a somewhat slower decline in growth rate than in the first example.

The ratio of marginal product of capital in the current year to equilibrium marginal product, which was shown earlier to be $(Y_E/Y_t)^{(1-\beta)/\beta}$, has a value of 1/.54 or 1.83. This is a high but perhaps more believable capital rental than in the first example. The percentage rate of change of marginal product $[d(\beta c_t K_t^{\beta-1})/dt](1/\beta c_t K_t^{\beta-1})$ reduces to $\dot{c}_t - (1-\beta)\dot{K}_t$ or $.03 - (1 - .5).1$ giving a 2 percent per year fall in capital rentals, which is a much more believable result than in the first example.

Part III

Technology and Trade

Chapter Seven

Agricultural Trade: Implications for the Distribution of Gains from Technical Process

Timothy Josling

Although one would guess that most of the world's agricultural output is consumed within a few hundred miles of its place of production, few countries can ignore the influence of international trade upon their farm sectors. Some crops are grown specifically for export: rich countries in temperate latitudes have established tastes for a variety of goods that can best be grown in tropical climates, and many northern industries use tropical raw materials. The rich countries differ among themselves in the availability and inherent productivity of agricultural land and the exchange of temperate zone goods among industrial economies has always been a large part of agricultural trade. In turn, the development of tropical countries often calls for imports of temperate products.

The peculiar characteristic of agricultural production—its close affinity with geographic and climatic conditions, allied to the improvement and diversification of diets—would suggest a continuing role for international trade in farm products. Even where production is largely for local food needs, the state of international markets makes its impact. Crops such as casava are finding outlets as animal feed in developed country markets. Countries plan their agricultural development programs on the availability of imports to complement local production, and on the market prospects for selling crops abroad. The trade tail wags the domestic dog.

The existence of an international market for farm goods has a significant impact on the way in which the gains from agricultural development are distributed. This impact is felt in various ways:

1. Participation in trade as either an exporter or an importer influences the extent to which productivity change benefits the consumers and producers within that country.

2. The trading system will transmit directly the effects of productivity change in one country to other countries participating in the same market.
3. The policies regarding exports, imports, and domestic markets may themselves be modified as a result of technical change at home or abroad, in turn influencing the distribution of gains and losses.
4. As a result, there may be pressure for international agreements to control these "external" effects or the policies arising from them.

Most of these implications can be demonstrated by examining the commodity markets. But international transmission of new techniques themselves is becoming a major factor in agricultural development, and this too has implications for domestic income distribution.

SIMPLE DISTRIBUTION MODEL

In a closed economy, technical change in one sector that lowers the total resource cost of a given level of output will tend to turn the terms of trade (the price ratio between this good and other goods) in favor of consumers. The good will be available at a lower price. The extent of this favorable price change will depend, among other things, on the price elasticity of demand for the good: the more elastic the demand the smaller the price change. The characteristic of low price elasticity is associated with goods that have only poor substitutes. The opening up of a market to trade will increase the range of goods that substitute for domestic production and at the same time increase the size of the market into which the domestic producer sells. Both effects will increase the elasticity of demand. This implies: (1) a smaller price fall following the adoption of the new technology, (2) a larger increase in production than in the "no-trade" situation, (3) a smaller gain to consumers, (4) a positive potential gain to consumers in other countries, as they benefit from the lower prices obtaining on the world market (whether the country increasing its output is an importer or an exporter of the good), and (5) a potential loss to other producers who find their own prices weakened.

This can be illustrated in a diagram (Figure 7-1) where the axes represent the profitability of a particular sector (producers' surplus) and the real income or satisfaction derived by consumers of that good (consumers' surplus). The line *W* is one of a family of iso-welfare lines, representing a particular level of social (consumers' plus producers') surplus. For any given (rising) marginal cost function and demand curve for the good, there will be some level of output which will maximize social surplus. This point is given by *A* on line *W*, such that

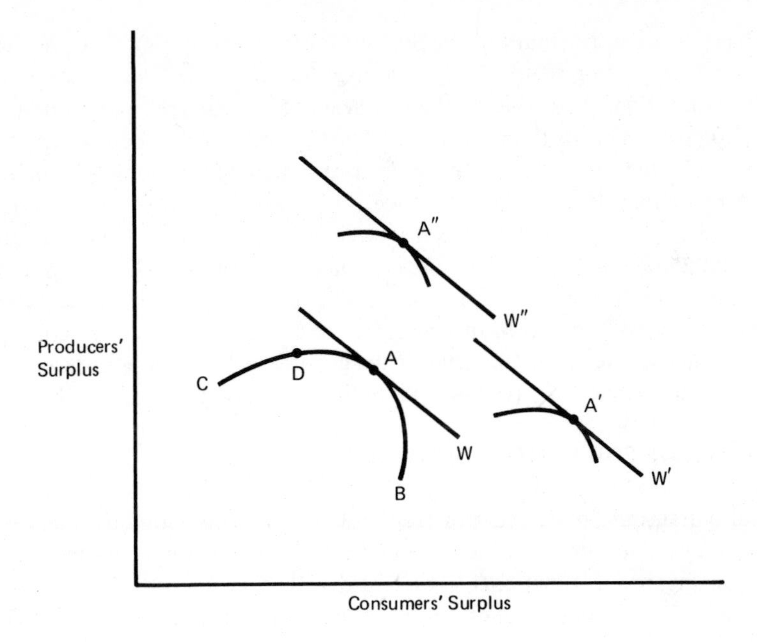

Figure 7-1. Distribution of Gains from Technical Progress in Case of Autarchy.

W = maximum ($CS + PS$). For socially suboptimal levels of output the welfare distribution is given by points along AC (lower levels of output) and AB (higher levels of output). In a closed economy, with no distortions between private and social costs or between private and social benefits, this point A will correspond to the competitive output. The producers' surplus will be less in this case than if output were restricted to the monopoly level (point D, Figure 7-1).

Assume an increase in productivity in the absence of trade. Potential welfare is increased. But the distribution of the benefits depends on the elasticity of demand. The new level of welfare may be at A' on W'—representing a loss to producers, or at A'' on W''—where the gains are shared between producers and consumers. For producers to be left worse off after adopting improved technology it is a necessary but not sufficient condition for the demand curve to be inelastic; profit may still increase if costs are reduced by more than gross returns.

Now imagine that the country has the opportunity to trade, either by importing or exporting the good in question. Redefine the line W and the point A to include the gains from trade at the initial level of technology. There will again be some output that maximizes welfare. Commencement of trade will itself have income distribution effects, consumers in importing countries and producers in exporting sectors being the main beneficiaries. Thus the optimum output distribution, A, will lie to the southeast of the autarchy optimum if the good is imported and to the northwest of that position if the good is exported.

If the sector now improves its productivity there is a potential increase in welfare. If the output increase is not large enough to alter the trade price (import or export) then the new welfare distribution will be vertically above that obtaining under the old technology. In Figure 7-2, the optimum output distribution moves from A to A' on W', the new welfare level. Any terms of trade change will shift A' to the southeast, to a point such as A'', whether the country is an exporter or an importer of the good. The producer will always gain from technical change more (or lose less) in the case of trade than autarchy.

IMPLICATIONS FOR OTHER COUNTRIES

Trade also transmits the effects of technical change across borders. Again it is useful to examine the distribution of these effects among consumers and producers. Figure 7-3 represents a welfare distribution diagram for a country which trades in the good in question but undergoes no increase in productivity.

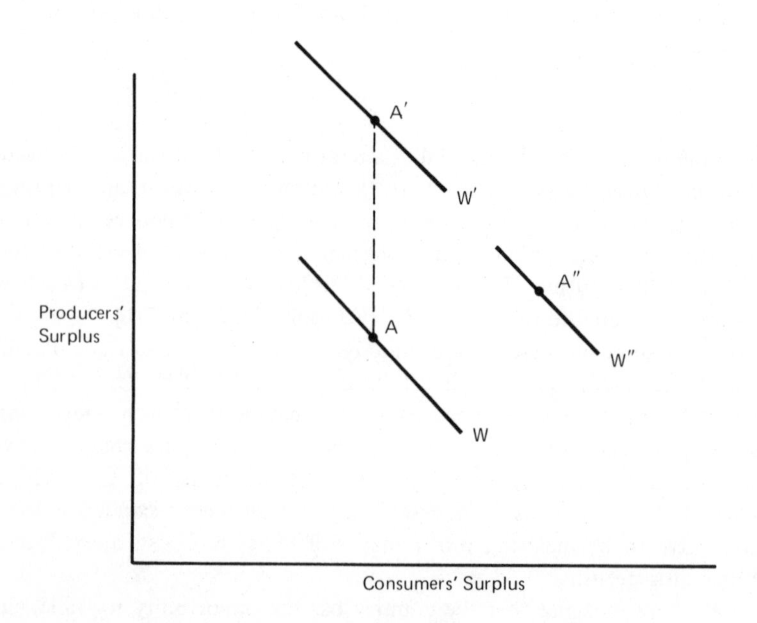

Figure 7-2. Distribution of Gains from Technical Progress in Presence of Trade

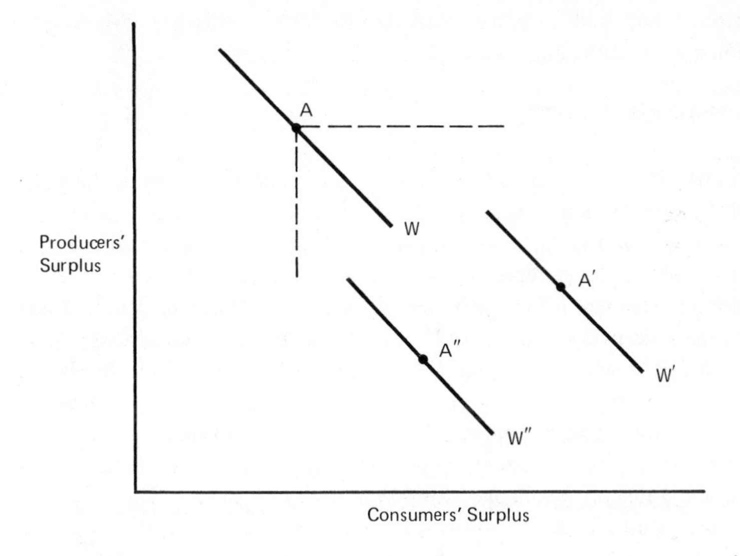

Figure 7-3. Distribution of Impact of Technical Progress Abroad

Technical change in another country will move the optimum output distribution to the southeast, favoring consumers at the expense of producers. If the country imports the good there will be some improvement in welfare, indicated by W', as the terms of trade move in that country's favor. The exporter will, however, find the terms of trade turning against him with the adoption of new techniques abroad, and will only be able to attain a somewhat lower level of welfare, W'', even after an optimal adjustment to the new situation.

This oversimplified model at least gives an indication as to what we might expect to observe in practice. Cochrane many years ago expounded a "treadmill" hypothesis whereby farmers were forced by competitive pressure to introduce new techniques that decreased total farm income and induced resource outflow;[1] any farmer not keeping up with the times suffered from lower relative prices without reaping the benefits of lower cost. One would expect to observe this phenomenon primarily where no trade possibilities exist. Trade liberates farmers from the confines of domestic price and income elasticity. Much of the thinking on farm policy confuses the parameters of domestic demand with those of the demand for domestic output. This is particularly true with respect to schemes that aim at controlling supply. We would also expect to observe demands from producers from protection against low cost goods from abroad in order to offset the income distribution effects of foreign technical change. This shows up largely as a pressure to fix domestic farm prices on domestic criteria such as parity with the nonfarm population, cost recoupment, inflation adjustments, and so on.

POLICY ADJUSTMENTS

Few countries are content to leave to the market the allocation of the gains from agricultural technology. Governments attempt to balance the considerable contribution that the farm sector can make to economic growth through the release of labor, the generation of investment capital and tax revenue, and the provision of cheaper food, with the desire of that sector to generate adequate and comparable living standards. The result has been a complex of intervention policies most of which have had the objective of either raising the demand for farm resources or of reducing the supply of such resources in agriculture. The former measures include import restrictions, export subsidies, direct payments, subsidies on nonfarm inputs, state trading, market discrimination, mixing regulations, multiple exchange rates systems, and so on. These are properly called "protection," and if data was available one could calculate the degree of effective protection given by such policies as the extent to which demand for farm resources (value added) was artificially raised.

The other set of measures would include research and extension, farm wage legislation, rural employment projects, social security systems, credit schemes, amalgamation and structural grants, acreage limitation, income subsidies, rural education programs, and land improvement payments. Each of these changes the supply conditions of farm resources and should be distinguished from market protection policies. Protection policies have become the focus of attention in international discussions of agricultural trade, and are likely to be under even closer scrutiny in the years ahead. Fortunately there is a coincidental trend toward disillusionment with the efficacy of such policies and a discernible move toward emphasis on adjustment rather than protection.

How have countries reacted to the challenge of farm productivity when trade markets have been available? As one would expect from the simple analysis above, the tendency has been to increase the elasticity of demand facing domestic producers. Strategy in an importing country is quite straightforward: as domestic production increases threaten acceptable price levels, demand can be increased by control of imports. This can take the form of our increased level of price protection at the border by raising tariffs and levies, or an equivalent degree of protection through the manipulation of quotas and market sharing agreements. Alternatively, the government may sponsor or support international agreements on minimum prices, or exert diplomatic activity to curtail export subsidies and aids in other countries.

The United Kingdom experience in the 1960s illustrates these choices. With domestic productivity increasing at about 3 percent, it was found necessary to accommodate the extra output without decreasing farm prices, or without increasing the cost to the exchequer of maintaining the guaranteed prices under the deficiency payment policy. The reaction was to enter into agreements with suppliers to maintain the import price level even at the expense of some income loss to the country as a whole. The pentalateral agreement with cereal producers, the bacon market sharing scheme, the butter import quota policy, and the establishment of voluntary quotas on cheese all had the effect of allowing domestic expansion to continue without depressing prices.

An exporting country in a similar situation would find itself obliged to expand export aids, to press for multilateral or bilateral access agreements, to seek international price agreements, and to expend considerable diplomatic energy to reduce protection in other countries. Exporters such as France and the Netherlands found an alternative solution in the establishment of a protected European market where their productive agricultural sectors could displace both nonmember suppliers and other community farmers, and where the joint financial resources of six countries were available for exporting surpluses. The United States has used a combination of diplomatic exhortation abroad, generous aid and export subsidy policies, and domestic output control, but appears to be preparing itself now for an abandonment of the policy of direct farm price support. Other countries such as Denmark, emphasized two-price policies whereby the domestic consumer and taxpayer underwrote the increase in farm productivity.

Policy reaction to other countries' productivity increases has been equally predictable. As was suggested above, an improvement in technology abroad distorts domestic income distribution. But a convenient defensive device is at hand: the variable levy and the flexible export subsidy (or restitution) enable a country, at some extra cost, to regulate the distribution effects. This can be seen in Figure 7-4. If a market is supported by a variable levy then any improvement in the terms of trade (decrease in the world price) shows up purely as an increase in government levy revenue.

Allow this to increase producer and consumer income in proportion to the relative tax burden, as shown by the stippled line in Figure 7-4. The new level of welfare attained is W', above W, but not as high as if protection were given with a fixed levy, since the cost of protection has increased somewhat. Similarly, an exporter can offset the world price decline by increasing the level of subsidy payment. Hence distribution of welfare between producers and consumers will be at A'' on welfare level W'', again being determined by the relative tax burdens of the two groups. Compared with the situation in the absence of a flexible protective policy (Figure 7-3), the producer is effectively isolated from the world price fall, though he bears some of the cost as a taxpayer. If one assumes that the tax system is itself a reflection of a desirable income distribution, then points A'', A' are "satisfactory" outcomes; the policy has a built-in redistributive mechanism.

This analysis is suggestive of the motivation of the European

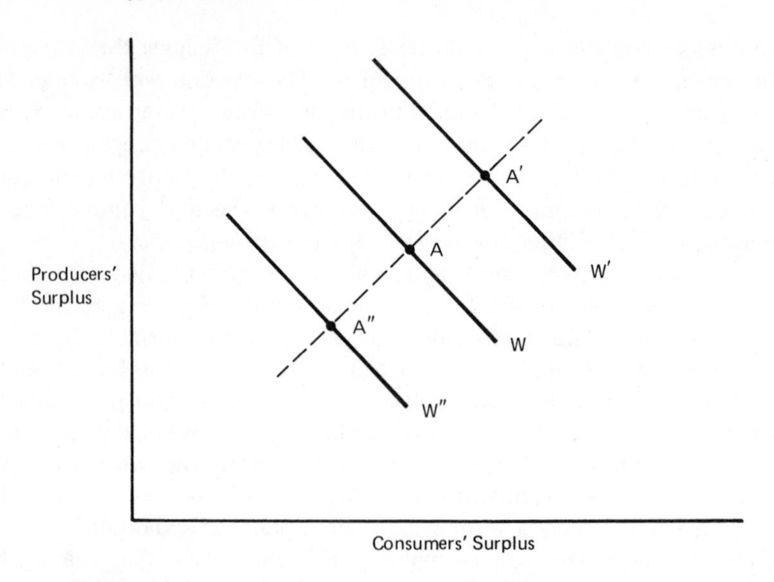

Figure 7-4. Automatic Redistribution of Impact of Foreign Technical Change by Support Policy

Community to adopt a variable levy and export restitution policy for their Common Agricultural Policy (CAP). Their desire as a Community (if not as individual governments) was to provide an economic environment in which European agriculture could be restructured and rationalized, in isolation from pressures transmitted through the world market. Though the overt preoccupation of the Europeans in the early 1960s was with the influence of export subsidies and support policies in other countries on the world price level, the underlying reason for rejecting trade prices as a guide to domestic production was the gap between European farm technology and that of the major world market suppliers. EEC price levels could approach those on the world market only when the technological gap had been closed. By that time, argued the architects of the CAP, world prices would themselves have responded to the increased food demand from the overpopulated third world.

But all did not go according to plan. World support agreements, proposed in the Kennedy Round, which would have had the effect of cushioning the impact of technology in other countries on European price levels were not introduced. In the one "successful" negotiation (for an International Grains Arrangement to follow the lines of successive Wheat Agreements) the EEC itself as an exporter of wheat found the limitation on export subsidies implied by the minimum price to be too restrictive. Prices soon fell below the floor of the IGA and signalled the demise of the only long running series of Commodity Agreements for a temperate zone farm commodity.

The United States objected to the Communities' attempt to introduce variable levies on a wide range of commodities through the introduction of reference prices, and to curtail variable export subsidies. Technology within Europe generated surpluses in goods, which the domestic market could not absorb. This in turn led to the extensive use of intervention buying in European markets and to the subsidization of exports, while the system of variable levies for such products as wheat and butter became measures necessary for the containment of domestic support costs rather than for the support of farm prices per se.

Other countries had similar "back-up" measures. In the United States, the familiar Section 22 of the Agricultural Adjustment Act had been strengthened in 1951 to allow the executive to override international agreements in using quotas to defend domestic farm prices. The GATT eventually recognized the inevitability of such a defense in the 1955 waiver. Target prices and parity prices were relieved of some of the pressures from international trade, and the distribution of gains from productivity increase was accomplished by the domestic support and taxation policies rather than by the operation of the unbridled market.

There does not appear to be a comprehensive study on the magnitude of the potential income transfer effect of technology through agricultural trade. To explore the transfer mechanism for each country would require a study of domestic and trade policies in agricultural markets. Individual case studies are available. Hayami and Ruttan documented the implications for Japanese producers and consumers of improved rice varieties in Taiwan—developed, ironically, by Japanese scientists.[2] The Japanese government was obliged finally to restrict rice imports so as to offset the income distribution effect of cheap foreign rice.

Another example of some topicality is the impact on other countries of the enlargement of the protected European market for farm goods. This enlargement can be thought of as granting to the producers in Denmark, Ireland, and the United Kingdom the protection available to the present EEC members to expand output by using available technology without the constraint of consequent price reductions.

Assuming no radical changes in the pricing policy of the EEC, it is likely that production of most commodities will increase as a result of the adoption of the CAP by the new members. Recent projection work has indicated the possible size of this shrinkage in the European market over the next decade. Using material from the FAO/UNCTAD study on equilibrium agricultural prices,[3] it is possible to suggest the magnitude of the income distribution effects that other countries will have to accept or modify through their own policies. In Table 7-1, the "enlargement effect" has been separated from the secular trend in trade arising from income and population changes and from technical change unrelated to European price policy. The distribution of gains and losses is based on FAO projections of demand and production by country.

Table 7-1. Impact of EEC Enlargement on Size of European Market and on World Price Levels, 1980[a]

Product	*Change in European Market due to Enlargement*[b]	*Consequent Impact on World Price*[c]
Wheat	312	−1.3
Feed grains	459	−0.5
Beef	296	−6.2
Lamb	−65	9.5
Pigmeat	163	−0.7
Butter	278	−13.6

[a]Estimates based on J. Ferris et al., *op. cit.*, and FAO, *op. cit.*

[b]Thousand metric tons. Positive figures indicate a decrease in net imports or an increase in net exports. The enlargement effect is the difference between projected trade position of the nine-country EEC in 1980 and the projected trade position of the present members and three new members in 1980 if the community had not been enlarged.

[c]Percentage price increases (negative figures are price falls) relative to 1980 "equilibrium" prices without enlargement.

Differences among countries in price elasticities of domestic supply and consumption are not included: the assumption is of uniform elasticities constrained to be consistent with that implied for the world market as a whole. Since the external effects of EEC enlargement are expressed simply as changes in the net import or export position of Europe, without regard to the pattern of trade, the figures in Tables 7-1 and 7-2 can be thought of as arising from a change in technology in Europe rather than a policy change. Likewise, for each country in Table 7-2 the implications are similar no matter where in the world the extra production is generated.

Table 7-2 indicates the rough magnitudes of the changes that other countries may expect to face as a result of the market changes in Europe. Since these effects will be felt only gradually over the next seven years, their impact may be obscured by other developments. In most cases the net effect on real income levels is likely to be small, as producer loss is offset by increase in consumer incomes. The effect on export earnings or import costs is more significant. The United States, for instance, finds export earnings decrease by about $540 million, even though the net effect on the economy is a gain of about $20 million in real income arising directly through the price changes. Australia, Canada, and Latin America, as net exporters, suffer in real income terms if policies do not change in the interim.

THE FUTURE OF FARM TRADE

If the interpretation of agricultural protectionism as a means of controlling the allocation of losses and gains from technology is valid, then we should not

Table 7-2. Impact on Selected Countries of the Changes in World Price Levels arising from EEC Enlargements, 1980[c] (# millions)

	Real Income Increase			
	Producers	*Consumers*	*Net*	*Balance of Trade*[a]
Developed Countries				
Australia	−29.8	15.4	−14.4	−29.1
Canada	−44.5	41.7	−2.8	−30.8
Japan	−10.3	15.3	5.0	−3.6
New Zealand	−2.8	5.8	3.0	0.1
U.S.A.	−384.8	393.0	8.2	−232.6
Developing Countries				
Argentina	−84.1	50.1	−34.0	−77.4
Latin America[b]	−157.7	149.6	−8.1	−105.5
Africa	−56.6	58.9	2.3	−33.1
Near East	−24.8	41.1	16.3	1.9
Asia	−110.3	130.7	20.4	−78.4
Central Plan Economics				
U.S.S.R.	−213.0	239.0	26.0	−131.8
East Europe	−94.7	96.0	1.3	−68.0
Asian CPE	−109.5	122.1	12.6	−53.7

[a]Value of production minus value of consumption. Negative figures indicate a decrease in export earnings or an increase in import costs.

[b]Excluding Argentina.

[c]Estimates based on FAO production and consumption estimates, and terms of trade changes from T ble 7-1.

expect such defenses to be reduced in the near future. But the proliferation of variable levies and export subsidies (not only in the EEC) has undoubtedly increased instability on the world market. When goods are exported from a country with a variable export subsidy to one with a variable levy, no "equilibrium" price exists. Indeed, one might conceive of a "policy induced surplus" as existing for those commodities where requirements of importers and exporters do not coincide.

Consider some volume of foreign supplies an importing country will welcome because it does not depress the price to domestic producers below an acceptable level. Similarly in an exporting country there will be some volume of production available for export induced by an acceptable producer price in that country. If the importer will accept less than the exporter has to sell, then a surplus exists. Price changes cannot clear the market since both producers and consumers are isolated from such changes. In the absence of domestic policy changes the world market becomes unstable and the isolationist policies are apparently vindicated. Releasing consumers from the constraints of such policies would improve the functioning of the international market.

One may expect increasing pressure on governments to modify the method of farm support on domestic as well as on commercial policy grounds, but one must assume that attempts to improve the stability of farm incomes will continue. The EEC will, for instance, undoubtedly move more toward income support by direct methods and towards lowering the cost of grain and of dairy products to the user or consumer. In this respect the United States is in advance of the EEC. Enlargement of the Community will add to these pressures as the impact of the CAP begins to be felt.

Modifications in the level of protection—as opposed to its method—are more amenable to direct bargaining among governments. Perhaps a binding of the level of support for key commodities is a necessary first step. But it is much more likely that governments will choose to modify the protection they grant to farmers for internal reasons. It is not apparent that the political visibility of farm groups declines with their numbers. It is, however, the case that there is a growing disenchantment with the costs of agricultural protection and in particular with the distribution of these costs and the related benefits. Prices have been reduced, payments to farmers limited, supply controlled, and taxes on output levied in the past. It is not the case that all governments are caught on the treadmill of higher farm protection; but the pace by which such adjustments can be made depends on developments in the nonfarm economy. It may not be fast enough to prevent the increase of international tension.

Chapter Eight

Agricultural Trade and Shifting Comparative Advantage

Robert Evenson

Standard international trade theory is well suited, in some respects, to the analysis of trade in agricultural commodities. The basic concept of comparative advantage is designed to take into account the diversity in natural or geoclimate resources between nations as well as the endowments of more conventional economic resources. An extensive literature has been developed in recent years to analyze both the shifts in production functions in one country and the effects of such shifts on trade in a comparative statics framework. We do not, however, have a very satisfactory theory of the generation of technical change or of shifts in actual comparative advantage. Nor are we well equipped with studies of the transfer of technology generated in one region or nation to other producing regions.

The consequence of this inability to specify the economic factors determining the generation and transfer of new technology is that with real world data, international trade models perform very poorly in terms of predicting changes in trade patterns and flows. Of course, the difficulties of specifying the numerous types of trade restrictions contribute to the problems in this area as well. An attempt is made in this chapter to develop an improved specification of the basic features of technology transfer in the production of cereal grains. This specification is based on several recent studies of the role of agricultural research in creating new technology. An econometric investigation of the indirect role of research in determining export performance in the cereal grains is also undertaken.

TECHNOLOGY TRANSFER: A SPECIFICATION OF THE DETERMINANTS OF CHANGE IN COMPARATIVE PRODUCTIVITY

Consider first an international equilibrium in cereal grains production. It is characterized by a set of cereal grain prices in each country, not all of which need be world prices because of trade restrictions. Each country will have a set of factor prices determined by factor supply and demand conditions and factor market distortions. And producers in each country will be planning to produce and to either import or export an equilibrium quantity of each cereal grain. Weather conditions will determine actual production and trade in any given year.

This equilibrium will be characterized not by a single set of techniques of production but by numerous techniques, even if all producers are as economically efficient as possible. This is the consequence of technology specificity to economic, geographic, biological, and climatological conditions. Producers in all countries have a set of alternative techniques of production from which to choose. This set of techniques includes cereal grain varieties, which differ in a number of characteristics such as disease resistance, lodging properties, photosynthetic response to plant nutrients, and photoperiod sensitivity. It also includes alternative implements for tillage, seeding, and harvesting as well as alternative procedures for the sequential performance of tasks associated with production.

Producers will select that set of techniques which will maximize profits if they have "perfect knowledge." The profit maximizing set will differ according to: (1) relative factor prices, (2) geoclimate conditions, and (3) the managerial skills of the farm manager. Profit maximization does not imply that all producers will be utilizing the same techniques or that all firms will be organized with the same scale of operation or other organizational features. The technology of relevance to each producer is that set of techniques which would be in his profit maximizing set under a feasible range of product and factor prices. Technological change, as used in this chapter, refers to a change in—or more specifically, an addition to—that set of techniques. Technical change refers to a change in the set of techniques actually used.[a]

Strictly speaking, then, we would have to specify a different production function for each producing firm, for a given technology set, since some degree of uniqueness exists for each firm:

$$1) \quad O_i = F_i(X_i)$$

In 1), O is an output vector, X an input vector. In a world where each producer has complete knowledge of the technology set relevant to him and where he knows all prices and knows how to maximize subject to the right constraints, comparisons between alternative technology sets or technique sets are somewhat arbitrary. The prices of unique factors such as particular types of land (and associated climate factors) or of particular managerial skills will be

[a]These definitions require further specification for operational purposes. For example, one might wish to define technology more strictly as the set of techniques relevant at prevailing factor prices. In that case, the technology set and the technique set are equivalent in a perfect knowledge setting.

determined in part by the technology sets, but one cannot say that one firm is using a higher (or lower) level of technology than another.

The technology sets or the technique sets of producers will have varying degrees of commonality. Certain general managerial principles will be common to wheat producers throughout the world. For the most part, however, these sets will differ significantly for producers in different countries. For example, the wheat producers of Canada and India do not make use of common varieties. Nor do they use similar harvesting implements. By the same token, a change in the technology or the technique set of the Canadian producer is unlikely to represent a similar change, or a change at all, for the Indian producer.

One of the consequences of technology specificity is that the search for new technology cannot efficiently be directed to all producers throughout the world. In practice the directed search (research) for new technology is keyed to the economic and geoclimate characteristics of particular geographic and political regions. In the United States, for example, the organization of the agricultural research system is based primarily on political boundaries. Each state has a State Agricultural Experiment Station (Connecticut and New York each actually have two stations) that receives the major portion of its funding from the state government. It is charged basically with discovering technology relevant to its political constituency.

In practice, most states choose to direct their research activities toward the discovery of technology that is specific to geoclimate regions, which differ from the region defined by the state boundary. Branch experiment stations are located in specialized regions of the state and cooperative research ventures between states are undertaken to direct research toward geoclimate regions common to several states. The federal government locates its research centers and designs its research effort to fill in gaps in state research programs in such a way as to provide research programs geared to technology discovery relevant to all major geoclimate regions.

This pattern of agricultural research organization is pursued in virtually every country in the world. In fact, a good deal of criticism is directed toward the overregionalization of research effort, which results in small, inefficient research stations isolated from the main centers of research. Most modern research systems have gone through a cycle of organization in this regard. Numerous branch and specialized stations have been established during the major building phase of the systems. At a later point, these stations have been closed in a consolidation program.

This form of organization is based partially on the recognition that there often are political advantages to locating research centers to serve all major groups. This is not the only basis for such organizations, however. A national research system, with the objective of maximizing the economic value of the new technology it discovers, for a given research expenditure, would be organized on a regional basis. As long as diminishing returns to technology discovery specific to each particular group of producers holds, it will be efficient to allocate research effort to several groups. The optimal allocation to groups or to geoclimate regions will be determined by the economic size of the geoclimate region and by the diseconomies of research conduct in small isolated stations.

Now, consider the question of technology transfer in a world in which the research systems are so organized. The discovery and improvements of new techniques of production as a result of the efforts of researchers in one station or even in one national system will be of quite different value to different groups of producers. Or, to put it in terms of technology transfer, even if all producers have complete information, new techniques will be transferred and utilized over a limited range of conditions. The extent of direct transfer of techniques will depend on the nature of each technique, on economic and geoclimate conditions, and on the extent of existing alternative or substitute techniques. A new variety of wheat, for example, will be adopted only in areas of relatively similar climate and soil types. The size of that area will depend on the number of alternative varieties that exist. The earliest "green revolution" wheat varieties were introduced over an extraordinarily wide range of geoclimate conditions, largely because of a lack of good alternative varieties. As these alternative varieties were produced (generally using the early varieties as parent material), the geographic area over which a single variety has been produced has been markedly reduced.

To this point, technology has been defined in terms of sets of techniques. For certain purposes, this is the most useful definition. If the role of information in the adoption process is the chief concern, for example, it is appropriate to focus on existing, well defined techniques. On the other hand, most discussions of international technology transfer are based on a somewhat broader but rather ill defined concept of technology. Advocates of heavy investment in extension activities in contemporary less developed countries usually suggest that extension effort does more than simply provide information to enable producers to more intelligently adopt technology, and that some modification of technique will be accomplished as well.

The current emphasis on "adaptive" research in the less developed countries is grounded on an even broader concept of technology transfer. The advocates of this research emphasis argue that, while the direct transfer of technique between countries is quite limited, a form of indirect transfer is very important. Adaptive research in the less developed countries can modify developed country techniques and produce techniques suited to producers in less developed regions. In this way the findings of researchers in the developed countries are transferred to the less developed countries.

To clarify this somewhat broader concept of technology transfer we require the definition of geoclimate and economic regions. We first define a set of 32 major geoclimate regions of the world, based on the work of Papadakis[7] (see Table 8-3 below). Within each major region we define subregions, which are based on political and economic factors as well as geoclimate factors.[b] This procedure delineates some 234 cereal producing subregions in the world. Within each subregion a further division into microregions (which are relatively homogeneous with respect to geoclimate and economic factors) can be made. As a working approximation, it will be supposed that national research systems are organized to discover and to adapt new technology generally suited to each subregion.

Within each microregion, an approximate aggregate production function can be defined as:

$$2) \quad O_m = T_m(F_m(X_m))$$

In this production function, output per farm is expressed as a function of a vector of conventional inputs per farm, X_m, adjusted by a scaling factor, T_m, based on the existing technology set available to the producers in the microregion. This scaling factor is arbitrarily set equal to one for a given base period. If in the base period a farm is utilizing that set of techniques which maximizes profits, it has a scaling factor equal to one.

This scaling factor provides a basis for two types of measurement. It can measure a change in the technology set, T_m, relative to the base and it can measure economic "slack," defined as the difference between the average scaling factor for farms in the microregion and the current profit maximizing factor.[c]

Technology transfer can be expressed in terms of the relationship between changes in the technology set for the subregion and the technology set for the microregion:

$$3) \quad \Delta T_m = G_m(C_m, EX_m, SC_m, \Delta T'_m, \Delta T'_{j+m}, \Delta T_s)$$

Expression 3) simply states that, for a given time period, a change in the technology set for the subregion, ΔT_s, is conveyed to the microregion by information supply activities in the microregions, extension, EX_m, and schooling, SC_m. These activities and the normal managerial efforts of producers accomplish a certain amount of technology modification and "subinvention" that adds to and refines the subregional technology set, indicated by $\Delta T'_m$. In expression 3), the subinvention in microregions other than region m, $\Delta T'_{j+m}$, is depicted as contributing to the microregion technology set. The term C_m measures the extent to which the specific geoclimate conditions in the microregion reduce the economic value of the technology produced in the subregion. The subregion technology change is measured in economic units based on its

[b]This definition is somewhat arbitrarily based on country boundaries. The part of each separate country falling in each geoclimate region is considered a subregion.

[c]Economic slack can be arbitrarily divided into technique choice errors and allocative errors, given technique choice.

implementation in geoclimate conditions which are best suited to it. In other words, after a certain amount of time–and with significant extension effort, producer learning, and subinvention–the C_m coefficients measure the proportionality between an increment in subregional technology and the value of the technology to each microregion.

Our chief interest in this chapter is with transfer between subregions located in different countries and between major geoclimate regions. It is this transfer that influences comparative advantage. This is a more complicated process than is involved in the transfer of technology to microregions within a subregion. As we have noted, the subregion is the basis for the organization of the research system. In the following section, data is presented showing that subregion research activity is quite varied. A number of important less developed subregions conduct virtually no research, while subregions in many of the developed countries have major research programs.

In transfer between subregions, the role of indigenous modification or adaptation of the transferred technology is significant. The definition of geoclimate regions required for analysis of international transfer necessarily encompasses a reasonably broad range of conditions. As a consequence, the direct transfer of technology–as embodied in crop varieties, for example–is quite limited. The really significant transfer requires modification and adaptation.

A direct transfer relationship might be specified as follows:

$$4) \quad \Delta T_s^{(d)} = H(EX_s, C_s(T_s), \Delta T_{(r-s)})$$

As with expression 3), for a given time period, a change in the technology sets in other subregions will be transferred to subregions s by extension and related activity in subregion s; but because of geoclimate and economic factors in the subregion, only a proportion C_s, which is a function of the prior technology set in the subregion, will be transferred. Thus, even with extension effort and time for the attainment of perfect knowledge by producers, a subregion will benefit from technology discovered in other similar subregions by a factor of proportionality, which is higher the lower the prior increase is in technology in the subregions. Leading subregions–that is, those with high rates of technology discovery in prior periods–may have very little technology directly transferred from other subregions. Subregions without indigenous research systems will realize higher transfer rates, but geoclimate and economic factors will limit it.

Expression 4) could be specified as:

$$4a) \quad \Delta T_s^{(d)} = b_1 C_s T_s (1 - b_2 EXP^{-b_3 EX_s}) \Delta T_{(r-s)}$$

in which transfer to the subregion is $b_1 C_s T_s \Delta T_{(r-s)}$ when extension activity in the subregion is relatively high and the proportion $(1 - b_2)$ of this when no extension activities are undertaken.

The available evidence suggests that direct transfer of this sort is important only in some of the less developed subregions without significant indigenous research systems. Indirect transfer through adaptive research is of much more significance. A somewhat modified formulation is required for indirect transfer. In addition to actual techniques, other types of knowledge are transferred. While we do not have good measures of specific techniques produced in each subregion, certain measures of knowledge are available: that is, measures of research findings in the form of numbers of carefully screened research publications are available.

A general specification of indirect transfer to a subregion would be:

$$5) \quad \Delta T_s^{(t)} = I(R_s, D_s(T_s), R_{(r-s)})$$

In this expression, the indigenous subregion research activity, R_s, takes advantage of research findings in similar subregions to produce or discover new technology relevant to the subregion. Research findings serve as inputs into a kind of production function by this view. This quasi-production function is obviously complex, but some evidence is now available in support of the hypothesis that such a functional relationship does exist. In the following section, econometric tests of the following specific form of 5) are cited:

$$5a) \quad \Delta T_s = D_s + b_1 R_s + b_2 (1/1 + b_3 EXP^{-b_3 R_s}) R_{(r-s)}$$

Little evidence is available to suggest that appreciable technology transfer between major regions takes place. Presumably much of this transfer is embodied in the human or intellectual capital of the researchers and in the findings of the less applied research.

COMPARATIVE PRODUCTIVITY AND THE INTERNATIONAL RESEARCH SYSTEM

The relative emphasis on efforts to discover new technology has been quite unevenly distributed throughout the world. Largely for this reason, and because of the limitations on technology transfer, the relative productivity gains have also been uneven. As Table 8-1 shows, in 1965 the less developed regions of the world invested relatively little in research. The less developed countries (including Argentina, Chile, and Israel) spent only 11 percent of the world's research budget and 20 percent of the extension budget in 1965. Expenditures for research expressed as a percent of the value of agricultural commodities produced in the less developed regions were less than one-third the level attained in the developed countries.

Table 8-1 does reflect considerable emphasis on extension in the less developed countries, but, as noted earlier, extension activity may effect some limited direct transfer, but it is not effective in facilitating indirect transfer.

The data presented in Table 8-2 are in some ways more informative

Table 8-1. Agricultural Research and Extension, 1965—Interregional Comparisons

Region	*Exp. on Research (Million $)*	*SMY*	*Exp. on Extension (Million $)*	*No. of Ext. Workers*	*Percent of Agr. Prod. spent on*	
					Res.	*Ext.*
1. North America	390.2	15,283	204.4	9,137	1.01	.53
2. Northern Europe	190.0	8,232	106.4	17,480	.93	.53
3. Southern Europe	23.1	2,236	25.1	5,335	.38	.41
4. Oceania, S. Africa, Rhodesia	86.7	3,671	(43.0)	(7,950)	1.61	(.80)
5. Eastern Europe and U.S.S.R.	(233.2)	15,340	(144.0)	(33,400)	.64	(.39)
6. Latin America	20.6	2,431	22.9	3,883	.17	.19
7. Middle East and North Africa	33.3	1,608	(33.0)	(15,500)	.55	(.55)
8. South and Southeast Asia	36.0	4,220	(45.9)	28,892	.24	.31
9. East Asia	65.7	5,195	47.4	18,443	.79	.57
10. Sub-Sahara Africa	33.5	1,344	28.0	23,820	.45	.38
Developed Countries[a]	985.7	49,262	559.2	87,428	.874	.496
Less Developed Countries[a]	126.6	10,298	140.9	76,412	.259	.289
World Total	1,112.3	59,560	700.1	163,840		

[a]Developed countries = categories 1, 2, 3, 4, 5 plus Japan; Less developed countries = 6, 7, 8, 9, 10 minus Japan.

Source: Kislev and Evenson [3].

Table 8-2. Agricultural Research Publications Abstracted in Selected International Abstracting Journals, 1948-1968

	Publications by orientation					*Annual Publications per $100 million Agricultural Production (1965 dollars)*		
	Plant Phys.	*Phytopath & Soils*	*All Crops*	*All Lvstk*	*Total Agr.*	*Crops*	*Lvstk*	*Total*
North America								
1948-51	2,130	3,758	6,549	10,000	16,549	7.0	9.8	8.3
1955-61		6,854	9,446	10,608	20,053	8.2	8.9	8.3
1962-68	8,831	8,383	12,743	11,265	24,009	9.3	8.2	8.9
Northern Europe								
1948-54	1,748	1,194	3,458	9,888	13,346	7.2	11.3	13.5
1955-61		1,454	4,084	9,958	14,042	7.4	8.9	11.7
1962-68	7,721	2,691	5,491	10,807	16,298	8.6	7.8	11.3
Southern Europe								
1948-54	245	480	1,026	981	2,007	4.2	6.9	6.1
1955-61		365	987	1,016	2,003	3.7	5.2	5.3
1962-68	830	513	1,169	1,387	2,556	4.3	5.1	5.9
Oceania, So. Africa & Rhodesia								
1948-54	172	393	1,254	1,316	2,570	14.1	7.8	10.1
1955-61		822	1,350	1,906	3,256	12.1	8.8	10.1
1962-68	1,358	915	1,545	2,291	5,836	10.5	9.5	10.0

Table 8-2 (cont)

	Publications by orientation					*Annual Publications per $100 million Agricultural Production (1965 dollars)*		
	Plant Phys.	*Phytopath & Soils*	*All Crops*	*All Lvstk*	*Total Agr.*	*Crops*	*Lvstk*	*Total*
Eastern Europe & U.S.S.R.								
1948-54	705	213	1,739	1,217	2,956	1.2	1.6	1.6
1955-61		1,003	4,283	2,532	6,815	2.3	2.2	2.7
1962-68	6,160	3,144	9,683	5,116	14,799	4.7	3.6	5.1
Latin America								
1948-54	70	209	858	228	1,086	1.8	1.1	1.6
1955-61		291	983	202	1,185	1.6	.9	1.5
1962-68	420	610	1,288	479	1,767	1.8	1.7	1.8
Middle East & North Africa								
1948-54	33	47	284	202	486	1.0	1.7	1.3
1955-61		133	360	303	633	1.2	2.1	1.3
1962-68	690	359	646	405	1,051	1.7	2.4	2.0
South & Southeast Asia								
1948-54	243	484	1,889	592	2,481	2.7	27.5[a]	3.5
1955-61		792	2,521	745	3,266	2.8	30.2[a]	3.5
1962-68	1,603	1,594	4,330	1,335	5,664	4.3	46.5[a]	5.5

East Asia								
1948-54	110	146	926	322	1,248	2.5	14.7	3.3
1955-61		419	1,596	589	2,186	3.4	10.7	4.3
1962-68	2,233	519	1,801	724	2,526	3.4	6.8	4.3
Sub-Sahara Africa								
1948-54	2	18	274	62	334	1.0	1.2	1.0
1955-61		105	419	155	574	1.5	2.8	1.8
1962-68	56	249	651	248	899	1.9	3.9	2.2
Developed Countries								
1948-54	5,044	6,176	14,777	23,724	38,501	4.2	7.9	6.7
1955-61		10,902	21,569	26,607	48,176	5.0	6.8	8.6
1962-68	27,074	16,083	32,115	31,529	63,694	6.5	6.6	7.6
Less Developed Countries								
1948-54	414	748	3,480	1,084	4,564	1.9	2.7	2.1
1955-61		1,336	4,460	1,407	5,867	2.1	3.1	2.3
1962-68	2,828	2,894	7,232	5,478	9,710	2.8	4.5	3.2

[a]Data on livestock output is very limited for the region.

than the limited expenditure data available. Table 8-2 summarizes, by major political region, the number of scientific publications selected for inclusion in three major international abstracting journals.[d] These publications have been screened by the editorial boards of the abstracting journals and are measures of research activity that are in some ways superior to data on research expenditures. They are not subject to exchange rate biases and, because of the screening process, at least some quality adjustment has been made.

They have an important advantage for purposes of this chapter in that they enable a comparison of research activities over time. For example, they show that the less developed regions increased their share of the world's total from 10.6 percent in the 1948-54 period to 13.2 percent in the 1962-68 period. If Eastern Europe and U.S.S.R. are excluded from these computations, the less developed country share increased from 11.4 percent to 16.6 percent. The extraordinary increase in research publications from the Soviet bloc countries is a major feature of the table.

It should be noted that the publications classified as oriented to crops and livestock are measuring commodity oriented research effort. The editorial boards have assigned each publication to a specific commodity. The publications in plant physiology, phytopathology, and soil sciences have not been so allocated and thus reflect more basic research.

Table 8-3 summarizes publications data by geoclimate regions of the world. The coverage is quite complete, except for the People's Republic of China. The 33 geoclimate regions are grouped in nine major region types. Each region contains from two to 22 of the 234 subregions delineated from the Papadakis climate classifications. The notes to Table 8-3 provide further definitions.

One of the major features of the climatological classification is the high correlation with level of development. The Tropical Region type (#1), for example, encompasses eight regions and 87 subregions in more than 35 countries, but includes only three developed subregions. The only climate type with an appreciable inclusion of both developed and less developed subregions is the Mediterranean.

The measures of research activity reported in Table 8-3 are total publications (from the same sources as in Table 8-2) from 1942 to 1970, per adjusted subregion. This measure deflates research by an indicator of the specific research problems in the region. The adjusted number of subregions takes into account differences in the size of the subregions (see notes to Table 8-3) and each cereal group is considered a subregion in the table.

The table shows quite clearly that the developed country regions have invested much more heavily in research than have the less developed countries. The leading regions in cereal grains research in publications per

---

[d]The journals are *Plant Breeding Abstracts*[14], *Dairy Science Abstracts*[13], and *Biological Abstracts.*[12]

subregion are primarily the developed regions. Of the less developed regions, only the cool winter tropical (1.9) and monsoon subtropical (4.2) regions have research programs that compare at all favorably. The leading developed regions invest from five to seven times as much as most of the less developed regions by this measure.

The cereal grain yield levels and rates of change shown in the table are crude indicators of productivity. The developed regions have a clear advantage in these measures also. Yield levels are much higher, especially in the humid continental and marine climate regions, which cover much of Northern Europe, Japan, and the United States. Fertilizer use is markedly higher in these regions, accounting for a good part of the difference. Increases in fertilizer use probably account for a substantial part of the yield increases in the regions as well.

The positive simple correlation between research effort per subregion in cereal grains and the changes in yield levels are quite apparent in the table. The simple correlation coefficient is .513. A regression of yield changes on research per subregion and the ratio of basic research in plant physiology, plant pathology, and soil science in the region yields:

$$\Delta YID = 1.24 + \underset{(.0003)}{.0011\, R/SR} + \underset{(.111)}{.174\, B/R} : R^2 = .32$$

(standard errors in parentheses)

This specification is quite incomplete since it does not incorporate a measure of change in fertilizer application or of other inputs. Sadan[9] has argued that the aggregate production function is relatively separable into "mechanical" and "biological" sets of inputs. The biological inputs are basically fertilizer and the technology embodied in varieties. Yields per hectare, they argue, are not greatly affected by changes in the mix of machines and labor in the performance of tasks. If so, then a model of yield determination based on biological inputs only is reasonable.

Table 8-4 reports regressions based on such a model. The observations are geoclimate region totals. They provide very strong support to the hypothesis that both applied plant breeding and agronomic research, and the more basic plant physiology, phytopathology, and soil science research activities, are important determinants of crop yields.

These regressions complement those reported in Kislev and Evenson[2] based on wheat and maize yield determination. The Kislev-Evenson specification did not utilize fertilizer data but were based on country data and specified a technology borrowing relationship between subregions. Those results indicated that, if a subregion did not perform research, little or no indirect transfer from other subregions took place. Hayami and Ruttan[8] have also provided some evidence in support of the role of research and related activities as determinants of international productivity levels.

Table 8-3. Geoclimate Region Research in Cereal Grain Production

Region #	Publications (1942-70) per Subregion					Cereals Publications		Adjusted		Cereal Grain Yields		
	Wheat	Barley	Maize	Sorghum	Rice	per Subregion	per 100 ha.	Number of Subregions	LDC Share	1950-51 (Kg/ha)	1966-67 (Kg/ha)	Ratio
1. *Tropical*						48.3				11.00	13.79	1.253
1.1 Humid equatorial	–	–	30.2	11.6	111.8	51.6	1.06	15.91	1.00	11.92	14.33	1.20
1.2 Humid tropical	1.5	.2	15.1	2.1	121.7	28.1	4.67	5.00	.86	16.98	24.62	1.45
1.3 Dry equatorial	–	–	4.7	1.1	22.5	8.2	1.30	4.06	1.00	10.61	14.53	1.37
1.4 Hot equatorial	8.4	–	19.3	13.6	224.5	68.7	1.32	10.22	.95	10.57	13.58	1.28
1.5 Semiarid equatorial	.0	–	4.1	32.2	8.6	8.6	.80	6.35	1.00	8.46	10.69	1.26
1.7 Humid tierra	20.4	20.4	30.6	26.0	20.8	24.1	1.38	16.19	1.00	12.38	12.91	1.04
1.8 Dry tierra	–	–	42.4	–	18.1	52.8	3.56	2.06	1.00	14.49	10.11	.70
1.9 Cool winter tropical	–	–	18.5	87.4	353.1	144.9	.59	5.58	.86	10.39	13.77	1.33
2. *Tierra Fria*						52.1				7.93	12.84	1.619
2.1 Tropical highlands	8.0	6.7	132.9	28.2	–	52.1	1.23	8.72	1.00	7.93	12.84	1.619
3. *Desert*						15.6				9.22	12.05	1.307
3.1 Hot tropical	.0	–	2.0	–	4.5	2.3	1.57	3.00	1.00	28.28	31.86	1.13
3.2 Hot subtropical	20.9	11.8	–	–	6.7	15.8	.69	16.94	1.00	8.99	11.80	1.31
3.7 Continental	1.4	1.6	.0	.0	93.5	24.5	1.78	4.00	.60	9.98	11.83	1.19
4. *Subtropical*						54.9				6.83	9.01	1.320
4.1 Humid	30.4	4.7	51.6	1.6	63.0	28.4	1.24	9.22	.75	12.50	15.65	1.25
4.2 Monsoon	116.6	128.1	69.7	144.9	52.0	102.7	.84	6.91	.66	6.41	8.16	1.27
4.3 Hot	105.7	46.7	47.6	156.8	6.6	68.7	.87	6.05	1.00	5.21	7.41	1.42
4.4 Semiarid	–	–	10.0	5.0	–	7.5	18.29	2.00	1.00	14.21	17.93	1.26
5. *Pampean*						97.3				13.61	16.73	1.229
5.1 Pampean	99.5	99.0	168.4	36.6	–	97.3	1.27	4.53	.20	13.61	16.73	1.23

6. *Mediterranean*						39.6				10.14	13.03	1.284
6.1 Subtropical	72.9	71.3	33.5	11.7	104.9	55.4	3.28	18.68	.45	10.38	13.10	1.26
6.2 Marine	14.0	2.2	34.4	12.0	.0	16.8	1.27	7.24	.25	9.20	13.32	1.45
6.5 Temperate	77.3	18.9	45.5	4.0	23.5	37.4	1.24	11.27	.17	11.93	15.86	1.33
6.7 Continental	67.0	27.7	133.4	8.3	1.6	47.5	1.34	19.68	.30	10.79	14.48	1.34
6.8 Subtrop. semiarid	46.9	22.8	21.3	6.0	–	26.7	.94	14.26	.50	8.64	9.75	1.13
6.9 Contin. semiarid	4.6	3.0	9.0	1.0	–	5.8	.25	4.61	.66	6.16	6.48	1.05
7. *Marine*						120.1				17.01	28.13	1.654
7.1 Warm	11.5	5.4	–	–	–	8.4	20.56	2.00	.00	25.13	35.48	1.41
7.2 Cool	78.9	236.3	92.9	–	–	136.1	5.97	6.81	.00	22.12	34.82	1.57
7.6 Cool temperate	97.1	145.8	158.9	20.3	–	120.3	4.54	21.71	.03	18.44	28.86	1.57
7.7 Cold temperate	90.6	144.8	187.9	–	–	133.9	5.13	8.00	.00	9.62	20.79	2.16
8. *Humid Continental*						256.2				19.61	34.02	1.735
8.1 Warm	152.4	151.2	450.5	92.2	417.0	254.3	5.54	7.62	.00	24.43	42.54	1.74
8.2 Semiwarm	164.3	124.1	703.0	283.5	622.3	291.5	2.75	12.16	.00	18.77	33.55	1.79
8.3 Cold	52.0	17.0	–	–	–	34.5	.86	2.00	.00	7.98	11.90	1.49
9. *Steppe*						357.9				11.57	18.26	1.578
9.2 Semiwarm	606.5	346.6	818.6	304.2	24.7	450.3	2.27	12.92	.00	12.29	21.14	1.68
9.3 Cold	636.4	348.5	111.9	12.0	–	382.3	1.42	7.28	.00	10.11	14.82	1.47
9.4 Temperate	38.2	35.5	–	–	–	36.9	1.79	4.34	.00	11.85	17.36	1.47

Notes: Publications data from R.E. Evenson and Y. Kislev.[3] Subregions are defined as $n(1-d) + d$ where n is the number of individual countries in the region, and

$$d = \sum_{i=1}^{n} A_i - \overline{A} \,/(2A_i - 2)\,\overline{A}.$$

A_i is the acreage of the crop in country i. The term $d = 0$, when all countries in the region have the same acreage, approaches 1 as acreage in the region is concentrated in one country. Cereal grain yields are computed by simply totaling cereal production of the different grains without price weighting. While prices vary considerably by country, international prices per Kg are approximately the same for all cereals.

Table 8-4. Regression Analysis: Geoclimate Yield Determination

Regression #	*(1)*	*(2)*	*(3)*	*(4)*	*(5)*	*(6)*
			LN (Output)			
Dependent Variable	*Wheat*	*Barley*	*Maize*	*Sorghum*	*Rice*	*All Cereals*
R^2	.996	.991	.998	.997	.997	.990
LN (Acres)	.917	1.050	.865	.912	.985	1.20
	(.020)	(.02)	(.016)	(.019)	(.025)	(.015)
LN (Fert/ha)	.037	.054	.033	–.014	.018	.037
	(.007)	(.011)	(.007)	(.019)	(.008)	(.006)
LN (Res/SR)	.087	.009	.115	.115	.033	.056
	(.005)	(.005)	(.005)	(.014)	(.008)	(.005)
LN (Res/SR)*RB	.00005	.00008	.00012	.00034	–.000006	.00005
	(.000004)	(.00001)	(.00001)	(.00004)	(.000004)	(.000004)
Regional Dummies	x	x	x	x	x	x

Notes: Observations: 1948-1968 for regions with significant production.
Regressions: Weighted by acreage.
Res/SR: Publications summed from 1942 to year of observation per subregion in the regions.
RB: The ratio of publications in plant physiology, plant pathology, and soil science to total applied crop publications.
Fert/ha: A price weighted average of nitrogen, phosphorus, and potash application per cropped acre; not a crop specific measure.
Regional Dummy Variables: Included in all regressions. This has the effect of converting all variables to deviations from mean values.

EXPORT PERFORMANCE IN CEREAL GRAINS AND TECHNOLOGY TRANSFER

International trade theorists have developed a number of hypotheses regarding the commodity composition of international trade. Following the well known findings of Leontief of several years ago, a number of modifications to the simple Heckshser-Ohlin theory have been developed. Vernon[11], Baldwin[1], and Keesing[5] have tested variants of the product cycle hypothesis and find some support from trade data. In an interesting paper, Hufbaur[4] tested several hypotheses of commodity composition and concluded that it was not really possible to discriminate between the leading theories.

The specification of technology transfer developed in this paper can be seen as a version of the product cycle theory, although the stress on geoclimate factors is not usually given in most product cycle discussions. In this section, two rather simple partial equilibrium specifications of the determinants of relative levels of cereal exports by exporting countries are tested. No attempt is made to develop a general equilibrium commodity composition model.

Cereal grains, of course, are important export commodities, especially in a number of rice exporting developing countries. According to standard trade theory, since cereal grains are produced by labor intensive methods in less developed regions, these regions might be expected to have a comparative advantage in their production. Of course, adverse climate conditions could offset their low wage advantage. In the previous section, however, it was shown that the less developed subregions had significantly lower yield increases than did the developed regions, and that their relatively low investment levels for research were a major contributing factor. It is not surprising, in view of this, that the cereal grain export performance of the developed countries has been much better than that shown by the less developed countries.[e]

The basic hypothesis under test here is related to one used by Leamer.[6] A general expression for the equilibrium level of trade (or the trade potential, as it is known in the literature) in a particular commodity, k, in country i, is:

$$6)\quad X_i = F_i(Y_i, N_i, T_i, U_i, R_i)$$

That is, given equilibrium world prices, differences in export performance are related to Gross National Product (Y_i), geoclimate or natural factors (N_i), the technology set in use by producers (T_i), the utility structure of consumer demand (U_i), and trade restrictions (R_i). It is a practical impossibility to measure a number of these factors, but if we specify the change in exports over a reasonably short time period we may be able to bypass the problem of obtaining measures of N_i, U_i, and R_i.

[e]See Sisler[10] for an excellent discussion of the trends in trade.

In general, these factors remain relatively constant over time and, depending on the form of 6), might not enter an expression showing the change in equilibrium exports as a function of the changes in GNP and in technology.

$$6a)\quad \Delta X_i = F_i(\Delta Y_i, \Delta T_i)$$

This rather simple and crude hypothesis was tested with data from 30 cereal grain exporting countries with three periods of change: 1951-52 to 1957-58, 1957-58 to 1962-63, and 1962-63 to 1969-70. Technological change was specified as a function of research per subregion. The results were:

$$6b)\quad \Delta X_{ic} = 422.6 + \underset{(.011)}{.055\, R/SR} - \underset{(899)}{145\, \Delta Y_i} \; (R^2 = .25)$$

Cereal research does appear to be influencing export performance, but the variance explained is low and the change in GNP variable is not significant.

An extension of the basic specification to a trade interdependence or trade flow model would be expressed as:

$$7)\quad X_{ij} = F_i F_j g(R_{ij}, WT)$$

In 7), the trade flow—that is, exports from country i to country j—is expressed as the product of the trade potential of each country and of flow specific trade restriction (R_{ij}) and total world trade (WT). Again, the change in trade between two countries is a more tractable empirical specification. A reasonable specification might be:

$$7a)\quad \Delta X_{ij} = h(\Delta T_i, \Delta T_j, \Delta Y_i, \Delta Y_j, \Delta T^*_{ij}, \Delta Y^*_{ij})$$

In 7a), $\Delta T_{ij}{}^*$ and $\Delta Y_{ij}{}^*$ reflect a hybridization of the trade flow model to include changes in technology and GNP in countries other than i and j.

A crude approximation to 7a) was estimated for 235 trade flow changes in cereal grain trade between 1963-64 and 1969-70:

$$\frac{\Delta X_{ij}}{X_{ij}} = 1.28 - \underset{(.004)}{.010\, \Delta Y_i} + \underset{(.0009)}{.0020\, R_i} + \underset{(.0001)}{.00012\, \Delta Y_j}$$

$$\underset{(.0007)}{-.0006\, R_j} - 1.3\, DCM \; (R^2 = .172)$$

(*DCM* is a dummy for trade between common market countries.)

These results, as with the earlier results, have the "right" signs, but the standard errors are relatively high and R^2 is low.

These two relatively crude specifications do support the basic proposition that research activity influences export performance through technology and discovery in indirect transfer. The relatively low percent of variance in export performance "explained" by the models is partially due to the major influence that weather factors have on production. It also suggests that more complicated specifications are probably required to more fully identify the determinants of trade flows and of export performance. In particular, trade restrictions and trade subsidies will probably have to be dealt with explicitly.

SUMMARY

The policies toward investment in agricultural research and extension by most of the less developed regions of the world in the past 25 years have led to a significant decrease in comparative productivity in cereal grain production. Direct technology transfer has, on balance, not been of enough significance to alter the pattern of technological change set by research investment and indirect technology transfer. This chapter provides some evidence that the decline in relative productivity in most of these countries has diminished their export performance as well.

The so-called green revolution in wheat and rice production might appear to some to contradict this conclusion. It might be argued that the widespread transfer of the Mexican wheat varieties and the IRRI rice varieties shows that direct technology transfer can be significant. The pessimistic conclusion that less developed subregions must develop strong research capabilities to realize significant gains may not be warranted. The international development community has long held that relatively small changes in the organization of agricultural production, along with strong extension programs carried out with the proper missionary zeal, were enough to realize significant gains in productivity.

Enough evidence is not yet in to allow a definitive answer, but two points bear mentioning.

First. The widespread direct transfer of technology between subregions is not inconsistent with the transfer specification offered here; in fact, it is to be expected, when a number of subregions fail to develop significant indigenous research programs. Here we might note that the direct transfer of the wheats and rices actually took place almost entirely within geoclimate regions as defined in Table 8-3.

Second. The green revolution experience itself demonstrates the principle of indirect transfer very well. The countries gaining most in the green revolution were those with significant indigenous research capabilities. They were in a position to screen varieties and determine optimal regions of production, hence they speeded up introduction of the new varieties. More important, however, those subregions with indigenous research capability quickly responded by taking advantage of indirect technology transfer. They recognized the value of implementing the genetic principles incorporated in the new varieties as well as the new varieties themselves in their indigenous breeding programs. In several countries, "second generation" wheat and rice varieties produced by these programs have displaced the original Mexican and IRRI varieties.

The conclusion that there really are no good substitutes for the development of strong, science based research systems in a geoclimate subregion is not as pessimistic as it first appears. A number of subregions in the tropical and subtropical climate zones have developed such systems; others are moving toward the building of such systems. The less developed regions are now rapidly increasing their share of world research (though progress is very spotty, with some less developed regions making little progress). Many developed country research systems have ended the post World War II expansion in research.

The long run implications of a continuation of this shift in investment pattern are significant. The potential for expansion of production in most of the less developed regions via indigenously produced technology is huge. Wise government policy will accelerate the investment in research to exploit this potential. The green revolution itself, while something of a temporary departure from the long range trend, demonstrates some of the potential impact, not only on production, but on trade patterns as well. With continued progress in the developing countries, comparative advantage will be significantly altered. The tropical and subtropical climate regions are likely to become significant competitors with the temperate zone regions for the cereal grain markets of the world.

Notes

Notes

Chapter One
Free Trade in Agricultural Products: Possible Effects on Total Output, Prices, and the International Distribution of Output

1. United Nations, FAO. Committee on Commodity Problems. *A World Price Equilibrium Model.* CCP 72/WP, 3. Rome, 1971.
2. United Nations, FAO. *Agricultural Commodity Projections, 1970-1980.* (2 vols.) Rome, 1971.
3. D. Gale Johnson. *World Agriculture in Disarray.* Fontana World Economic Issues. London: Fontana, 1973; New York: St. Martin's Press, 1973, pp. 44-51.
4. W.F. Roenigk. *Agriculture in the European Community and the United States, 1958-68.* USDA. ERS-Foreign 307. Washington, D.C., 1971, p. 5.
5. Earl O. Heady and Luther G. Tweeten. *Resource Demand and Structure of the Agricultural Industry.* Ames, Iowa, 1963, p. 448.
6. George E. Dudley, James R. Donald, and Russell G. Barlowe. "Yield and Acreage Implications for U.S. Cotton." *Cotton Situation.* CS247. August 1970, pp. 17-23; Leroy J. Hushak. "A Welfare Analysis of the Voluntary Corn Diversion Program, 1961 to 1966." *American Journal of Agricultural Economics* 53 (2) (May 1971): 173-181.
7. U.S. Department of Agriculture. *The World Food Budget 1970.* Foreign Agricultural Economic Report No. 19 Washington, D.C., October 1964, p. 45.
8. Donald W. Regier and Ol Halbert Goolsby. *Growth in World Demand for Feed Grains, 1980.* USDA. Foreign Agriculture Economic Report No. 63. Washington, D.C., 1970, p. 87.
9. D. Gale Johnson, *op. cit.*, pp. 138-142.
10. U.S. Department of Agriculture. *The Agricultural Situation in the Far East*

and Oceania: Review of 1970 and Outlook for 1971. ERS-Foreign 315. April 1971, p. 12.

11. M.S. Rao. "Protection to Fertilizer Industry and Its Impact on Indian Agriculture." Unpublished paper. Department of Economics, University of Chicago, 19 .
12. "Agriculture and Foreign Economic Policy." *Journal of Farm Economics* 46 (5) (December 1964): 926-927.
13. United Nations, FAO. *Monthly Bulletin of Agricultural Economics and Statistics* 19 (September 1970): 43. (The price supports ranged from $73 in Mexico to $95 per ton in Pakistan for 1969/70.) International Wheat Council. *Review of World Grains Situation 1968-69.* London, November 1969, p. 33.
14. Anthony S. Rojko and Arthur B. Mackie. *World Demand Prospects for Agricultural Exports of Less Developed Countries in 1980.* USDA. Foreign Agricultural Economic Report No. 60. Washington, D.C., 1970, p. 45.
15. United Nations, FAO. *Monthly Bulletin of Agricultural Economics and Statistics* 19 (September 1970): 45.
16. United Nations, FAO. *Provisional Indicative World Plan for Agricultural Development.* Chapter 14, p. 117. Rome, July 1969.
17. Calculated from United Nations, FAO, *World Price Equilibrium Model, op. cit.*, pp. 23 and 26.
18. *World Agriculture in Disarray, op. cit.*, pp. 242-246.

Chapter Two
The Impact of U.S. Agricultural Policies on Trade of the Developing Countries

1. *Partners in Development: Report of the Commission on International Development.* New York: Praeger, 1969.
2. For an excellent discussion of this topic see Ian Little, Tibor Scitovsky, and Maurice Scott. *Industry and Trade in Some Developing Countries: A Comparative Study.* London: Oxford University Press, 1970.
3. Arthur B. Mackie, A. Nicholas Filippello, John E. Hutchison, and James F. Kiefer. *World Agricultural Trade in Selected Agricultural Commodities, 1951-65.* Vol. II: *Food and Feed Grains.* FAER No. 45, ERS, USDA, June 1968.
4. Delane Welsch and Sopin Tongpan. *Rice in Thailand,* Staff Paper P71-32, Department of Agricultural and Applied Economics, University of Minnesota, December 1971. (Unpublished data on Thai rice prices provided by Delane Welsch.)
5. Food and Agricultural Organization of the United Nations. *Production Yearbook, 1970.* Vol. 24, 1971.
6. Willard W. Cochrane. *The World Food Problem: A Guardedly Optimistic View.* New York: Thomas Y. Crowell, 1969.
7. Anthony S. Rojko, Francis S. Urban, and James J. Naive. *World Demand Prospects for Grains in 1980 with Emphasis on Trade by the Less Developed Countries.* FAER No. 75, ERS, USDA, December 1971.

8. The section on oilseeds was drawn upon data contained in Arthur B. Mackie, Tom E. Full, and Jon E. Falck. *World Trade in Selected Agricultural Commodities, 1951-65.* Vol. V: *Oilseeds, Oil Nuts, and Animal and Vegetable Oils.* FAER No. 47, ERS, USDA, August 1968.
9. Anthony S. Rojko and Arthur B. Mackie. *World Demand Prospects for Agricultural Exports of Less Developed Countries in 1980.* FAER No. 60, ERS, USDA, June 1970.
10. The section on cotton was drawn from Richard S. Magleby and Edmond Missiaen, *World Demand for Cotton in 1980 with Emphasis on Trade by Less Developed Countries*, FAER No. 000, ERS, USDA, January 1971.
11. Rojko and Mackie, *op. cit.*
12. Arthur B. Mackie and J. Lawrence Blum. *World Trade in Selected Agricultural Commodities, 1951-65.* Vol. IV: *Sugar, Fruits, and Vegetables.* FAER No. 44, ERS, USDA, June 1968.
13. Larry J. Wipf. "Tariffs, Nontariff Distortions, and Effective Protection in U.S. Agriculture." *American Journal of Agricultural Economics* 53 (3) (August 1971).
14. Wipf, *op. cit.*, pp. 430-32.
15. James P. Houck. "The Green Revolution: Its Impact on Trade and Agricultural Policy in Developed Nations." Staff Paper P71-20. Department of Agricultural and Applied Economics, University of Minnesota, November 1971.
16. D. Gale Johnson. "Sugar Program: Costs and Benefits." *Foreign Trade and Agricultural Policy.* Technical Papers, Vol. VI. National Advisory Commission on Food and Fiber, August 1967.
17. Donald C. Horton. "Policy Directions for the United States Sugar Program." *American Journal of Agricultural Economics* 52 (2) (May 1970).
18. D. Gale Johnson, *op. cit.*, pp. 185-196.
19. D. Gale Johnson. *Comparative Advantage and U.S. Exports and Imports, of Farm Products.* Paper No. 72:1. Office of Agricultural Economics Research, University of Chicago, February 15, 1971. The program cost estimates are based on higher world prices that would result from increased imports by the United States.
20. Thomas H. Bates. "The Long-Run Efficiency of United States Sugar Policy." *American Journal of Agricultural Economics* 50 (2) (August 1968): pp. 521-535. Donald C. Horton. "Policy Directions for the United States Sugar Program." *American Journal of Agricultural Economics* 52 (2) (May 1970): pp. 185-196. See also R.H. Snape. "Sugar: Costs of Protection and Taxation." *Economica* XXXVI (141) (February 1969): pp. 29-41.
21. Harry G. Johnson. "Sugar Protectionism and the Export Earnings of Less Developed Countries: Variations on a Theme by Snape." *Economica* XXXIII (129) (February 1966): pp. 34-42.
22. R.H. Snape. "Some Effects of Protection in the World Sugar Industry." *Economica* XXX (117) (February 1963): pp. 63-73.

23. P.L. Strickland, W.H. Brown, W.C. McArthur, and W.W. Pawson. *Cotton Production and Farm Income Estimates Under Selected Alternative Farm Programs.* FAER No. 212, ERS, USDA, September 1971.
24. Wipf, *op. cit.* The calculated rates of protection were much lower in 1968 because of unusually high world market prices. With present much lower world prices, we would expect current rates of protection to be as high if not higher than in 1963.
25. *Rice Situations.* RS-19-ERS, USDA, March 1972.
26. A recent study by Warren R. Grant and D.S. Moore, *Alternative Government Rice Programs: An Economic Evaluation* (AER No. 187, ERS, USDA, June 1970), concludes that rice production in the United States in a free market situation would be 138.7 million cwt. at an equilibrium price of $3.40 per cwt. for rough rice. This is a much larger amount than the peak production of 104 million cwt. produced in 1968 and way above the 1970 level of production of 83 million cwt. This increase is predicted in spite of a sharp drop in net returns from rice production in the short run (actually negative returns) and a significant reduction in land values required in the long run. The author finds these results hard to accept for such a protected commodity.
27. Bela Belassa. "Tariff Protection in Industrial Nations and Its Effects on the Exports of Processed Goods from Developing Countries." *Canadian Journal of Economics* (August 1968).
28. Arthur B. Mackie. *Foreign Economic Growth and Market Potentials for U.S. Agricultural Products.* FAER No. 24, ERS, USDA, April 1965.
29. D. Gale Johnson, "Where U.S. Agricultural Comparative Advantage Lies," Chapter 3 in D. Gale Johnson and John A. Schnittker, *U.S. Agriculture in a World Context* (New York: Praeger, 1974).
30. H.S. Houthakker. "Domestic Farm Policy and International Trade," *American Journal of Agricultural Economics* 53 (5) (December 1971): 764.
31. Dale E. Hathaway. *Trade Restrictions and U.S. Consumers.* Paper presented at the U.S. Trade Policy and Agricultural Exports Conference, Ames, Iowa, June 2, 1971.
32. Willard W. Cochrane. "Agricultural Aspects of U.S. Economic Relations with Developing Countries." *United States International Economic Policy in an Interdependent World.* Vol. II. Papers submitted to the Commission on International and Investment Policy. Washington, D.C., July 1971, p. 264.
33. FAO. *International Commodity Arrangements and Policies.* FAO Commodity Policy Studies No. 16. Special Studies Program No. 1. Rome, 1964; Joint Staff Study of the International Monetary Fund and the International Bank for Reconstruction and Development. *The Problem of Stabilization of Prices of Primary Products.* Washington, D.C., 1969.
34. *The Problem of Stabilization of Prices of Primary Products, ibid.*
35. R.C. Porter. "Who Destabilizes Primary Product Prices?" *The Indian Economic Journal* XVI (4) (April-June 1969).

36. Herbert G. Grubel. "Foreign Exchange Earnings and Price Stabilization Schemes." *The American Economic Review* LIV (4) (June 1964).
37. Alasdair I. McBean. *Export Instability and Economic Development.* Cambridge, Mass.: Harvard University Press, 1966, p. 32.
38. *Ibid.*, p. 341.
39. See, for example, *Future United States Foreign Trade Policy*, Report to the President submitted by the Special Representative for Trade Negotiations (Washington, D.C., January 14, 1969); and *United States International Economic Policy in an Interdependent World*, Report to the President submitted by the Commission on International Trade and Investment Policy (Washington, D.C., July 1971).
40. John Schnittker. "A Look Ahead–Trade Policy Recommendations." *United States International Economic Policy in an Interdependent World.* Vol. I. Papers submitted to the Commission on International Trade and Investment Policy. Washington, D.C., July 1971, p. 905.
41. There is some convincing evidence that exporting agricultural products is one way a developing country can extract an economic surplus from the agricultural sector with which to finance general economic development: George L. Hicks and Geoffrey McNicoll. *Trade and Growth in the Philippines: An Open Dual Economy.* Ithaca: Cornell University Press, 1971.

Chapter Three
The Impact of Price on Rice Trade in Asia

1. Saleh Afiff and C. Peter Timmer. "Rice Policy in Indonesia." *Food Research Institute Studies* X (2), 1971.
2. Randolph Barker. "Annual Research Review: Agricultural Economics." Mimeographed. International Rice Research Institute (IRRI). Los Baños, February 1, 1973.
3. Zvi Griliches. "Specification Bias in Estimates of Production Functions." *Journal of Farm Economics* (February 1957).
4. Yujiro Hayami and Vernon Ruttan. *Agricultural Development: An International Perspective*. Baltimore: Johns Hopkins Press, 1971.
5. Irving Hoch. "Estimation of Production Function Parameters Combining Time-Series and Cross-Section Data." *Econometrica* (January 1962).
6. Hendrik S. Houthakker. "An International Comparison of Household Expenditure Patterns, Commemorating the Centenary of Engel's Law." *Econometrica* (October 1957).
7. T.H. Lee. "Government Interference in the Rice Market in Taiwan." In *Viewpoints on Rice Policy in Asia.* International Rice Research Institute (IRRI), 1971.
8. Moon Pal Yong. "Farm Producer Response to Price Changes: The Case of Korean Farmers." Working Paper 7216. Korea Development Institute, Seoul, 1972.
9. Yair Mundlak. "Empirical Production Function Free of Management Bias." *Journal of Farm Economics* (February 1961).

10. Brian Phelan. "Thai Neglect." *Far Eastern Economic Review* (September 10, 1973).
11. C. Peter Timmer. "On Measuring Technical Efficiency." *Food Research Institute Studies* IX (2).
12. C. Peter Timmer. "Objectives and Constraints in the Formation of Indonesian Rice Policy: A Proto-type Essay." Stanford Rice Project Working Paper No. 2. Food Research Institute, September 1973. Mimeo.
13. C. Peter Timmer and Walter P. Falcon. "The Political Economy of Rice Production and Trade in Asia." In *Agriculture in Development Theory* (Lloyd Reynolds, Ed.). New Haven: Yale University Press, forthcoming.
14. Richard Weisskoff. "Demand Elasticities for a Developing Economy: An International Comparison of Consumption Patterns." In *Studies in Development Planning* (Hollis B. Chenery et al., Eds.). Cambridge, Mass.: Harvard University Press, 1971.

Chapter Four
The Interaction of Growth Strategy, Agriculture, and Foreign Trade: The Case of India

1. For a review of this position, see John W. Mellor, *The Economics of Agricultural Development*, Ithaca: Cornell University Press, 1966, Chapter 6; and George S. Tolley and George D. Gwyer, "International Trade in Agricultural Products in Relation to Economic Development," in Herman M. Southworth and Bruce F. Johnston (Eds.), *Agricultural Development and Economic Growth*, Ithaca: Cornell University Press, 1967.
2. This view is presented in a general policy context in Uma J. Lele and John W. Mellor, "Jobs, Poverty, and the 'Green Revolution,' " *International Affairs* 48 (1) (January 1972).
3. The conflicting objectives of growth and their implications to choice of growth strategy are discussed at length in John W. Mellor, *India and the New Economics of Growth*, Twentieth Century Fund, forthcoming.
4. We detail the nature of an employment oriented strategy in three closely related papers: Lele and Mellor, *op. cit.*, January 1972; Uma J. Lele and John W. Mellor, "Technological Change and Distributive Bias in a Dual Economy," Revised Occasional Paper No. 43, Dept. of Agricultural Economics, Cornell University USAID Employment and Income Distribution Research Project, June 1971; and John W. Mellor and Uma J. Lele, "Growth Linkages of the New Foodgrain Technologies," *Indian Journal of Agricultural Economics* XXVIII (1) (Jan.-Mar. 1973).
5. Data are for the lowest two deciles of the Indian income distribution. See Mellor and Lele, "Growth Linkages," *op. cit.*, Table 3. For a more

complete analysis of demand relations, see B.M. Desai, "Analysis of Consumption Expenditure Patterns in India," Occasional Paper No. 54, Dept. of Agricultural Economics, Cornell University USAID Employment and Income Distribution Research Project, August 1972.

6. For a full exposition of this position in the context of growth theory, see John W. Mellor, "Models of Economic Growth and Land Augmenting Technological Change in Foodgrain Production," in Nurul Islam (Ed.), *Agriculture in the Development of Low Income Nations*, London: Macmillan and St. Martin's Press, forthcoming.
7. For an exposition of intersectoral capital flows, see John W. Mellor, "Accelerated Growth in Agricultural Production and the Intersectoral Transfer of Resources," *Economic Development and Cultural Change* 22 (1) (October 1973). For a full analysis of the question and application to Taiwan, see Teng-hui Lee, *Intersectoral Capital Flows in the Economic Development of Taiwan, 1895-1960*, Ithaca: Cornell University Press, 1971.
8. This potential is discussed at length in Mellor and Lele, *op. cit.*, Note 4.
9. See the discussion of this question in the context of small scale industries in Jan H. van der Veen, "A Study of Small Industries in Gujarat State, India," Occasional Paper No. 65, Dept. of Agricultural Economics, Cornell University USAID Employment and Income Distribution Research Project, May 1973.
10. For a detailed exposition of the extreme difficulty of encouraging exports in the context of centrally directed resource allocation, see Jagdish N. Bhagwati and Padma Desai, *India, Planning for Industrialization*, New York: Oxford University Press, 1970. For the special problems of small scale industry in a nonmarket context, and the low capital intensity of small scale industry, see van der Veen, *op. cit.* (Note 9). For the need for decentralized decision making in agriculture, see Mellor, *op. cit.* (Note 1).
11. For a review of these models in the context of choice of growth strategy, see Mellor, in Islam, *op cit.* (Note 6).
12. See P.C. Mahalanobis, "Some Observations on the Process of Growth of National Income," *Sankhya* 12 (September 1953); P.C. Mahalanobis, "The Approach of Operational Research to Planning in India," *Sankhya* 16 (December 1955); and S. Chakravarty, *Capital and Development Planning*, Cambridge, Mass.: M.I.T. Press, 1969.
13. For a detailed analysis by industrial sector, see Mellor, *op. cit.* Chapter V, (Note 3).
14. S.B. Lindar. *An Essay on Trade and Transformation.* New York: John Wiley, 1961.
15. E. Hecksher. "The Effect of Foreign Trade on the Distribution of Income." In *Readings in the Theory of International Trade*, Philadelphia: American Economic Association, 1949; and Bertil Ohlin. *Interregional and International Trade.* Cambridge, Mass.: Harvard University Press, 1933.

16. Data are from United Nations, Department of Economic and Social Affairs, Statistical Office, *Yearbook of International Trade Statistics*, New York, various issues.
17. *Ibid.*
18. *Ibid.*
19. *Ibid.*
20. *Ibid.*
21. Government of India, Planning Commission. "Approach to the Fifth Plan, 1974-79." Delhi, January 1973.
22. *Ibid.*, p. 14.
23. *Ibid.*, pp. 21-22.
24. *Ibid.*, p. 22.
25. See Bhagwati and Desai, *op. cit.*, p. 369 (Note 10).
26. See United Nations, *op. cit.*, various issues (Note 16).
27. *Ibid.*
28. *Ibid.*
29. See Bhagwati and Desai, *op. cit.*, pp. 429-431.
30. See Heckshe r, *op. cit.* and Ohlin, *op. cit.* (Note 15).
31. For details and sources, see Mellor, *op. cit.*, Chapter V, (Note 3).
32. These data are based on an unpublished work by Uma J. Lele, "An Analysis of the L.D.C.'s Exports of Manufactured Goods." See also the analysis by Bharadwaj confirming a rise in the capital intensity of exports vis-à-vis imports replacement in 1958-59 compared to 1953-54, in Ranganath Bharadwaj, *Trade: A Study Suggested by the Input-Output Analysis*, University of Bombay, 1962.
33. See Lele, *op. cit.* (Note 32).
34. Rank correlation coefficients between capital intensity and export growth from 1964 and 1969 were statistically significant at the 90 percent level. See Lele, *ibid.*
35. *Ibid.*
36. This is, in essence, Lindar's hypothesis that countries with similar per capita incomes and hence similar consumption patterns will trade with each other (see Lindar, *op. cit.*, 1961). In a test of Lindar's hypothesis, Lele finds no correlation between propensities to import and income differences between India and pairs of regions (see Lele, *op. cit.*, unpublished). For this purpose, the world was divided into ten regions, each relatively homogeneous for per capita income. For each region the average propensity to import from India was calculated by dividing the imports into the region from India by region GNP, then the Spearman rank correlation coefficient was calculated between the ranking of propensities to import of each region and the difference between the regions and India's GNP per capita. Similarly, India's imports fıom the region were calculated. In both cases the rank correlation was not significant at the 5 percent level. With the exception of miscellaneous manufactures and machinery and transport equipment which account for only one-sixth of India's export growth in the past two decades, the better

performers in exports are commodities going primarily to high income countries, although the growth in trade with the Eastern Bloc countries may reflect some affinity with respect to demand for quality of goods between the areas.

37. Kou-shu Liang and T.H. Lee. "Process and Pattern of Economic Development in Taiwan." Unpublished paper, 1972.
38. Bhagwati and Desai, *op. cit.*, pp. 130-134 (Note 10).
39. Manmohan Singh. *India's Export Trends.* Oxford: Clarendon Press, 1966, pp. 50-55. Also, Bhagwati and Desai, *op. cit.*, pp. 385-388; and General Agreement on Trade and Tariff, *International Trade*, 1969, p. 82.
40. See United Nations, *op. cit.*, various issues (Note 16).
41. *Ibid.*
42. *Ibid.*
43. Indian Cotton Mill's Federation. "The Indian Cotton Textile Industry." *Cotton and Allied Textile Industries* 8 (Bombay, 1967): 20.
44. *Ibid.*
45. *Ibid.*

Chapter Five
Agricultural Trade in the Economic Development of Taiwan

1. J.R. Hicks. *Essays in World Economics.* Oxford: Clarendon, 1959, pp. 185-188.
2. Teng-hui Lee. *Intersectoral Capital Flows in the Economic Development of Taiwan, 1895-1960.* Ithaca: Cornell University Press, 1971.
3. H.B. Chenery and Bruno Michael. "Development Alternatives in an Open Economy: The Case of Israel." *Economic Journal* 72 (March 1962): 79-109.
4. Irma Adelman and H.B. Chenery. "Foreign Aid and Economic Development: The Case of Greece." *Review of Economics and Statistics* 48 (February 1968): 1-18.
5. H.B. Chenery and Alan Strout. "Foreign Assistance and Economic Development." *American Economic Review* 56 (September 1966): 679-733.
6. C. Michalopoulos. "Imports, Foreign Exchange, and Economic Development: The Greek Experience." In *The Open Economy: Essays on International Trade and Finance*, edited by P.B. Kenen and R. Lawrence. New York: Columbia University Press, 1968, pp. 289-312.
7. Kuo-shu Liang. *Foreign Trade and Economic Development in Taiwan: 1952-1967.* Ph.D. dissertation, Vanderbilt University, 1970, pp. 36-44.
8. Jaroslav Vanek. *Estimating Foreign Resource Needs for Economic Development.* New York: McGraw Hill, 1967.
9. R.I. McKinnon. "Foreign Exchange Constraints in Economic Development and Efficient Aid Allocation." *Economic Journal* 76 (June 1964): 388-409.

10. R.I. McKinnon. "Rejoinder." *Economic Journal* 76 (March 1966): 170-71.
11. B.I. Cohen. "Foreign-Exchange Constraints in Economic Development and Efficient Aid Allocation: Comment." *Economic Journal* 76 (March 1966): 168-69.
12. H.B. Chenery and Peter Eckstein. "Development Alternatives for Latin America." *Journal of Political Economy* 78 (August 1970): 966-1006.
13. Anthony M. Tang. "Policy and Performance in Agriculture." In *Economic Trends in Communist China*, edited by A. Eckstein, W. Galenson, and T.C. Liu. Chicago: Aldine, 1968, pp. 459-507.
14. Robert M. Solow. "A Contribution to the Theory of Economic Growth." *Quarterly Journal of Economics* 70 (February 1956): pp. 65-94.
15. Ryuzo Sato. "The Harrod-Domar Model vs. The Neo-Classical Growth Model." *Economic Journal* 74 (June 1964): 380-387.
16. T.H. Lee and Kuo-shu Liang. "The Structure of Protection in Taiwan." *Economic Essays*, The Graduate Institute of Economics, National Taiwan University 2 (November 1971), pp. 75-89.
17. Han-yu Chang. "Quantitative Comparison of the Living Standards between Taiwan's Farmers and Nonfarmers." In *Studies on the Structural Change in Taiwan's Agriculture*, edited by T.H. Lee (In Chinese). Taipei: JCRR, 1972, p. 19.
18. W.F. Hsu and H.Y. Chen. *Agricultural Marketing in Taiwan.* Taipei: Mimeographed. (February 1972), p. 12.
19. T.H. Lee. "Government Interference in the Rice Market," *Economic Essays* 2 (September 1971), pp. 45-68.
20. Hla Myint. *The Economics of the Developing Countries.* London: Hutchinson, 1964, p. 158.

Chapter Seven
Agricultural Trade: Implications for the Distribution of Gains from Technical Process

1. Willard Cochrane, *Farm Prices, Myth and Reality* (St. Paul: University of Minnesota Press, 1958).
2. Yujiro Hayami and Vernon W. Ruttan, *Agricultural Development: An International Perspective* (Baltimore: The Johns Hopkins Press, 1971), Chapter 9.
3. Food and Agricultural Organization of the United Nations, *Implications of the Enlargement of the EEC for Agricultural Commodity Projection, 1970-80*, CCP 72/WP.6, December 1971.

Chapter Eight
Agricultural Trade and Shifting Comparative Advantage

1. R.E. Baldwin. "Determinants of the Commodity Structure of U.S. Trade." *A.E.R.* LXIX (1969).

2. R.E. Evenson and Y. Kislev. "Research and Productivity in Wheat and Maize." *J.P.E.* Forthcoming.
3. R.E. Evenson and Y. Kislev. "Investment in Agricultural Research and Extension: An International Survey." *Economic Development and Cultural Change*. Forthcoming.
4. G.C. Hufbaur. "Factor Endowments, National Size and Changing Technology." In *The Technology Factors in International Trade* (ed. R. Vernon). New York: Columbia University Press, 1970.
5. D.B. Keesing. "Population and Industrial Development: Some Evidence from Trade Patterns." *A.E.R.* (June 1968).
6. E.F. Leamer. "The Commodity Composition of International Trade in Manufactures." Harvard Institute of Economic Research, Discussion Paper No. 236.
7. J. Papadakis. *Agricultural Climates of the World.* Buenos Aires, 1966.
8. V.W. Ruttan and Y. Hayami. *Agricultural Development: An International Perspective.* Baltimore: Johns Hopkins University Press, 1971.
9. E. Sadan. "Partial Production Functions and the Analysis of Farm-Firm Costs and Efficiency." *American Journal of Agricultural Economics* 52:62-70.
10. D. Sisler. "Agricultural Trade and Development." International Conference of Agricultural Economics, Proceedings, 1970.
11. Vernon. "International Investment and International Trade in Product Cycle." *Quarterly Journal of Economics* 80:190-207.
12. *Biological Abstracts.* Philadelphia, Pa.
13. *Dairy Science Abstracts.* Commonwealth Bureau of Dairy Production. London, England.
14. *Plant Breeding Abstracts.* Commonwealth Bureau of Plant Breeding and Genetics. Cambridge, England.

Index

Africa: meat, 33
Agricultural Adjustment Act, 177
agriculture: fertilizer impact in Evenson, 193; free trade in Johnson, 7; international forum in Abel, 56; LDC exports, 18; natural endowment factor, 153; P.L. 480, 50; price formulation in Taiwan, 142; production in Joslins, 169; protection and projection, 13; raw materials, 24; resource use, 20; Taiwan land reform, 116, 117; Taiwan performance, 132; technology and policy, in Joslins, 174; trade barriers, 15; U.S. resource allocations, 56
Argentina: effect of free trade, 14; grains, 24; meat, 33; wheat market, 38
Australia, 15; consumer exploitation, 13; grain production, 25; rice export, 39; sugar, 32; wheat, 14, 17

Baldwin, R.E., 197
bananas, 18
Belassa, B., 42
Brazil: wheat, 38
Burma, 24; rice, 57

Cambodia, 24
Canada: consumer exploitation, 13; effect of free trade, 14; grain production, 25; price protection, 5
capital: allocation, 113; elasticity in Korea, 160; and equilibrium in Korea, 151; flows in Korea, in Tolley, 151; flow of in Taiwan, 138; formation, 119–121; formation and equilibrium values, 155; in Taiwan, 116; transfers, 22
cereal grain: export performance, 181
Ceylon: fertilizer and rice yield data, 69; rice, 57
Chenery, H.B. and Eckstein, P., 119; foreign capital and Taiwan, 123; model, 128
China: tobacco, 35
Cochrane, W., 173
coffee: free trade, 18
commodity: exports in Korea, 150; noncompetitive, 21; and P.L. 480, 50; price stabilization, 51; Taiwan exports, 136; and technology transfer, 184, 187, 192; U.S. restrictions, 35
construction: in Korea, 148
consumers: welfare of in Abel, 44
consumption, 19; response to rice in Timmer and Falcon, 80; rice, 58
cotton, 28; synthetics, 18
Cuba: tobacco, 35

Dahomey, 16
dairy products, 15; protection, 36
debt: burden, 23
developing countries: capital accumulation in Korea, 158; farm/trade policy, 5; U.S. wheat policy, 47
Dominican Republic: tobacco, 35

EEC: consumer exploitation, 13; effect of free trade, 14; protection rate, 42; farm technology, 176; price protection, 5; sugar imports, 33; technology changes, 178
equilibrium: concept of, in Evenson, 182; concept of, in Tang and Liang, 118–120
exports: balance-of-payments equilibrium in Korea, 149; and cereal research, 198; and free trade concept in Johnson, 18; meat, 33; oilseeds, 28; and P.L. 480, 50; primary commodities, 51; sugar world trade, 32; Taiwan in Tang and Liang, 124;

Taiwan trade-oriented economy, 135; textiles, 110; tobacco, 35; wheat, 20; world grain picture, 25

FAO: projections, 13
fertilizer: functional relationship to rice price, 78; inputs and rice yield, 66; and rice prices, 58; subsidy, 16; yield increase, 193
food: production and free trade, in Johnson, 19; production and policy, 146; production in Western Europe, 7; free trade, in Johnson, 3, 4; in Taiwan, 130
foreign aid: aspects, in Abel, 22
foreign exchange, 35; agriculture and trade, 93; commodity price stabilization, 51; India textiles, 112; in Korea, 147; and processed product barriers, 42; in Taiwan, 118–122, 144
free trade: defined by Johnson, 3; farm inputs and outputs, 19; and specific crops, 18

GATT, 53, 177
government: Bank of Korea, 148; collective bargaining in Taiwan, 142; and farm protection, 180; research efforts, 183; research sponsorship, 200; Taiwan commodity policy, 118; U.S. commercial exports, 43; wheat programs, 37
grains: and low price elasticity, 4; and U.S. policy, 24
Green Revolution, 17, 184; and P.L. 480, 50; and technology transfer, in Evenson, 194; USDA trade prospects, 26
growth: equilibrium income in Korea, 156; in Korea, in Tolley, 147; in Mellor and Lele, 93; in Ranis and Fei, 145; strategy, 110; Taiwan industrialization, in Tang and Liang, 126

Hathaway, D.E., 45
Hayami, Y. and Ruttan, V., 66, 177
Heady, E. and Tweeten, L., 7
Hong Kong, 29
Horton, D.C., 38
Houthakker-Weisskoff formulation, 61
Hufbaur, G.C., 197

imports: fruits and vegetables, 33; substitutions, 112
income: distribution effects, in Joslins, 173; distribution elasticity in Taiwan, 129–131, 146; rate of growth, 161
India: employment, 94; protection, in Johnson, 16; tobacco, 35; textile exports, 110; wheat, 17
Indonesia: consumption response parameter, 82, 83; fertilizer and rice yield data, 69; rice, 57, 58; tobacco, 35; wheat, 38
industrialization: policy reform in Taiwan, 146, 137
International Coffee Agreement, 53
International Grains Arrangement, 176
Ireland: consumer exploitation, 13
Italy: rice export, 39

Japan: consumer exploitation, 13; effect of free trade, 14; fertilizer and yield data, 69; price protection, 5; protection rate, 42; rice, 58; rice export, 39; sugar import, 33; textile export, 110
Johnson, D.G., 38
Johnson, Harry, 39

Keesing, D.B., 197
Kennedy Round, 176
Kenya: wheat, 38
Kindleberger, C.P., 131
Kislev, Y. and Evenson, R.E., 193
Korea: capital and product flow analysis, 160–164; domestic infrastructure, 149; equilibrium income, 156; fertilizer and rice yield data, 69; income growth, 162; investment, 158; Korean Development Institute, 151; processed raw materials, 153; rice, 58; textile export, 110; and Vietnam related income, 148
Krueger, Anne, 151

labor: mobilization, 113; Taiwan government policies, 139
land reform: Taiwan, 144, 116
LDC: agricultural exports, 18; constraint model, in Tang and Liang, 129; grain imports, 25; policies of industrial nations, 19; research expenditure, 187; and restrictive trade policies, 54; self-sufficiency, 35
Leamer, E.F., 197
Lee, T.H., 137
Libya, 16

Mackie, A.B., 43
McKinnon, R.I., 118; model, 128
Malawi: tobacco, 35
Malaysia: rice, 58
Mali, 16
management: commonality, 183; in Korea, 156
market: access, 52; international commodity agreements, 56; sharing and manipulations, in Joslins, 174; in Taiwan, 118, 136; and technical change, 170; U.S. and LDCs, 43; world cotton, 48
meat: price and agriculture free trade, 13;

U.S. quotas, 49; world trade, 33
methodology: analysis of technology transfer, in Evenson, 185; capital and product analysis, 160–164; Cobb-Douglas function, 62, 160; consumption functions, in Timmer and Falcon, 76; Harrod-Domar construct, 129; production function in Korea, by Tolley, 154; projection of real income in Korea, by Tolley, 152; in Tang and Liang, 118; time series, in Timmer and Falcon, 60; trade flow model, in Evenson, 198; trade simulations, 71
Mexico: wheat, 7, 38

New Zealand, 15; consumer exploitation, 13; sugar, 32

Oceania: effect of free trade, 14
OECD: projections, 13
oilseeds, 28
output: mix and stability, 53

Pakistan, 16; cotton, 29; textile export, 112; wheat, 17
Papadakis, J., 184
peanuts: protection, 37
Pearson Commission Report, 22
Philippines, 17; fertilizer and rice yield data, 69; rice, 57; tobacco, 35
P.L. 480, 50
policy: agriculture, in Joslins, 174; central farm in Taiwan, 133; concept of liberalization and compensation, 45; and food supply, 5; import substitution, 24; industrial countries, 19; reforms in Taiwan, in Tang and Liang, 138; rice research project, 62; U.S. agriculture, 35; U.S. national interest, 46; U.S. rice, 48; U.S. sugar, 39
Portugal: cotton, 29
price: and dairy products, 15; elasticity and demand, 170; and grain products, 13; and Houthakker-Weisskoff formulation, 61; in Korea, in Tolley, 149; and price stabilization, 52; and rice data, 72; and rice marketing, 78; and self-sufficiency, 83; supports, 17; and consumer price, in Johnson, 4, 5
production: capacity in Taiwan, 124; domestic in Korea and transportation, 149; economies of scale, 154; grain, 14; and research, 200; response and rice price, in Timmer and Falcon, 60; rice, 89; rice yields, in Timmer and Falcon, 67; and technology transfer, 187; and trade, in Joslins, 171; wheat, 37; wheat in South Asia, 20
profit maximization, 61; concept of, in Evenson, 182
protection: of agriculture, in Johnson, 16; cost of, 5; cotton tariffs, 48; in Hathaway, 45; Indian production, 16; in Joslins, 175; and processed products, 22; and specific commodities, in Abel, 49; sugar and cotton, 39; and U.S. commodities, 36

quotas: and industrial countries, 19

Ranis, G. and Fei, J.C.H., 131
Regier, D. and Goolsby, O., 13
resource allocation: adjustments, in Abel, 45; adjustments in Korea, 150; cotton adjustment, 48; and food production, 4; and free trade, 20; investment availability, 128
Rhodesia: tobacco, 35
rice, 17; IRRI variety transfer, 199; Japan's rice import restriction, 177; production, 48; simulation, 72, 76; substitution and production, 88; in Taiwan, 142; trade, 77; U.S. export, 39; U.S. policy, 24
Rojko and Mackie, 17, 20; LDC and cotton, 31
rubber, 18

Sadan, E., 193
Samuelson, P., 153
Sato, R., 129
Schnittker, J., 54
self-sufficiency: concept of, 80; in Mellor and Lele, 93; production structure in Taiwan, 130; and rice market, 62; and wheat, 38
Snape, R.H., 39
South Africa: sugar, 32
South Vietnam, 25
strategy: for Taiwan development, 145; textile growth and development, 111; U.S. trade and LDCs, 44
subsidy: and crop production, 4; export, 17; fertilizer, 16; policies, in Joslin, 175; rice, 40; trade and Evenson recommendation, 199; variable levies, 179
sugar, 18; crop in Taiwan, 142; Taiwan Sugar Corp., 143; U.S., 38, 49; world trade, 32
supply: farm products, 16
Sweden: protection rate, 42
synthetics, 52

Taiwan: agriculture structure, 132; fertilizer and rice yield data, 69; food, 130; rice, 58; in Tang and Liang posit, 115; textile export, 110

tariffs, 46; commodities, 41
technology: and agricultural growth, 24; analysis and microregions, 186; defined by Evenson, 182; grain production, 25; income transfer effect, 177; India textile, 112; Taiwan, 116; trade level, 171; transfer of, 154; and transfer, in Evenson, 181
Thailand, 24; rice, 57; wheat, 38
tobacco, 34
trade: as complement to foreign aid, 53; and farm policy, 173; impact, in Joslins, 169, 172
transportation: and commodities, 15
Turkey: wheat, 17

UAR, 29
UNCTAD, 55
United Kingdom: consumer exploitation, 13; protection rate, 42
United States: agricultural research station, 183; consumer exploitation, 13; diplomacy, 175; effect of free trade, 14; expenditures in Korea, 150; export flow, 24; grain production, 25; LDCs and trade policies, 55; noncompetitive commodities, 21; price protection, 5; protection rate, 42; rice production, 40; sugar import, 33
Uruguay: meat, 33
USDA: grain trade prospects, 26; projections, 13; trade barriers in Far East, 15
USSR: consumer exploitation, 13; price protection, 5; sugar imports, 33

Vernon, 197

weather: climatological classification, 192; drought in 1965-66, 25; and production, 182; production, in Evenson, 199; and rice, 58, 62
welfare: distribution, 170-172
Westphal, L. and Tolley, G.S., 151
wheat: and less protectionist policies, 46; Mexican variety transfer, 199; production in South Asia, 20; subsidy and production, 14; U.S. policy, 24
Wipf, L., 36

Zambia: tobacco, 35

List of Contributors

D. Gale Johnson
University of Chicago

Martin E. Abel
Professor, Department of Agricultural and Applied Economics,
University of Minnesota

C. Peter Timmer
Walter P. Falcon
Food Research Center, Stanford University

John W. Mellor
Uma Lele
Cornell University

Anthony M. Tang
Professor of Economics, Vanderbilt University

Kuo-shu Liang
Professor of Economics, National Taiwan University

George S. Tolley
Department of Economics, University of Chicago

Timothy Josling
Reader in Economics, London School of Economics, London, England

Robert Evenson
Associate Professor of Economics, Yale University

About the Editor

George S. Tolley is Professor of Economics at the University of Chicago, on leave as Deputy Assistant Secretary for Tax Policy of the U.S. Treasury. Prior to joining the Chicago faculty in 1966, he held an executive position in the U.S. Department of Agriculture with responsibilities for economic development of non-metropolitan parts of the economy. From 1956 to 1965, he was on the faculty of North Carolina State University. He obtained M.A. and Ph.D. degrees from the University of Chicago. He has taught as Visiting Professor at the University of California, Berkeley and at Purdue University and in 1965 to 1966 was Vice President of the American Farm Economic Association, which has cited several of his publications for excellence.

His activities include serving on: President Nixon's Task Force on Urban Renewal, Advisory Board on Water Resources Planning of the Government of Iran, Inter-University Committee on Urban Economics, National Academy of Sciences Committee on Water, National Academy of Sciences Committee on Automotive Pollution, and the Committee of the Social Science Research Council on Agricultural Economics.

He has served as consultant to the Ministry of Agriculture of the Republic of Korea, Minister of Planning of Panama, International Bank for Reconstruction and Development, University of Puerto Rico, Appalachia Commission, and the President's Commission on Rural Poverty.

Dr. Tolley is author and editor of numerous publications and has been associated with societies and associations covering broad spectrums of activities. His fields of research and writing include agricultural economics, economic development, urban economics, natural resources and environmental problems, monetary fiscal policy and consumer demand.